Attacked On All Sides

Attacked On All Sides

* * *

*The Civil War Battle of Decatur, Georgia, the
Untold Story of the Battle of Atlanta*

David Allison
With chapters by Lisa Rickey and Blaise J. Arena

ISBN-13: 9781977761903
ISBN-10: 1977761909
Library of Congress Control Number: 2017915794
CreateSpace Independent Publishing Platform
North Charleston, South Carolina

This book is dedicated to all those who suffered because of the Battle of Decatur, and their families who suffered with them. It is also written with gratitude to those who invented the Internet and Google, without which this book would not have been possible.

Acknowledgements

This book would not have been possible without the help and support of many, to whom I extend my sincerest gratitude.

I would be remiss if I did not first acknowledge that it was Lisa Rickey's incredible work uncovering and documenting Howard Forrer's all-too-short life (see Chapter 8) that inspired me to do this book. Lisa, you have my heartfelt thanks for opening my eyes to the possibilities of this type of storytelling.

Bill McIntire and Jamie McQuinn of the Dayton Metro Library graciously provided numerous photographs of and documents about Howard Forrer for Lisa's chapter. There is nothing greater than a great library, and great librarians. Thank you Bill and Jamie.

Phillip L. Crane of the Lower Muskingum Historical Society in Waterford, Ohio, went through the society's collections to find an original copy of Betty K. Rose's 2010 article on Isaiah R. Rose of the 63rd Ohio Infantry, which he graciously provided. I am in your debt, Mr. Crane.

The chapter about Solomon Spitler of the 63rd Ohio would not have been possible without the kind assistance of Paula Spitler of Linden, Virginia, who provided me with family documents detailing Solomon's Civil War service, wounding at the Battle of Decatur, and subsequent death in an army hospital. Because of Paula's efforts, Solomon's sacrifice for his country can now be brought to a wider audience.

Atlanta-based historical researcher Don Evans provided great help searching the Georgia State Archives and providing archival materials from the DeKalb History Society, including the 1866 map of the Decatur courthouse square. I thank you sincerely, Don.

Baird Holm LLP of Omaha, Nebraska, graciously provided me with information from its archive about the Civil War experiences of the firm's founder, Colonel [later general] Milton Montgomery of the 25th Wisconsin Infantry. My sincere thanks to Rick Putnam and Meredith Williams.

The Special Collections office of the LSU Libraries at Louisiana State University helped me obtain the memoirs of Confederate General Samuel W. Ferguson, which provided a detailed first-person account of the Battle of Decatur.

The Chicago History Museum's Research Center graciously provided the papers of John A. Nourse of the Chicago Board of Trade Battery, which includes another dramatic first-person account of the battle.

Scott Mingus of York, Pennsylvania, provided me with his incredible account of the escape of Augustus Dusenberry of the 35th New Jersey Infantry from a Confederate prison and winter trek over the Appalachian Mountains to safety back in Federal lines. Thank you so much, Scott.

The Wisconsin Historical Society has an awesome online archive which gave me access to the E.B. Quiner Scrapbooks, which contained a great deal of useful information. The Society has my sincere thanks.

Finally, it would not have been possible for me to do this book in the pre-Internet era. The ever-growing digital database that is now available allows access with just a few clicks to many obscure, out-of-print books, photographs, and historical documents that are tucked away in obscure archives. (I would particularly like to call out Fold3.com, which was an invaluable source of pension records which allowed me to document the terrible human toll the Battle of Decatur took on the families of some of the Federal soldiers who died there.) This, combined with the ability to communicate via e-mail, makes today a truly golden age for Civil

War (and other types of) historical research. The fact that I did this book without getting on a plane is remarkable. Everyone who aspires to understand history owes a debt of gratitude to the creators of the Internet and Google.

If I have neglected to here acknowledge anyone else who assisted me, I deeply regret my oversight. You have my sincere thanks as well.

David Allison

Art credits

The photograph of the third DeKalb County courthouse was kindly provided by the DeKalb History Center.

The photograph of Milton Montgomery of the 25th Wisconsin Infantry was kindly provided by the Library of Congress.

The Dayton Metro Library graciously provided images of Howard Forrer of the 63rd Ohio Infantry. My thanks to Bill McIntire and James McQuinn.

Ronald S. Coddington kindly gave his permission to reproduce images of members of the 35th New Jersey Infantry from the September/October 1988 issue of Military Images magazine.

The Ohio History Connection in Columbus, Ohio, provided images of members of the 63rd Ohio Infantry.

The U.S. Army Heritage and Education Center in Carlisle, Pennsylvania, provided the photograph of Captain Daniel T. Thorne and Private Alfred Piffley.

The photographs of John F. Brobst, and John and Mary Brobst, are courtesy of the University of Wisconsin Press.

The Library of Congress provided photographs of General John W. Sprague, the Sultana, and Joseph Wheeler.

Contents

Introduction

"I begin to regard the death & mangling of a couple of thousand men as a small affair, a kind of morning dash – and it may be well that we become so hardened."

--GENERAL WILLIAM T. SHERMAN WRITING IN A LETTER TO HIS WIFE ON JUNE 30, 1864, DURING THE ATLANTA CAMPAIGN THREE WEEKS PRIOR TO THE BATTLE OF DECATUR.[1]

"There is a class of events which by their very nature, and despite any intrinsic interest that they may possess, are foredoomed to oblivion. They are merged in the general story of those greater events of which they are a part, as the thunder of a billow breaking on a distant beach is unnoted in the continuous roar."

--AMBROSE BIERCE[2]

The battle fought during the American Civil War at Decatur, Georgia, on the Friday afternoon of July 22, 1864, was a small affair, what General Sherman might have called an afternoon dash, but one which killed and mangled only several hundred men. The Battle of Decatur was foredoomed to oblivion as a sideshow to the great and famous Battle of Atlanta. That epic pageant, fought simultaneously that hot summer afternoon six miles to the west of Decatur and involving tens of thousands of combatants, is portrayed vividly in the Atlanta Cyclorama and numerous books. Amidst the later historic drama of the death struggle for Atlanta in the summer of 1864, the Battle of Decatur was seemingly forgotten almost before the gun smoke cleared and the dead were buried. There are no great markers or monuments to it. Most residents of Decatur or Atlanta today don't know that thousands of Confederate soldiers once charged across the railroad near Agnes Scott College and up the hill to the courthouse, where hundreds of U.S. soldiers and six army cannons poured death into their ranks.

The Battle of Decatur didn't affect the Battle of Atlanta, the larger Atlanta Campaign or much less the greater Civil War. It was a profitless waste of blood and lives. So why write a book-length history of a forgotten three-hour fire fight which accomplished nothing militarily and had no impact on history? Among the many published accounts of the Battle of Atlanta, the Battle of Decatur is often given only a brief mention or even omitted altogether. That is the impetus for this book. The tale has elements of a great story: A smaller force attacked by a much larger force. Tremendous human courage and tragedy. A bayonet charge. A Medal of Honor won. These events and many others like them occurred. The Battle of Decatur is also worthy of remembering if only to honor the sacrifice of those lives it ended, shattered, or forever changed. Historian Ron Chernow said in a 2017 interview about his then-just-published biography of the great Civil War general and later president Ulysses S. Grant – about whom so much has been written -- that his goal for his new book was to "zero in on the silences."[3] This is what I attempt to do here.

The Battle of Decatur is linked to one of the great horrors of the Civil War, Georgia's Andersonville prison. Most of the Federals captured by the Confederates at Decatur were sent to that hell-hole, and many met their deaths there. The battle is also linked to the greatest maritime disaster in American history, the Sultana explosion, in which a sidewheel steam ship carrying freed Federal prisoners of war back to their homes blew up on the Mississippi River, claiming more lives than the sinking of the Titanic. And most don't know the battle's connection to modern American pop culture: American Idol star Kelly Clarkson's great-great-great grandfather and uncle fought in the battle. One survived, the other died.

Other participants in the Battle of Decatur went on to lead notable post-war lives and to become nationally prominent figures who shaped late 19th century American political, business and military events. Among the Federals, Colonel (later General) John W. Sprague, who commanded the Federal forces during the battle, later helped settle the American northwest as a founder of the city of Tacoma, Washington. Jeremiah Rusk, second in command of one of the Federal regiments in the battle, later became governor of Wisconsin and the first-ever U.S. secretary of agriculture. That regiment's commanding officer, Milton Montgomery, founded what's now the oldest law firm in Omaha, Nebraska. Other participants became members of Congress or state politicians. One became a close business associate of the great steel magnate Andrew Carnegie. Among the Confederates, General Joseph Wheeler after the war helped to reconcile the North and South as a member of Congress and played a role in one of the U.S. Army's first overseas invasions in Cuba. Decatur resident Mary A.H. Gay, who was in the town at the time of the battle, later wrote a book based on what she saw that inspired Margaret Mitchell's creation of the character Scarlett O'Hara in "Gone With The Wind," one of the top-selling novels of all time.

Much of the recent popular American discourse about the Civil War has focused on its racial aspects. Readers interested in this topic as seen through the lens of the Battle of Decatur may want to read the Civil War letters of Chauncey H. Cooke, an abolitionist soldier in the 25th Wisconsin who wrote quite a bit about the former slaves he encountered during the war and his perceptions of the detrimental impact slavery had on Southern culture. Cooke went into the hospital just before the Battle of Decatur and so did not take part in it, but his regiment did and his best friend John Christian was killed there. Readers may also be interested in the immediate post-war experience of John W. Sprague. Just after the war ended, Sprague was appointed the Freedmen's Bureau's first agent in Arkansas. His role there is explored at some length in "The Freedmen's Bureau and Reconstruction: Reconsiderations," published by Fordham University Press in 1999. For the Confederate perspective, there is Decatur resident Mary A.H. Gay's "Life in Dixie During The War," a good example of the Lost Cause genre of literature which portrays her view of the Confederacy's noble aims and a paternalistic view of slavery. For a modern, scholarly appraisal of Gay and her writings, I would point readers to Michelle Gillespie's chapter on Gay in "Georgia Women: Their Lives and Times," Volume 1, published by The University of Georgia Press in 2009. For the perspective of a Confederate soldier who supported slavery (although he owned no slaves), readers may wish to read the letters of William L. Nugent, one of Wheeler's cavalry officers who was in the Battle of Decatur. A collection of Nugent's letters, "My Dear Nellie," was published by the University Press of Mississippi in 1977.

This book begins by describing the Decatur of 1864, then introduces some of the notable participants on each side of the conflict. I next show how wartime events brought these individuals together to clash at the Battle of Decatur. We then follow the aftermath of the battle on some of those who took part in it, as well as on their families, and see what some participants did with their lives after the war. Contributors Lisa Rickey and Blaise J. Arena provide profiles of two participants in the battle, Howard Forrer of the 63rd Ohio Volunteer Infantry and John C. Fleming of the Chicago Board of Trade Battery. Forrer was shot dead in Decatur, whereas Fleming survived the battle and war. Their life stories are microcosms of the Civil War experiences of tens of thousands of other Civil War participants.

Now, let us step back in time to the 1860s.

David Allison

I

Setting the Stage: Decatur in 1864

In the spring of 1864 the American Civil War was beginning its fourth year. In Virginia, Federal forces led by General Ulysses S. Grant were locked in a bloody death match with Confederates commanded by General Robert E. Lee. On the other side of the Appalachian Mountains in Chattanooga, Tennessee, General William T. Sherman was massing Federal forces to invade Georgia, the Confederate heartland, his aim being to capture of the strategic railroad and manufacturing city of Atlanta. Opposing Sherman and determined to stop him was a Confederate army led by General Joseph E. Johnston. Meanwhile, in Washington, D.C., and around the North, despite the previous year's Federal victories at Gettysburg and Vicksburg, opposition to President Abraham Lincoln's prosecution of the war was reaching critical mass and he doubted he would win re-election in the upcoming November 1864 elections. Lincoln needed a decisive success that would convince the North that its enormous sacrifices in blood and treasure would yield victory over the Confederates. All but giving up hopes that Grant would be able to defeat Lee before the election, Lincoln's administration looked to Sherman to capture Atlanta and secure his re-election.

At the beginning of May 1864, Sherman launched the Atlanta Campaign. His 100,000-man army pushed south out of Chattanooga and confronted a Confederate army estimated at between 50,000 and 70,000 men. Sherman's strategy was to move up close to the Confederates, entrench, and then use his forces' numerical superiority to outflank the Confederates by marching around behind their positions to cut their supply lifeline, the railroad leading back to Atlanta. Sherman did this repeatedly, forcing Johnston to retreat out of one strong defensive position after another until, by the beginning of July 1864, the Confederate army retreated across the Chattahoochee River, putting Sherman on Atlanta's doorstep. Sherman, fearing that the Confederates in Atlanta might be reinforced by the railroad entering the city from the east, on July 17, 1864, sent part of his army across the Chattahoochee at Roswell, with the goal of cutting the railroad between Decatur and Stone Mountain. This movement brought the Federal army into Decatur on July 19. In the Confederate capital of Richmond, Confederate President Jefferson Davis decided Johnston lacked the will to stop Sherman, and relieved Johnston of command. In Johnston's place, Davis placed General John B. Hood, a Texan famed for his rash fighting spirit. Hood was personally scarred by battle, having had his left arm crippled at the Battle of Gettysburg and then losing his right leg at the Battle of Chickamauga. Hood almost immediately struck Sherman's advancing army, which was by that time across the Chattahoochee and approaching Atlanta's outskirts, at the Battle of Peachtree Creek on July 20. The Confederate attack failed to stop the Federals. Undeterred, Hood again attacked, this time hitting the Federal army that had reached Decatur and was then fast approaching Atlanta from the east. This would become known as the Battle of Atlanta, and includes the Battle of Decatur.

Up until this time Decatur had escaped the ravages of the Civil War. When the war had begun three years before, many young men from the Decatur area enlisted in the Confederate army and went to the front in Virginia. But prior to the arrival of the Federals on July 19, probably the most notable wartime event in Decatur was that the town was chosen by the famous Confederate cavalry general, John H. Morgan, as the place to reorganize his unit after his escape from imprisonment in Ohio. Morgan's chief of staff, Lieutenant Colonel Robert A. Alston, was from Decatur. Morgan, a notorious Confederate cavalry raider, had in July 1863 led his troopers north on what would become his most famous exploit, a spectacular foray aimed at raising Confederate morale. Morgan led his forces across the Ohio River into Indiana and Ohio where they left a thousand-mile trail of destruction. With Federal pursuers on his tail, Morgan's luck finally ran out on July 26, 1863, when his tattered remaining forces gave up and surrendered, just 60 miles south of Lake Erie, the farthest point north ever reached by Confederates. Morgan and his men were imprisoned in Columbus, Ohio. But in November, the daring Morgan and six of his officers tunneled out of the prison and escaped south, reaching Confederate lines by December 8, 1863. Facing possible court martial by Confederate leaders because of the failure of his recent raid, Morgan came to Decatur in February 1864 and began trying to assemble the remnants of his old unit. "Apparently Morgan's personal magnetism still worked. Men flocked into Decatur from throughout the South to help form a new command," wrote Edison H. Thomas in a history of Morgan's great raid. [1] Decatur resident Mary Gay noted the excitement at the time. "In the winter of 1864 there seems to have been a lull in hostilities between the armies at 'the front,'" she wrote in her post-war memoir "Life In Dixie During The War." "Morgan's men were rendezvousing near Decatur. Their brave and dashing chief had been captured, but had made his escape from the Ohio penitentiary, and was daily expected. Some artillery companies were camping near, among them Waddell's. There was also a conscript camp within a mile or two; so it is not to be wondered at that the young ladies of Decatur availed themselves in a quiet way of the social enjoyment the times afforded, and that there were little gatherings at private houses at which 'Morgan's men' and the other soldiers were frequently represented." [2] Morgan remained in Decatur until April 1864, when he led his group to Virginia to fight Yankees. It was there in September that Morgan's luck finally ran out and he was killed.

When the Civil War finally came to Decatur in July 1864, it was a 41-year-old "country town," as one Federal officer described it, and very different from the sophisticated urban community of hipsters, chic restaurants and luxury apartment towers that it is today. Up until the early 1800s this section of Piedmont Georgia was still occupied by Native

Americans of the Creek and Cherokee nations. But as growing numbers of white settlers with their black slaves moved into the area from eastern Georgia, the Creeks and Cherokees ceded their lands and moved away. The first white settlers had begun moving into the Decatur area in the early 1800s. DeKalb County was formed at the end of 1822, and a year later at the end of 1823 Decatur was incorporated as the county seat and courthouse town. Courthouse squares were a central defining architectural feature of the 19th century South. "A highway traveler in much of the Middle West and South must thread his way through a busy square every twenty or thirty miles. He is likely to carry in his memory a composite picture of these squares -- a rectangular block surrounded by streets, with the courthouse, often the grandest and most ornate building in the county, standing alone in the middle of the square and the town's leading business houses enclosing the square symmetrically on all four sides." [3] This description fits Decatur perfectly.

A post-war photograph of the DeKalb County courthouse in Decatur at the time of the Civil War. The clock tower was added after the war.

Decatur's second courthouse had burned in 1842, so a third was built, meaning the courthouse there during the Civil War would have been 21 or 22 years old by 1864. [4] The third courthouse was a two-story brick structure which faced to the east, with two squared granite columns on the eastern end framing a doorway into the first floor. Stairs climbed up on each side of that first-floor doorway to a doorway to the second floor. Each floor had five windows, each with wooden shutters. A clock tower would later be added on the eastern end of the building but was not there during the Civil War. [Editor's note: A sketch made of the courthouse during the Civil War entitled "Sprague's Brigade Protecting The Wagon Trains of Sherman's Army At Decatur, Georgia, July 22, 1864" appears to show six windows on each floor and multiple columns on the eastern end. This is erroneous, as photographs clearly show five windows and only two columns.] There were four large offices on the ground floor. The courthouse was surrounded by plenty of open space. "The court house square was surrounded by hitching racks for horses and teams. There were long poles of timber, resting on posts, placed about five feet above the ground, and county people or others coming to town on horses or in buggies or wagons hitched their horses or mules to these racks. During court weeks and every Saturday the square was surrounded with teams thus hitched." [5] On the blocks surrounding the square were dry goods and grocery stores, saloons, a post office, hotels and private homes. [6] An 1864 map prepared by the Federal army shows solid lines of buildings facing the courthouse on the blocks to the east and west.

To understand the Battle of Decatur, it helps to understand the layout of the town as it then existed in 1864. So let us imagine we are standing there in the courthouse square. Here's what we would have seen. There were no tall buildings, only low-rise structures of wood and brick. Looking north from the square ran the Shallow Ford Road, as it was then called (today it is Clairemont Avenue and Clairmont Road) because it followed the old Shallow Ford Indian Trail north to a crossing on the Chattahoochee River at the textile mills at Roswell. A mile

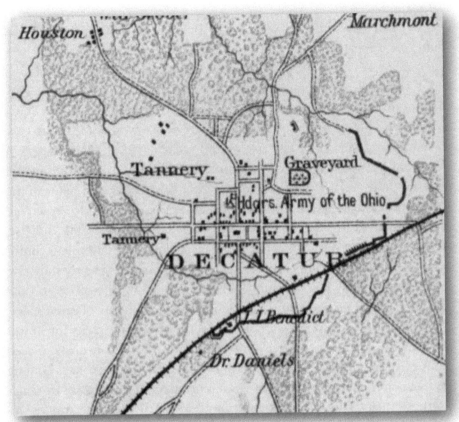

A map of the Decatur area prepared by U.S. Army engineers during the Civil War.

and a half north of the courthouse square another road led off the left, or west. This was the Pace's Ferry Road (today North Decatur Road), so called because it led to Buckhead and then to Pace's Ferry on the Chattahoochee. A block east of the square another road led north out of town to the northeast to Lawrenceville, today's Church Street. A short distance up Church Street a road led off to the right to the town cemetery. Just beyond that was the Presbyterian Church, a brick building that had been constructed in 1846.

On the northwest side of the square at the corner of the Shallow Ford Road was a large building, the residence of Ezekial Mason. In the early days of the Civil War, "Here, day after day, a band of devoted women met to make the uniforms for the DeKalb Light Infantry,"[7] noted Decatur

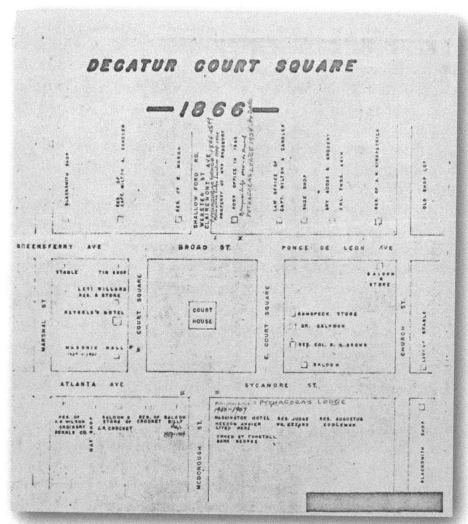

A map of the Decatur square prepared in 1866, two years after the Battle of Decatur but probably changed very little from the time of the battle.

resident Mary Gay. Gay's own home was on a large lot a short distance further north of the square. Across the street, in the northeast corner of the square where today Clairemont Avenue meets Ponce de Leon Avenue, was the post office.

A map of the courthouse square prepared in 1866 provides a good idea of what it probably looked like two years earlier during the Civil War.

On the block just east of the courthouse and facing it was a "Ramspeck" store, two homes and a saloon. On the block just west of the courthouse and facing it was the Masonic Hall, Reynold's Hotel, the Levi Willard residence and store, and a tin shop. On the blocks south of the square and facing it were homes, two saloons and the Washington Hotel.

Looking eastward from the square, if you went two blocks east and turned right you would see the Decatur Methodist Church, which had been formed in 1826.

Looking southward from the square, the ground slopes downward. As they do today, McDonough Street led due south, with what's now East Trinity Place branching off toward the southeast. A short distance down from where these two roads split was the jail, on the western side of McDonough Street. It had been erected in 1849 and was two stories and reportedly built of granite blocks. [8] Past the jail the ground continues sloping downward a couple of hundred yards before rising up to a ridge, just below the crest of which was the Georgia Railroad, running east to west, and the railroad depot. Decatur and all of north Georgia had been transformed in the 1840s with the coming of railroads. In 1836 the state of Georgia had decided to build a railroad linking the port of Savannah to the Midwest. One rail line called the Central of Georgia was built westward from Savannah to Macon, while another called the Macon & Western continued northward. Meanwhile, another known as the Western & Atlantic would be built southward from Chattanooga. Simultaneously, the Georgia Railroad was being constructed westward from Augusta. The three lines from the north, south and east would meet at a spot south of the Chattahoochee River known as Terminus, which later changed its name to Marthasville. Decatur was changed forever in 1845 when the Georgia Railroad, which had been extended from Augusta to Madison, Georgia, reached Decatur and linked to the Western & Atlantic six miles to the west in Marthasville.

At the bottom of the hill south of the courthouse and between it and the railroad, where Decatur High School is today, was a large marshy area, the headwaters of Pea Vine Creek. If you climbed up to the railroad embankment and looked to the right, or westward, you would see another landmark, the "Hoyle House." Just to the southwest of the square was the home of Decatur resident Benjamin Franklin Swanton, "described as one of the nicest houses in Decatur." [9]

Significantly for later military events in Decatur, leading south out of town were three roads: today's Columbia Drive leading to the southeast, today's Candler Road leading due south (and then known as the McDonough road because it leads to McDonough, Georgia), and a road leading southwest toward Atlanta, today's Ansley Street and Oakview Road.

Viewed from back in the courthouse square, running westward was today's DeKalb Avenue, the road to Atlanta, the upstart new boomtown six miles to the west that had been founded just 14 years before.

How did Decatur appear to soldiers during the Civil War? Just two days before the Battle of Decatur, the 72nd Indiana Volunteer Infantry of the Mounted Lightning Brigade, which was part of Garrard's Cavalry, rode into the town late on the evening of July 20, having been east toward Stone Mountain tearing up the railroad. A member of the 72nd Indiana described Decatur was "a most beautiful place." "The town is situated on high, rolling ground, well-shaded (an item of vast importance in southern cities) and has 1,000 inhabitants," [10] the regimental history notes.

Now let's learn more about some of the Federal soldiers who descended on Decatur.

II

The Federals

Three infantry regiments of the U.S. Army fought in the Battle of Decatur. These were the 63rd Ohio Volunteer Infantry, the 25th Wisconsin Volunteer Infantry, and the 35th New Jersey Volunteer Infantry. Together with another regiment, the 43rd Ohio Volunteer Infantry, the four regiments made up the Second Brigade of the 4th Division of the 16th Army Corps. (The 43rd Ohio would make an appearance in the Battle of Decatur just as it was ending but did not take an active part in the battle itself.) As of May 1, 1864, the day the brigade left Huntsville, Alabama, to start the Atlanta Campaign, the four regiments had a total of 2,548 soldiers. [1] Two artillery units, The Chicago Board of Trade Battery and a section of Battery C of the First Michigan Artillery also played key roles in the Battle of Decatur. Let's learn more about these units.

The 63rd Ohio Volunteer Infantry

Of the three Federal regiments that fought at Decatur, the 63rd Ohio Volunteer Infantry was the most veteran, having been formed in January 1862. The 63rd had thus been in service nine months before the 25th Wisconsin was mustered (September 1862) and almost a year and a half before the 35th New Jersey was formed (September 1863). [2] The 63rd was composed of recruits from Columbus, Marietta and Chillicothe, Ohio, through the consolidation of the 22nd Ohio (seven companies) and 63rd

Ohio (four companies), with John W. Sprague named its colonel. [3] Late in January 1862 the troops were issued muskets which had been flint locks but had been converted to cap locks. On February 18, 1862, the regiment embarked on an Ohio River steamer and were sent to Paducah, Kentucky, then to Cairo, Illinois, and then down the Mississippi River to the village of Commerce, Missouri, where U.S. General John Pope was battling the Confederate M. Jeff Thompson. (One of the other Federal units with the 63rd was the 43rd Ohio, which would come to the 63rd's aid at Decatur two years later at the Battle of Decatur.) On March 3, 1862, the Federals approached the well-fortified Confederate line near New Madrid, Missouri. Here the young men of the 63rd came under fire for the first time. "We formed in line of battle and the shot and shells began to fly quite briskly over us at a distance of over a mile from their main works," Second Lieutenant Oscar L. Jackson would note in his diary. "Some came very near us. It was our first experience under fire but the boys took it very cooly." [4] Several days later the 63rd and 43rd were skirmishing with the Confederates, the firing "sharp and brisk. These were the first musket balls I had heard whiz," Jackson wrote. "They had not the unearthly sound of rifled cannon shot, nor the death-like crashing of heavy shells, to all of which I have this day been exposed." Over the next week any of the recruits of the 63rd who thought they were still playing soldier realized the deadly reality of their line of work. Writing on March 13, Jackson noted "dead bodies were being carried off the field and wounded men passing on litters to the ambulances. One man a few yards from me had his right leg shattered, cut off by the surgeon and he carried to the hospital and his shattered leg left lying on the ground. The groans were terrible and they made me grit my teeth and grasp my sword the tighter... Terrible scenes and many hairbreadth escapes were passing before our eyes. Once a large piece of shell buried itself in the ground just beside my thigh as I lay on the ground." The 63rd would spend the rest of March 1862 in the New Madrid area. [5] Near the end of the month the regiment was issued new Austrian-made rifled muskets with distinctive stocks of white maple, which the 63rd used until the end of the war, including the Battle of Decatur. [6]

As April 1862 began, 160 miles southeast of the 63rd Ohio, big things were happening at an obscure spot in western Tennessee on the Tennessee River known as Pittsburg Landing, not far north of the Mississippi state line and about 100 miles east of Memphis. After driving the Confederates out of Kentucky and western Tennessee, U.S. General Ulysses S. Grant, commander of the Army of the Tennessee, was concentrating forces at Pittsburg Landing with the aim of capturing the nearby town of Corinth, Mississippi, through which ran the railroad connecting Nashville, Tennessee, and the Mississippi River. Corinth was the junction of "the two most important railroads in the Mississippi Valley – one connecting Memphis and the Mississippi River with the East, and the other leading south to all the cotton states," Grant wrote in his memoirs. [7] "If we obtained possession of Corinth the enemy would have no railroad for the transportation of armies or supplies until that running east from Vicksburg was reached. It was the great strategic position at the West between the Tennessee and the Mississippi rivers and between Nashville and Vicksburg."

The Confederates were fortifying Corinth and collecting an army there under General Albert Sidney Johnston. While Grant was waiting for reinforcements to arrive at Pittsburg Landing, Johnston saw a chance to strike first and drive Grant's forces into the Tennessee River. As the morning of April 6 dawned, the Confederates launched a surprise attack, what would become the famous Battle of Shiloh. The vicious contest was waged all day, with Johnston receiving a fatal wound as he led the rebel attack. The Confederate command passed to General Pierre G.T. Beauregard, who called off the attack at nightfall. Overnight, the Federals were reinforced, and on the morning of April 7 they launched a strong counterattack, driving back the Confederates who realized they were beaten and retreated. Thus ended what was until then the bloodiest battle of the Civil War, with 13,000 Federal casualties and nearly 11,000 Confederate casualties. The road to Corinth was now open for Grant's forces.

Back in Missouri, the 63rd Ohio was ordered on April 16 to join the Federal forces massing for the attack on Corinth. Boarding transport boats on April 17, the regiment steamed up the Mississippi River to Cairo, Illinois, where its steamer stopped to load coal. While waiting there, the 63rd's Oscar Jackson saw coffins containing the bodies of officers killed at Shiloh. With its steamer refueled, the 63rd continued its voyage up the Tennessee River, passing the Shiloh battlefield on April 23 and landing a few miles upriver at Hamburg, Tennessee, which is northeast of Corinth. The next day the 63rd began moving westward toward Corinth. The Federals would spend the next month besieging Corinth, which the Confederates finally abandoned on May 30, 1862.

The contest for northern Mississippi and Alabama wasn't over, though, and in September 1862 the 63rd would take part in the Battle of Iuka, Mississippi, where the Confederates were driven from that town. "A battle field is a strange, melancholy sight after the conflict is ended," the 63rd's Oscar Jackson would note at Iuka. "As you walk over it, some strange curiosity impels you to examine the countenances of the fallen and the nature of their wounds. On an eminence perhaps the bodies of friend and foe lie mixed indiscriminately, showing where the struggle was warmest. A little farther on and you find them scattered and as you reach broken or wooded ground, you hunt for them as for strawberries in a meadow. Then the different postures of the dead. Some fall dead instantly. Others struggle into the dark region of the hereafter; whilst many, placing themselves in fantastic or grave positions, appear to leave life as if it all was a farce, or in calm meditation." [8] The 63rd would soon get a much bigger taste of death. On Friday, October 3, 1862, the Confederates attacked them at Corinth with the battle continuing anew the next day. On October 4 the Ohioans were in the thick of the bloody fighting. About 10 o'clock in the morning, the 63rd was in line of battle facing the Confederates who were sheltering in woods, when they came out into the open.

"The rebels began pouring out of the timber and forming storming columns. All the firing ceased and everything was silent as the grave," Oscar Jackson recalled. "They formed one column of perhaps two thousand men in plain view, then another, and crowding out of the woods another, and so on. I thought they would never stop coming out of the timber. While they were forming, the men were considerable distance from us but in plain sight and as soon as they were ready they started at us with a firm, slow, steady step... In my campaigning I had never seen anything so hard to stand as that slow, steady tramp. Not a sound was heard but they looked as if they intended to walk over us." Jackson could see that his men were affected by the oncoming Confederates. "I noticed one man examining his gun to see if it was clean; another to see if his was primed right; a third would stand a while on one foot then on the other; whilst others were pulling at their blouses, feeling if their cartridge boxes or cap-pouches were all right and so on, but all the time steadily watching the advancing foe."

"Boys, I guess we are going to have a fight," the 22-year-old Jackson told his men, reminding them that to their rear they were supported by other Federal soldiers, and that they had good bayonets on their rifles. The Federals were ordered to lie down to reduce their exposure to the Confederates' fire, and then when the Confederates got close enough to rise and fire by companies. When the Confederates had gotten to about 30 yards away, Jackson ordered his men, "Company H, get up." Touching his sword to a three- or four-foot-tall bush in front of him, he said, "Boys, give them a volley just over this. Ready! Aim! Fire!" The whole Federal line exploded, cutting down the Confederates. "As the smoke cleared away, there was apparently ten yards square of a mass of struggling bodies and butternut clothes. [Editor's note: Many Confederate soldiers wore homemade uniforms that were died a brownish tan color, known as butternut.] Their column appeared to reel like a rope shaken at the end," Jackson recalled. Company H delivered another volley right into the faces of the Confederates. The rebels retreated, but about 40 minutes later reformed and attacked again, coming at the Federals "with a yell on the double quick. Our men stood firm with loaded guns and fixed bayonets and gave them a volley that threw them somewhat into confusion, slaughtering them fearfully, but pressing on, and firing at us rapidly, they dashed themselves against us like water against a rock and were a second time repulsed and gave back," Jackson said. The battle continued, with Jackson's men fighting the Confederates hand to hand. One of Jackson's men killed a Texan with his bayonet, "which is a remarkable thing in a battle," Jackson said. [9] In his report of the battle, the 63rd Ohio's commander Colonel John W. Sprague described the Confederate fire hitting the 63rd as "furious," "terrific and deadly," and "murderous," but the 63rd gave it back. The ditch in front of the Federal works was nearly filled with dead and wounded Confederates. "Every officer and man of my command seemed to put forth superhuman exertions to hold our position," Sprague said. [10]

At last the rebels retreated. While the 63rd and the other Federals won "a most brilliant victory" in the second battle of Corinth, as Sprague described it, and repulsed the Confederates, the victory had come at a fearful cost to the 63rd: 24 dead, 105 wounded and three missing, or a total of 132 – which was far more than either of the three other regiments in its brigade (the 43rd Ohio lost a total of 90 at Corinth).[11] In Oscar Jackson's company alone, out of 34 officers and men, 23 – or two thirds – were killed or wounded. [12] Late in the battle, Jackson was himself shot in the face with a small bullet that hit just below his right eye and lodged in his skull. He was left unconscious and unattended with the many other wounded Federals believed to be dying and beyond help of the overworked army surgeons. But Jackson's black servant, a man named Mose, found Jackson and carried him in his arms to the field hospital and had him cared for, no doubt saving his life. [13] Jackson did not regain consciousness until two days later, but recovered and served until the end of the war.

The 63rd Ohio would spend the remainder of 1862 and most of 1863 chasing Confederates and performing garrison duty in northern Mississippi and Alabama and nearby areas of Tennessee. In January 1864, many of the soldiers of the 63rd would re-enlist, which earned them a month-long furlough to go home to Ohio to visit. In February 1864 the 63rd was sent back to Alabama, where it helped capture the town of Decatur on the Tennessee River. On April 1, 1864, the 63rd was made part of the Second Brigade, Fourth Division of the 16th Army Corps under General Grenville M. Dodge, which combined the 63rd with the 43rd Ohio Volunteer Infantry, the 25th Wisconsin Volunteer Infantry and 35th New Jersey Volunteer Infantry. [14] At the beginning of May the division was ordered to leave Decatur, Alabama, and move to Chattanooga, Tennessee, to join General William T. Sherman's forces massing for the Federals' campaign to capture Atlanta.

The 25th Wisconsin Volunteer Infantry

Nine months after the 63rd Ohio went into service, the 25th Wisconsin was mustered in on September 14, 1862. [15] The regiment was recruited by Jeremiah M. Rusk, who in 1861 had been elected to the Wisconsin state legislature. [16] The new recruits were collected at LaCrosse, Wisconsin. Unlike most Federal regiments, the 25th did not immediately march southward to fight Confederates. Rather, it headed northwest to the Minnesota frontier to deal with a Native American uprising. When that work was done, the 25th finally headed south in February 1863, traveling down the Mississippi River via steamer to Kentucky, later to Memphis, Tennessee, and then up the Yazoo River to a spot northeast of Vicksburg, Mississippi, where the unit arrived in June 1863. [17] The 25th would spend the next seven months chasing guerillas and performing other garrison duty. In February 1864 the 25th would take part along with the 35th New Jersey and other Federal regiments in the Meridian Expedition, in which General William T. Sherman led a Federal army eastward out of Vicksburg, Mississippi, across the state to the strategic town of Meridian, Mississippi, which was sacked. Back in Vicksburg, at the end of March 1864 the 25th began its movement to join the forces being gathered by Sherman near Chattanooga for the Atlanta Campaign. The 25th traveled by steamer up the Mississippi to Cairo, Illinois, and then up the Tennessee River to near Decatur, Alabama. On April 1, 1864, the 25th was made part of the Second Brigade, Fourth Division of the 16th Army Corps under General Grenville M. Dodge, which combined the 25th with the 43rd Ohio Volunteer Infantry, the 63rd Ohio Volunteer Infantry and 35th New Jersey Volunteer Infantry. [18] On April 16, 1864, the 25th marched into Decatur, Alabama, where it had a "sharp skirmish" with Confederates, losing two men wounded. Thus the 25th had been in service nearly a year and a half before it had been under any significant enemy fire. But its luck wasn't going to last. In late April the regiment was ordered to Chattanooga, traveling there from Huntsville via railroad and arriving in Chattanooga on May 5, 1864. With the start of the Atlanta Campaign the regiment immediately moved south into Georgia with the other Federal forces.

The 35th New Jersey Volunteer Infantry

Of the Federal regiments that fought at the Battle of Decatur, the last to form was the 35th New Jersey, which was mustered in in September 1863.[19] Rutgers University historian William Gillette described the political environment in which the 35th was raised. "In the course of the war New Jersey's military recruitment passed through different stages, which paralleled the experiences and problems of other northern states. In 1861, carried on a tidal wave of enthusiasm, more than ten thousand volunteers enlisted. This first response was so overwhelming that New Jersey authorities turned away many eager patriots in the early days... In 1862, however, the supply of volunteers slowed to a trickle. The Union army had achieved a few important gains in the East. This fact, combined with an improvement in the economy and better prospects for employment, made military service less attractive... By 1863 a full understanding of the realities and dangers of soldiering chilled the ardor of many able-bodied men of military age. In addition, as the war dragged on, critics denounced government officials for mismanaging the war, greedy businessmen for war profiteering, and craven politicians for using the war to seize the spoils." According to Gillette, New Jersey raised 14 infantry regiments by the end of 1861, 16 more in 1862, then just three in 1863. [20] By the summer of 1863, the Lincoln administration was growing desperate to raise more fighting men, and threatened governors of northern states that the Federal government would institute a draft unless the states raised required quotas of soldiers. Northern animosity to the war in general and a draft in particularly led to the New York draft riots in July 1863. Following the riots, New Jersey Governor Joel Parker persuaded Lincoln to delay the draft in New Jersey until the spring of 1864, according to Gillette. "Parker, in return, offered to make a concerted effort to secure enough volunteers to fill the state's quota. ... The delay of the draft allowed time for tempers to cool and for volunteers to enlist. Fear of the draft pressured many more men to enlist and galvanized counties and towns to raise higher bounties to lure volunteers. The state reached two-thirds of its quota, not a trifling achievement in comparison with many other states." [21] Among these was the 35th New Jersey.

Most of infantry regiments raised in New Jersey served in the eastern theater of the war. In contrast, the 35th was one of three New Jersey regiments that served in the western theater with General William T. Sherman's army, the other two being the 13th New Jersey and 33rd New Jersey. [22] The 35th New Jersey was a very different regiment than either the 63rd Ohio or 25th Wisconsin: Rather than being made up largely of Midwestern farm boys, many of the men of the 35th New Jersey were from cities. One company was raised in Trenton and Lambertville, New Jersey, the others in the north of New Jersey. [23] Another difference was that many of those who enlisted were only after the $300 bounty that New Jersey was offering enlistees in an effort to meet the state's quota of soldiers before a Federal draft was imposed on the state. The 35th 's roster records the names of dozens of enlistees who deserted, sometimes just days after they were mustered in! [24] New Jersey state records show that out of a total of 1,906 men who were mustered into the unit during the war, a shocking 450 deserted. [25] The roster even includes one William Egan who, on October 17, 1863 just a month after he enlisted and before the 35th even left New Jersey, was shot by an officer for insubordination! [26] Rutgers University historian William Gillette writes that, "Although the desertion rate among New Jersey servicemen was extremely high for a northern state (only New Hampshire, Connecticut, and Kansas outstripped New Jersey), most of New Jersey's troops stayed with their outfits. Their perseverance carried them through many brutal campaigns." [27] Another difference between the 35th New Jersey and the 63rd Ohio or 25th Wisconsin was that many of the 35th's volunteers were veterans, having seen service in other units during 1861 and 1862 where they had experienced combat. In addition, the 35th was distinguished by its fancy "Zouave" uniforms. The name "Zouaves" originally referred to Algerian military units who the French encountered when they invaded that north African county in 1830. Some European military groups later adopted elements of "Arab" inspired uniforms. [28] The 35th was known by the name of its commanding officer, Colonel John J. Cladek, as the "Cladek's Zouaves." New Jersey raised two Zouave units, the 35th New Jersey and the 33rd New Jersey. Like the 35th, the 33rd was part of Sherman's army and participated in the Atlanta Campaign.

The headquarters of the 35th was established in Flemington, New Jersey – a town about midway between New York City and Philadelphia – in September 1863 and the regiment was complete by mid October 1863 with 37 officers and 865 non-commissioned officers and men, for a total of 902. By this date, the bloodiest battles of the year – Gettysburg, Vicksburg and Chickamauga – were over and the 35th had not been in them. On October 19 the unit was transported to Washington, where it marched through the city and crossed the Long Bridge into Virginia. "They were a fine looking body of men, dressed in the Zouave costume, and were attended by a fine drum corps of stout young lads. Many of the men are veterans, and from their steadiness in marching and general appearance of good discipline, bid fair to become a good regiment for service," noted an October 21, 1863, report in the Newark Daily Advertiser. [29] But the 35th would not stay in the capital long. At the end of October 1863 it was assigned duty in "the West," as the region of the country on the other side of the Appalachian Mountains was then known. The unit was sent to Vicksburg, Mississippi, the key river city which had been captured by U.S. General Ulysses Grant in July 1863. The regiment then became part of the Army of The Tennessee and was attached to the 16th Army Corps. In February 1864, the 35th participated in the Meridian expedition, in which General William T. Sherman's forces left Vicksburg and marched eastward nearly across the state of Mississippi to the town of Meridian, an important railroad junction. In a warm-up for what would happen to Atlanta, Sherman sacked the town, destroying railroads and public property. During the raid the 35th saw some skirmishing, but no heavy combat. [30] The Federals then marched back to Vicksburg, arriving March 1. [31] On April 1, 1864, the 35th was made part of the Second Brigade, Fourth Division of the 16th Army Corps under General Grenville M. Dodge, which combined the 35th with the 43rd Ohio Volunteer Infantry, the 63rd Ohio Volunteer Infantry and 25th Wisconsin Volunteer Infantry. [32] A month later these regiments marched into Georgia.

$$* \quad * \quad *$$

The Chicago Board of Trade Battery

The artillery unit known as the Chicago Board of Trade Battery would play a big role in the Atlanta Campaign and later the Battle of Decatur (which would be fought exactly two years to the day after the battery was formed). As its name suggests, the battery was established in Chicago in July 1862 as the winds of war were blowing hot. (It was in Chicago a little over two years before this, in May 1860, that Abraham Lincoln had been nominated as the Republican candidate for the then-upcoming presidential election.) The weeks prior to the battery's organization had seen bloody fighting in Virginia, including the Seven Days Battles, the Battle of Mechanicsville, the Battle of Gaines Mill, and the Battle of Malvern Hill. On July 6, 1862, President Abraham Lincoln had issued a call for 300,000 volunteers to join the Federal army, and the Chicago Board of Trade Battery was among the very first of the volunteer organizations to respond. [33] On July 16, 1862, C.T. Wheeler, president of the Board of Trade, and nine other members of the business organization called for a general meeting of members at the Board's office "to pledge ourselves to use our influence and money to recruit a battery to be known as the Board of Trade Battery." The meeting was held on July 21, where

$5,121 was pledged and nine recruits enlisted for three years service. On the evening of the next day, July 22, an "enthusiastic meeting" was held and the muster roll grew to 63 names. [34] The battery was initially formed with six James rifled ten-pounder field artillery guns [Editor's note: the term "ten-pounder" refers to the shells fired by the guns which weighed 10 pounds.] The members of the battery were given distinctive silver badges for their uniforms. [35] A young Chicago man named John A. Nourse, his brother and some of their friends on that day enlisted in the battery. Nourse began keeping a diary that day of his experiences in the battery that tells us a great deal about his and the battery's wartime experiences. [36]

The battery headed to the front in September 1862, being transported south to Louisville, Kentucky. On October 11, 1862, it had its first engagement, firing one shot in a skirmish with Confederate General Nathan Bedford Forrest's cavalry. But the battery's first big battle would not come for two more months, when it would win "glorious distinction" in the bloody Battle of Stones River in Murfreesboro, Tennessee, on December 31, 1862. When the Federal line threatened to collapse, the men of the battery stood by their guns, firing "death-dealing shells" into the ranks of the on-rushing Confederates. "By 11 o'clock the enemy had learned that neither bravery nor numbers could carry the battery in their front, and all was quiet. Three of our men lay dead by their disabled guns. Ten wounded were taken to the rear. The battery having held its ground, it became the pivotal point on which the right and centre rested." [37] The battery would spend 1863 in service in Tennessee and Alabama attached to a division of cavalry. In late September 1863 it would fire the first gun opening the Chickamauga campaign, the Federal army's first effort to invade Georgia, which would end in the disastrous Federal defeat. John Nourse recorded on September 20 that the Chicago Board of Trade Battery was ordered towards Chattanooga with a wagon train of wounded. "Oh, the horrors of this day and night. I cannot write them." [38]

By early October 1863, the cavalry division in which the battery served for the first time encountered a foe it would meet again 10 months later in the Battle of Decatur -- General Joseph Wheeler's Confederate cavalry – in a fight on October 7 at Farmington, Tennessee, south of Nashville. The battery would spend the remainder of 1863 and first month of 1864 in service in Tennessee and Alabama. In February 1864 the battery went into winter camp in Huntsville, Alabama. There, on February 24, it would get brand new guns – a battery of 3-inch Parrott rifled cannons. These guns, named after their inventor Robert Parrott, were some of the most widely used cannons of the Civil War. Made of cast iron and with a three-inch rifled bore, they had a distinctive band of thick iron around their breach to keep them from bursting when fired. The guns fired projectiles weighing 10 pounds that could be solid, explosive shell or cannister (a metal can containing iron or lead pellets.) In late April, Federal forces commanded by General William T. Sherman began gathering in Chattanooga for the Federal army's next attempt to invade Georgia, beginning the Atlanta Campaign. The Chicago Board of Trade Battery was included, moving north into Tennessee to Chattanooga and then to La Fayette, Georgia, with other advancing Federal units.

Wars are ultimately fought not by military units, but by individuals, so let's learn about some of the officers and soldiers in the 63rd Ohio, 25th Wisconsin, 35th New Jersey and Chicago Board of Trade Battery who would later fight at the Battle of Decatur.

Private John F. Brobst, 25th Wisconsin Infantry

What was it like to be a private soldier in the Federal army who fought in the Battle of Decatur? We can get a wonderful glimpse through the letters of Private John F. Brobst of the 25th Wisconsin Infantry written to a girl at home whom he would ultimately marry, Mary Englesby. In September 1862, Brobst and five of his friends from Gilmanton, Wisconsin, were mustered into Company G of the 25th Wisconsin. Brobst was in his early twenties and not married. "He was of medium height and stocky build, and appeared capable of handling any task involving physical strength," writes Margaret Brobst Roth in an edited collection of Brobst's letters. "John had felt that it was his duty to volunteer for service. His stand on the question of abolition was undecided, but he did think it would be a disgrace to allow the rebellious southern states to secede." [39] After a brief campaign in Minnesota to put down a Native American uprising, the 25th was sent south to Mississippi, where Brobst and his pals would get their first taste of war during 1863, without seeing any major combat. In early 1864 the regiment and many others were ordered to begin moving to Chattanooga, Tennessee, where General William T. Sherman was gathering forces for the Atlanta Campaign that was launched at the beginning of May 1864.

Colonel Charles E. Brown, 63rd Ohio Infantry

Colonel Charles E. Brown, commanding officer of the 63rd Ohio Infantry regiment, lost a leg at the Battle of Decatur.

Colonel Charles E. Brown commanded the 63rd Ohio during the Battle of Decatur. He had just turned 30 years old a few weeks before the battle. Charles Elwood Brown had been born in Cincinnati, Ohio, on July 4, 1834. Orphaned at an early age, he was raised on the farm of his maternal grandfather just east of Cincinnati. In 1854 he graduated from Miami University just north of Cincinnati in Oxford, Ohio. It was there that he got to know classmate Benjamin Harrison, who would later become U.S. president. On his 23rd birthday – July 4, 1857 – Brown married Anna Elizabeth Hussey, the daughter of a doctor from Chillicothe, Ohio. Immediately after the marriage, Brown moved to Baton Rouge, Louisiana, to work as a tutor, and while there he studied law and was admitted to the bar and began practicing law. He returned to Ohio in 1859, practicing law in Chillicothe. In 1859 and 1860 he served as the prosecuting attorney for Ross County. [40] When the Civil War began in 1861, Brown volunteered and helped raise a company of recruits which would become Company B of the 63rd Ohio, and Brown was made the company's captain. The 63rd would see a lot of action in the early part of the war in the west, participating in the operations at New Madrid, Missouri, the capture of Fort Thompson and Island Number 10, the siege of Corinth, Mississippi, and battle at Iuka, Mississippi. At the second battle of Corinth – where 48 percent of the 63rd Ohio's soldiers were killed and wounded – Brown was cited in official reports for his coolness and daring under terrible fire from the Confederates. He was the only officer in the regiment not killed or wounded. [41] Brown's leadership was apparently recognized, as in the later part of 1862 and early part of 1863 he was occasionally given temporary command of the entire 63rd Ohio as its senior captain. In March 1863 he was promoted to lieutenant colonel and would once again occasionally command the entire regiment during periods in 1863 while the 63rd was involved in operations in northern Mississippi and Alabama. A year later, in March 1864, Brown was made the permanent commander of the 63rd. As such he oversaw its movement from Decatur, Alabama, to Chattanooga, Tennessee, for the beginning of the Atlanta Campaign. [42]

Colonel John J. Cladek, 35ᵗʰ New Jersey

John Julius Cladek must have been an interesting personality. At the time of the Battle of Decatur, he had just turned 40 and was in command of one of New Jersey's colorful Zouave units, the 35ᵗʰ New Jersey. Born in March 1824, Cladek was a Hungarian who as a young man served in the Hungarian War of Independence (1848-1849) where he was severely wounded while serving as an artillery officer in the Austrian army. [43] He emigrated to the United States at least by the outbreak of the Civil War in 1861, when he joined the New Jersey Militia as a lieutenant, a rank he may have received due to his prior military service. Just a few months later Cladek was made a captain in the 5ᵗʰ New Jersey Infantry. He left that unit in July 1862 due to illness, then in September 1862 joined the 30ᵗʰ New Jersey Infantry as a lieutenant colonel. Six months later in March 1863 he was made a full colonel. He served with the 30ᵗʰ New Jersey until the summer, when he became colonel of the 35ᵗʰ New Jersey.

Private Chauncey H. Cooke, 25ᵗʰ Wisconsin Infantry

When the Civil War erupted, Chauncey H. Cooke was a 15-year-old Wisconsin boy. In August 1862, now 16, he and a number of other boys from the county where he lived enlisted in the 25ᵗʰ Wisconsin Infantry. During the war, the well-educated and literate Cooke would write descriptive and detail-filled letters home to his family that he later preserved and published. These provide a wonderful look into the experiences of the Federal soldiers who fought at Decatur. Cooke stands out from many of the other young Northern men who went to war, many of whom cared nothing about slaves or slavery. Cooke, on the other hand, was "an idealistic teenager who marched off to preserve the Union and end the evil of slavery," notes William H. Mulligan Jr. in an introduction to a collection of Cooke's letters. "There is little doubt why Cooke enlisted. His father was a staunch abolitionist, and young Cooke, too, was an abolitionist who enlisted to end slavery." [44]

On February 28, 1863, the 25th began its journey south to the war. Cooke would spend the remainder of 1863 and the winter of 1864 in Kentucky, Mississippi and Alabama, and his letters vividly describe his eyewitness experience of slavery, which confirmed all that his father and upbringing had told him about its horrors. Welcomed by former slaves as one of the "Lincoln soldiers," he would find confirmation of what he had read in "Uncle Tom's Cabin," Harriet Beecher Stowe's anti-slavery novel that had been published 11 years earlier. While in Columbus, Kentucky, on the Mississippi River in May 1863, Cooke saw a steamboat from St. Louis at the wharf. "After unloading its freight, the deck hands, all darkies, joined in singing a lot of plantation songs," Cooke would write in a letter to his sister. "I sat on some cotton bales watching them and listening to their curious speech. They gathered on the forecastle of the boat and for more than an hour sang the most pitiful songs of slave life I ever heard. The negroes may not know much, but they sing the most sorrowful songs in the sweetest voices I ever heard." [45] Later that month the 25th would be transported by steamboat to Vicksburg, Mississippi, to take part in the Federal army's siege of that strategic river city. In a June 11, 1863, letter to his sister, Cooke noted how the city's residents were starving and sleepless due to the bombardment by Federal artillery, and that they had dug holes under their houses and in the bluffs to get away from the shot and bursting shells of the Union guns. His views on slavery continued to color his perceptions. "O, but the poor wretched whites that let the rich slaveholders drag them into this war. The negroes tell us the rich white man in the South looks down on the poor white trash who has no slaves, as much as he does on the black man. And the common soldier in the rebel army is awful ignorant. There ain't one in ten that can read or write, and they think the Dutch boys in our army were hired in Germany and came over just to fight them." [46] During the second half of 1863, after the Confederates surrendered in Vicksburg, the 25th would see more service in Mississippi and Arkansas, without any serious combat or big battles. But by the beginning of May 1864, Cooke and the 25th Wisconsin had been moved north into Alabama and were in Decatur and then Huntsville, Alabama, as General William T. Sherman began gathering Federal forces near Chattanooga for the start of the Atlanta Campaign.

Captain Augustus Dusenberry, 35th New Jersey

Augustus Dusenberry of the 35th New Jersey Infantry was captured by the Confederates at the Battle of Decatur and later survived a harrowing escape from a Confederate prison.

Augustus Dusenberry had quite a Civil War service record before joining the 35th New Jersey, which would ultimately bring him to Georgia and the Battle of Decatur [Editor's note: his name is misspelled as Dusenbury in some post-war publications but appears plainly as Dusenberry in service records as well as on his gravestone.]. He had been born in December 1837. When the Civil War began, at the age of 24 in May 1861 he joined the 9th New York Infantry, which was organized in New York City as "a two year regiment." It was also known as "Hawkins' Zouaves." The "Hawkins" referred to its commander, Colonel Rush C. Hawkins, and the "Zouaves" referred to the regiment's distinctive North African-influenced uniform. The unit became known for valor in battle and espirt de corps. Dusenberry was later promoted to corporal and then to sergeant major. At the epic battle of Antietam, Maryland, on September 17, 1862, when the Federal army defeated Confederate General Robert E. Lee's first attempted invasion of the North, Dusenberry was in the middle of some of the most bloody fighting, and he was captured and imprisoned in Richmond, Virginia. He was quickly paroled and exchanged on October 6 and rejoined the regiment. When the regiment reached the end of its two years' service term in May 1863, it was disbanded, but a large majority of its men at once re-enlisted in other units. [47] Dusenberry waited a few months but then on September 18, 1863, joined as captain of Company I of the 35th New Jersey for three years' service. Like the 9th New York, the 35th New Jersey was a "Zouave" unit with a distinctive uniform. [48]

Milton Montgomery, 25th Wisconsin Infantry

Milton Montgomery commanded one of the Federal infantry regiments at the Battle of Decatur, the 25th Wisconsin, and his life would change forever that day. By July 1864, Montgomery was 39 years old. He had been born in May 1825 in Ohio. In 1840 his family moved to Wisconsin, settling in the town of Sparta in the southwest of the state. Montgomery became a lawyer, married and had a son, named Carroll, in 1851. Montgomery was practicing law when the Civil War broke out in 1861. In the summer of 1862 he raised a company of volunteers that became part of the 25th Wisconsin Volunteer Infantry, and Montgomery was placed in command of the regiment with the rank of colonel. [49] The 25th was sent to Mississippi, where Montgomery commanded a brigade that included the 40th Iowa, 3rd Minnesota, 25th Wisconsin and 27th Wisconsin. [50] Today there's a bronze monument in the Vicksburg National Military Park with a relief portrait of Montgomery which was erected in 1913. [51]

John A. Nourse, Chicago Board of Trade Battery

For John A. Nourse, the Civil War began with lemonade, a sandwich, and a bouquet of flowers. [52] Nourse was a 17-year-old Chicago boy (born 1845) who in the summer of 1862 got swept up in the patriotic fervor sweeping Chicago. On July 22, 1862, the Board of Trade of Chicago began recruiting enlistees for a new artillery battery that it would pay for and equip. Nourse, his brother Frank and two friends, Thomas Wygant and William Taylor, enrolled their names, and the roster was filled before the day was over. Each enlistee would receive a bounty of $100. "As I was quite young and small," Nourse would recall, "a number of persons who were desirous of joining the company ridiculed me, stating that I would not stand the service, and that the U.S. officer would refuse me when he came to muster the command. One individual went so far as to offer me one thousand dollars, if I would withdraw my name in his favor. But as I felt very patriotic, money was no object."

The next day, after bidding goodbye to their father, mother, sisters and brother, Nourse and his brother reported to the Board of Trade. He and the other new recruits were marched to a nearby U.S. Army camp. "We were escorted by a full band provided by the Board of Trade as far as 22nd Street. We halted on our way at the residence of John Hancock, where we were each furnished with what lemonade we could drink, a sandwich, and a bouquet of flowers."

Nourse, who was a very thoughtful, educated and intelligent observer, would begin keeping a detailed diary of his Civil War experiences, which provides a window into the Chicago Board of Trade Battery's distinguished service in the war. The weeks following the battery's muster were filled with drilling, organizing, and equipping. On September 23rd, two months after the unit formed, it started south into Kentucky. During the latter part of 1862 it would move with the Federal army further south into Tennessee.

There, during three days spanning the end of 1862 and the beginning of 1863, it would fight its first major battle, the great Battle of Stones River, also known as the Battle of Murfreesboro, in which the battery would play a pivotal role in stopping the final Confederate attack. "This is a day long to be remembered," Nourse wrote on December 31. At one point, "As the rebels came up the hill, we just poured the articles of war into them. The ground was piled up with dead and wounded rebels after they returned to the woods." [53] Many of Nourse's comrades were shot down. "Andrew Finney and W.H. Wiley were instantly killed by a shell at gun No. 3. J.S. Stagg of No. 2 was killed by a round shot. Corpl. A.H. Carver, shot through the bowels, dead. Sergt. A.L. Adams, wounded by a shell on the ankle bone. J.W. Blume [sic, Bloom] burnt by powder. J.C. Camberg shot through the calf of the leg. W.H.S. Odell struck by the concussion of a shell. Lieut. T.D. Griffen [sic, Griffin] shot through the body." While Nourse emerged from the battle unharmed, "I received as close a call from the 'Johnnies' as I want. As I was holding my saddle horse, a bullet passed through his leg, and cut a crease in my pants." After a relatively quiet January 1 while the fighting raged on other parts of the battle field, on January 2 the Chicago Board of Trade Battery was called on to help save the day when a Confederate attack threatened to crush the left flank of the Federal line. [Editor's note: "Left" and "Right" are terms commonly used to describe the positions of forces on a battlefield from the perspective of a viewer to the rear of the forces. Thus, on Civil War battlefields, the Federal left would be opposite the Confederate right, while the Confederate left would be opposite the Federal right, as shown in the diagram below.]

Federal forces

Right

Left

Left

Right

Confederate forces

"At four o'clock, the rebels advanced their right, driving our troops before them like scattered sheep," Nourse wrote. In a scene that's now famous in Civil War history, Federal General James S. Negley quickly organized a counterattack. Riding up to the Chicago Board of Trade Battery, he asked for help. The battery got into position and began to blast away. "We opened lively and soon stopped the 'Butternuts' [Editor's note: Many Confederate soldiers did not wear grey uniforms, but home-made uniforms that were died a brownish tan color known as Butternut, hence they were often called "Butternuts"], who in turn fled faster than our men had done before, throwing away everything that impeded their flight, and muskets and equipment covered the ground. We followed them across the ford [across Stones River] within one mile of Murfreesboro, then darkness shut down its quiet cover over the sights of horror. General Negley rode over to us, saying 'I cannot bestow too many thanks upon the Board of Trade Battery as it has won the day.' The ground was littered with everything that could belong to a soldier, and the dead rebels lay so thick in the ground that we could not draw the guns across the field until the bodies had been removed, allowing us to pass."

Nourse and the battery would spend the rest of 1863 in service in Tennessee and Alabama. The battery would see its next major combat in September 1863 at great Battle of Chickamauga, Georgia, just south of Chattanooga. When not in combat, Nourse's daily concerns often revolved around basic things that are very important to any soldier: food, the weather, letters from home, and whether the battery was going to be on the move. His diary records the battery's movement, the weather, the coming and going of comrades, and thoughts of home. Early on the morning of November 24, 1863, he lay awake in camp in Maysville, Alabama, watching an eclipse of the moon. Two months later while in winter camp in Huntsville, Alabama, on the afternoon of February 1, 1864, on a beautiful day and surrounded by green fields, the men of the battery split into teams and played a game of baseball. The fun did not last long. The beginning of May 1864 brought the beginning of the Atlanta Campaign, and the Chicago Board of Trade Battery would be right in the middle of it, attached to a Federal cavalry division.

David S. Oliphant, 35th New Jersey Infantry

The Battle of Decatur would lead a young New Jersey man named David S. Oliphant to an epic adventure. Oliphant grew up in Monmouth County, New Jersey. He was born in June 1841 in Barnegat, New Jersey, one of six children. His parents were of Dutch ancestry, some of the many Dutch immigrants who chose New Jersey as a new home during the 1600s. The Civil War came just as David turned 20, and like many young men he was swept up by the war. He enlisted on August 7, 1861, in the 6th Regiment of New Jersey Volunteers, serving as a corporal and second sergeant. While with the 6th New Jersey he participated in many important battles, including the siege of Yorktown; Williamsburg, Virginia; Fair Oaks, Virginia; Savage Station, Virginia; Malvern Hill, Virginia; the Second Battle of Bull Run, Virginia; Chancellorsville, Virginia; and Gettysburg, Pennsylvania. At Second Bull Run he was taken prisoner by the forces of Confederate General James Longstreet, but was paroled and exchanged in time to take part in the Fredericksburg campaign. In October 1863 he was discharged so he could become a second lieutenant in Company D of the 35th New Jersey, which had just been formed. With the 35th he took part in the Meridian, Mississippi, expedition. During the Atlanta Campaign he was at the battles of Resaca, New Hope Church, Big Shanty, Kennesaw Mountain, and Ruffs Mill. So by the time of the Battle of Decatur he was no stranger to combat. [54]

Isaiah R. Rose, 63rd Ohio Volunteer Infantry

Isaiah R. Rose was a young Ohio farm boy who joined the Union Army with his younger brother, and both wound up fighting in the Battle of Decatur. Isaiah would survive the battle, while his brother did not. Isaiah Rose was born in June 1842 on a farm in Belmont County, Ohio, near the state's eastern border with Pennsylvania southwest of Pittsburgh. When he was small, his family moved a little south to the small town of Coal Run in Washington County. With the beginning of the Civil War, and now the age of 18, Rose enlisted in the U.S. Army, first serving three months in the 18th Regiment Ohio Volunteer Infantry. When that term was up, he enlisted in Company F of the 63rd Ohio Volunteer Infantry. His brother Thompson, who was two years younger, also enlisted in Company F. [55]

Jeremiah M. Rusk, 25th Wisconsin Volunteer Infantry

Jeremiah McLain Rusk's father was one of the pioneering white settlers of the Muskingum Valley in Ohio in 1829. At the time Ohio was the far west of the young United States. It was there in June 1830 that Jeremiah M. Rusk was born, the youngest of 11 children. Jeremiah, who became known to all as "Jerry" and later "Uncle Jerry," was blessed with a powerful physique and commanding presence, which would serve him well in his future life. He became an excellent horseman, and as a young man took a job driving stage coaches. Early in his life he became friends with another young Ohioan who would rise to national political prominence, future U.S. President James A. Garfield. Rusk later started a barrel-making business which he followed until 1853 when he moved westward with his wife and their two infant children to Viroqua, Wisconsin, a small town about midway between Milwaukee and Minneapolis. There he became a tavern keeper and ran a stage coach line. He also became the county's sheriff. Rusk's rise to national prominence began in 1861 when he was elected to the Wisconsin legislature. With the outbreak of the Civil War, Rusk received a commission from Wisconsin's governor to raise a regiment of infantry, which would become the 25th Wisconsin. [56]

John M. Shaw, 25th Wisconsin Infantry

John M. Shaw served as captain of Company E of the 25th Wisconsin. Born on December 18, 1833, in Maine, his family moved when he was 20 in 1853 to Galena, Illinois, driven by "financial reverses" to become part of the great American migration to the promising new lands of the west. A few months after arriving in Illinois, Shaw's father died, and at the age of 19 he became head of the family. "Continuing to live at Galena, in the household for which he felt responsible, he toiled for five years as book-keeper and shipping clerk for a wholesale grocery concern, in reality working as two men, for the salary of one," notes a biography of Shaw. [57] "Meantime he had never abandoned the idea of acquiring a legal education, and all his spare time was devoted to reading elementary law books," according to a history of the city of Minneapolis, where Shaw would go on to have a distinguished career after the Civil War. "In 1860 he was able to enter a law office in Galena, and in about a year was admitted to practice. In 1861 he removed to Plattsville, Wis., and opened an office. Before, however, he had fairly established a practice in that town, his patriotic feeling led him to obey the call of his country, and he enlisted in the 25th Wisconsin Regiment." [58] Shaw and his law partner, John G. Scott, raised what became Company E of the 25th Wisconsin Infantry, in September 1862. Scott became the company's captain, and Shaw was made its second lieutenant. Probably because of his bookkeeping talents, he was made an assistant quartermaster later in 1862 and then, no doubt because of his work at an attorney, he was made the regiment's acting judge-advocate of the general court-martial in Columbus, Kentucky, in 1863. In May 1864, when Captain Scott died, Shaw was promoted to captain and participated in the Atlanta Campaign. [59]

John W. Sprague, Second Brigade, Fourth Division of the 16th Army Corps

The officer who commanded the Federal forces at the Battle of Decatur, John Wilson Sprague, was born on April 4, 1817, in White Creek, New York, a small town in Washington County in upstate New York between Albany and Montreal. While young he moved with his father to nearby Troy, New York, where he attended the public schools. He also attended the Rensselaer Polytechnic Institute, but did not

A Civil War photograph of General John W. Sprague, seated center, and his staff.

graduate. At the age of 23, he started a wholesale and retail grocery business in Troy. After five years, he moved to Huron, Ohio, a town on Lake Erie west of Cleveland, where he was in the shipping business with sail boats and steamers. He married and the union produced a daughter, but his first wife died before they had been married a year. He remarried, the second union producing four sons. [60] When the Civil War began in April 1861, Sprague raised a company of volunteers and reported to Camp Taylor, near Cleveland. The company became part of in the 7th Ohio Volunteers, and Sprague was made a captain. The regiment was sent to West Virginia where, in August 1861, Sprague was captured by Confederate cavalry. He was taken as a prisoner to Richmond, Virginia, where he was kept for a month and a half, then transferred to Charleston, South Carolina, then to Columbia, South Carolina. Fortunately for Sprague, in January 1862 he was exchanged in a prisoner swap and sent home.

The governor of Ohio, David Tod, commissioned the newly freed Sprague colonel of the newly formed 63rd Ohio Volunteer Infantry, which was created by consolidating the 22nd Ohio with the 63rd Ohio, with the regiment keeping the latter's name. [61] Oscar L. Jackson, then a second lieutenant in the 22nd Ohio, thought it was "an injustice to the 22nd to obliterate it, but it was done in order to give Captain Sprague a colonelcy, as he had influence with Governor Todd (sic)." [62] During the next six months Sprague and the 63rd would move from Ohio to Kentucky and then to Missouri, where it saw its first actions at New Madrid, Fort Thompson and Island Number Ten. The regiment was then sent south to Tennessee to join General Ulysses S. Grant's army. The 63rd missed the bloody battle of Shiloh, but participated in the capture of the nearby town of Corinth, Mississippi, a strategic railroad junction. The first major baptism of fire for Sprague and the 63rd came on October 4, 1862, when Sprague commanded the 63rd in the bloody second battle of Corinth, Mississippi, where almost half of the soldiers of the 63rd were killed or wounded. "Colonel J.W. Sprague, whose regiment had the most exposed position, stood at his post cheering his men on when two-thirds of his officers and half his command had fallen, and in an incredibly short space of time reformed his men and brought them again into line," [63] recalled Colonel John W. Fuller. At an 1878 reunion of the "Ohio Brigade," then-General Fuller again called out Sprague. "I shall always recollect how well Sprague looked at that eventful moment. Tall, and commanding in appearance, with sword in one hand and pistol in the other, he stood as a painter likes to portray an officer in battle." [64]

Captain Oscar L. Jackson provides a vivid description of Sprague in combat that day. The 63rd had repulsed one Confederate attack, and then the rebels charged again. "Colonel Sprague had all the while been in the thickest of the fight," Jackson recalled in his diary. "I think I see him now rush to where the line wavered and with sabre sweeping the air, exclaim, 'What does this mean, men? Company ﹘﹘﹘, close up!' He then spoke and said, 'Men, it is your time to cheer now,' and with a hearty good will did they respond." [65] Sprague and the 63rd would spend the remainder of 1862 and most of 1863 conducting operations in northern Alabama and Mississippi. Jackson relates how, during a November 1862 raid at the small town of Prospect, Tennessee, just north of the Alabama state line, the 63rd camped at a farm and Sprague ordered the soldiers not to burn the farm's fence rails for fire wood. But a few hours later Sprague found out the farm was owned by a man then serving in the Confederate army, and countermanded the order "to the great suffering of all fences." On March 8, 1864, Sprague had a near miss with death. The 63rd conducted a daring, nighttime amphibious assault on the Tennessee River town of Decatur, Alabama, crossing from the northern bank in small row boats and quietly floating downstream to attack the town on the southern bank. Confederate sentinels, hearing the approaching Federals, fired a few shots at them, one of which struck Sprague's pistol, which deflected the bullet "and evidently saved his life," Jackson recalled. The sentinels then fled, and the Federals took the town. Just after the capture of Decatur, Alabama, General Grenville M. Dodge formed a new brigade composed of the 43rd Ohio, 63rd Ohio, 25th Wisconsin and 35th New Jersey, known as the Second Brigade, Fourth Division of the 16th Army Corps, and Colonel Sprague was named its commander. (The organization of this brigade determined which units would later fight in the Battle of Decatur, Georgia.) By this time Sprague had just turned 47 years old. On May 1, 1864, Sprague's brigade moved from Decatur, Alabama, to Chattanooga to join the main force of the Army of the Tennessee for the beginning of the Atlanta Campaign. [66]

Daniel T. Thorne, 63rd Ohio Volunteer Infantry

Daniel T. Thorne was a resident of Dayton, Ohio, who in the late summer of 1862 at the age of 34 began with others to recruit men for a new regiment. Thorne himself formally enlisted for three years on August 11, 1862. The volunteers became part of the 63rd Ohio and were transferred

Captain Daniel T. Thorne, left, with Private Alfred Piffley.

to the regiment, which was then in northern Mississippi. In recognition of his recruiting services, Thorne was made a captain in Company K. A short biography of him says, "He came to the army a civilian without any previous military training, but with a captain's commission, in a regiment that had then seen long and hard service in the field. He was placed in command of a company, a large part of whose members were old soldiers and he had thus a very difficult position to fill. He at once devoted himself faithfully to acquiring a knowledge of his duties as an officer." Thorne "was kind to his men, faithful in the performance of duty, and as soon as the occasion offered he showed himself a brave and gallant soldier" who "had acquired the confidence of his company, the respect of his fellow officers and was regarded as being one of the best officers in the regiment." [67] Thorne took part with the 63rd in operations in northern Mississippi and Tennessee, and in March 1864 took part in the capture of Decatur, Alabama. Two months later, Thorne would move with the 63rd to Chattanooga and then south into Georgia at the start of the Atlanta Campaign.

Now, let's learn about the Confederates who were opposing the Federals.

III

The Confederates

The Confederates who fought at the Battle of Decatur were mostly units of Wheeler's Cavalry, a famous mounted unit formed in 1862 when the then-Colonel Joseph Wheeler was given command of portions of seven Alabama and Mississippi regiments to conduct raids on Federal lines, destroy bridges, obstruct fords and otherwise delay the approach of the enemy. [1] Thanks to the favor of Confederate General Braxton Bragg, Wheeler was made a brigadier general in October 1862 and took full command of the cavalry of the Army of Tennessee a month later. [2] Wheeler's Cavalry rode thousands of miles during the Civil War, all through Kentucky and Tennessee, down through Georgia to Atlanta, south to Savannah during the March To The Sea, and then up into South Carolina and North Carolina as the Civil War neared its end. When thinking of cavalry, modern readers may think of riders on horseback with sabers. But this does not accurately describe Wheeler's horsemen. During 1863, especially, they would act like more traditional cavalry, raiding behind Federal lines and attacking and destroying Federal wagon trains loaded with supplies. But by the beginning of the Atlanta Campaign they acted more like mobile infantry (something like today's helicopter-borne airborne infantry) who used their horses to transport them to the battlefield, where they would fight dismounted like infantry.

Wheeler's Cavalry would see near continuous service at the battles of Perryville, Murfreesboro, Chickamauga, the siege of Knoxville, and the Confederate retreat from Missionary Ridge after the Federal army took

Chattanooga. Some of the very first shots of the Atlanta Campaign were fired in late April 1864 when soldiers of Wheeler's Cavalry skirmished with soldiers of the giant Federal army under General William T. Sherman who were already moving south out of Chattanooga. [3] Wheeler's Cavalry would then fight almost nonstop as the Federal army pushed the Confederates south from Chattanooga toward Atlanta, being in the battles of Ringgold, Rocky Face, Dalton, Resaca, Cassville, New Hope, Kennesaw Mountain, Peachtree Creek, and then Decatur. [4] The units that made up Wheeler's Cavalry as of July 10, 1864, (at the time of the Battle of Decatur) included: [5]

Martin's Division, led by Major General William T. Martin

Allen's Brigade
>1st Alabama, Lieutenant Colonel D.T. Blakey
>3d Alabama, Colonel James Hagan
>4th Alabama, Colonel Alfred A. Russell
>7th Alabama, Captain George Mason
>51st Alabama, Colonel M.L. Kirkpatrick
>12th Alabama Battalion, Captain Warren S. Reese

Iverson's Brigade
>1st Georgia, Lieutenant Colonel James H. Strickland
>2d Georgia, Colonel James W. Mayo
>3d Georgia, Colonel Robert Thompson
>4th Georgia, Major Augustus R. Stewart
>6th Georgia, Colonel John R. Hart

Hume's Division

Ashby's Brigade
>1st [6th] Tennessee, Colonel James T. Wheeler
>2d Tennessee, Captain William M. Smith

5th Tennessee, Colonel George W. McKenzie
9th Tennessee Battalion, Major James H. Akin

Harrison's Brigade
3d Arkansas, Colonel Amson W. Hobson
4th Tennessee
8th Texas, Lieutenant Colonel Gustave Cook
11th Texas, Colonel George R. Reeves

Kelly's Division

Dibrell's Brigade
4th Tennessee, Colonel William S. McLemore
8th Tennessee, Captain Jefferson Leftwich
9th Tennessee, Captain James M. Reynolds
10th Tennessee, Major John Minor

Anderson's Brigade
3d Confederate, Lieutenant Colonel John McCaskill
8th Confederate, Lieutenant Colonel John S. Prather
10th Confederate, Captain W.J. Vason
12th Confederate, Captain Charles H. Conner
5th Georgia, Lieutenant Colonel Edward Bird

Williams' Brigade
1st [3d] Kentucky, Colonel J.R. Butler
2d Kentucky (Woodward's regiment), Major Thomas W. Lewis
9th Kentucky Battalion, Captain John B. Dortch
Allison's (Tennessee) Squadron, Captain J.S. Reese
Hamilton's (Tennessee) Battalion, Major Joseph Shaw

Hannon's Brigade
53d Alabama, Lieutenant Col. John F. Gaines
24th Alabama Battalion, Major Robert B. Snodgrass

Ferguson's Brigade of Confederate cavalry was actually part of Brigadier Gen. William H. Jackson's Cavalry Division, not Wheeler's Cavalry, but it fought with Wheeler during the Atlanta Campaign and led the main Confederate attack at Decatur: [6]

>Ferguson's Brigade, Brigadier General Samuel W. Ferguson
>>2d Alabama, Lieutenant Colonel John N. Carpenter
>>56th Alabama, Colonel William Boyles
>>12th Mississippi Battalion, Colonel William M. Inge
>>Miller's (Mississippi) regiment, Colonel Horace H. Miller
>>Perrin's (Mississippi) regiment, Colonel Robert O. Perrin
>>Scout Company (Mississippi Cavalry), Captain Thomas C. Flournoy

The lives of Wheeler's horsemen were focused on fighting, riding and food. What did these Southern horsemen look like? "The cavalry under Wheeler, as well as most of the other cavalry units of Bragg's army, was possibly the most nondescript of all the fighting forces of the Confederacy," historian John P. Dyer notes in his biography of Wheeler. "At the outbreak of the war they had quit their farms and, mounting whatever animal they might have handy, had ridden to join the army. Part of them were formally mustered into service but some never were. Some of them had been issued horses, saddles, pistols, and sabers. Many equipped themselves at the expense of dead 'Yankees' on the field. Gaunt, bearded fellows, unaccustomed to discipline, they roved and raided friend and foe alike. If there was whiskey they got drunk. If there was food to be had for themselves or their horses, they took it with little regard for the source." [7]

Now let's look at some of the individual Confederates who would play prominent roles at the Battle of Decatur.

Mary A.H. Gay

Mary Gay would not be remembered today were it not for the book she published in 1892, 27 years after the Civil War ended. "Life in Dixie During The War" is a classic example of the Lost Cause genre that

Decatur resident Mary A.H. Gay, whose home was just north of the Decatur square, witnessed the Battle of Decatur and later wrote about it in her book, "Life in Dixie During The War".

sought to celebrate the antebellum South and the heroic cause of the Confederacy and the men who fought and died for it, like her half-brother Thomie Stokes. Many economically better-off Southern white women fervently supported the South's secession from the Union. Gay was one of these. A Decatur, Georgia, resident, at the time of the Civil War she lived with her mother and a couple of slave servants in a house just north of the town square. Through her writings we can gain insight into how this class of Southern women wanted to remember the Civil War and its aftermath, and what it was like to live in Decatur when the war came to her doorstep.

Mary Ann Harris Gay was born on her grandfather's farm near Macon, Georgia, in March 1829. Gay's grandfather was a slave owner whose brutal treatment of his slaves was described in an 1855 auto-biography of one of his former slaves that was published in England,

"Slave Life in Georgia: A Narrative of the Life, Sufferings, and Escape of John Brown". In a 2009 essay about Gay, Michelle Gillespie writes that "Brown's account, much of which has been verified in state and county records, provides a crucial foundation from which to grapple with Mary Gay's lifelong racist assumptions about slavery, slaves and race relations. Her later insistence on the benevolence with which she and her mother and sister acted as slaveholders during the Civil War may mark an implicit acknowledgment of her grandfather's cruel treatment of his slaves, as well as a pained reaction to John Brown's published portrait of her grandfather as a brutal master." [8] In the early 1830s Gay's widowed mother would move to the recently settled (1823) courthouse town of Decatur, Georgia, county seat of the newly formed DeKalb County, where her grandfather had business dealings. Her mother there married a lawyer and had a son, Thomas, followed by a second daughter, Missouria. The young family spent time in northwest Georgia. When Mary's step father died in 1850, mom and kids moved back to Decatur. The young Mary never married. In 1858 at the age of 29, Gay published her first book, a volume titled "Prose and Poetry." In a testament to her strong feelings about the righteousness of the South's cause, when the Southern states formed the Confederacy, Gay and some family members went to Montgomery, Alabama, to see the inauguration of President Jefferson Davis. Three years later the war would come to Gay's doorstep on July 19, 1864, when the Federal army arrived at Decatur, and General Kenner Garrard, then commanding cavalry, made the Gays' large lot his staff's headquarters.

General Samuel W. Ferguson

When Wheeler's Cavalry attacked at Decatur, commanding one of its brigades was a 29-year-old South Carolinian named Samuel Wragg Ferguson. Ferguson is a great example of the socio-economic class that led the South into the war. Late in his life Ferguson would pen a memoir, thanks to which we know about his fascinating life and how it led

Confederate General Samuel W. Ferguson commanded one of
the Confederate brigades at the Battle of Decatur. A native of
Charleston, South Carolina, he had witnessed the start of the
Civil War and was on hand when Fort Sumter surrendered.

him to the Battle of Decatur. Ferguson was born in Charleston, South
Carolina, on November 3, 1834, to a prominent and wealthy slave-owning family. They lived on a plantation, and his father was in the shipping business. The young Sam Ferguson was one of 11 children, only
five of whom would live to maturity. He enjoyed a privileged childhood,
beginning his education with a private tutor. "A servant accompanied
me to school, took my horse, and brought it for me in the afternoon,"
Ferguson would recall. (Contrast his education with the famous poverty
of Abraham Lincoln, who as a young man once walked six miles to bor-
row a grammar book from a neighbor.) [9] Later Ferguson would be sent
to a private school. His education would include Latin and Greek, and
private lessons in mathematics, French and line drawing. [10] Ferguson
had planned to attend the University of South Carolina in Columbia,
but instead received an appointment to the U.S. Military Academy at

West Point, a distinction apparently secured by his father. "I had promised my father to go, and I knew that his heart was set on it," Ferguson said.

Ferguson entered West Point in 1852. In his memoir he recounts frequently getting into trouble, yet he managed to not get thrown out. He graduated in 1857 a sergeant of cavalry, 18th in his class and having more demerits than any other man in his class. "I never held any office in the Corps [of Cadets], always behaved too badly for that." Writing of his life "at the Point", Ferguson would say "It was full of wasted opportunities, and youthful follies, and at the same time often seemed hard and monotonous, but I look back on it now with pleasure, and as perhaps the happiest part of my life." [11] At the time he graduated, the U.S. Army was organizing an expedition to the Mormons in Utah. Ferguson volunteered to take part and was accepted. He traveled by rail and riverboat to Kansas, where he had the opportunity to go on a buffalo hunt. He then would join the army column headed west, crossing the Rocky Mountains in winter. In the spring they would march down into the valley of the Great Salt Lake and into Salt Lake City, where the issue with the Mormons was resolved peacefully. Ferguson would spend some months in the west before being recalled east to become a lieutenant in the Dragoons. He returned to Charleston in time to spend his first Christmas there since 1851, and spent several months at home. In a testament of Ferguson's elite social standing, in the spring he was invited to travel to Virginia to be a groomsman in the wedding of William Henry Fitzhugh Lee, son of Robert E. Lee. Soon afterward he was ordered to a frontier post in Oregon, which he reached by steamship via Havana, the Isthmus of Panama and San Francisco. After a monotonous life in the garrison, at Christmas 1860 Ferguson learned of the election of Abraham Lincoln and the movement by Southern states to secede. He started immediately to return home to South Carolina. While in San Francisco awaiting a steamer, Ferguson would speak with James McPherson, then an officer in the U.S. Army engineers, who "tried very hard to persuade me not to resign" from the U.S. Army, Ferguson recounted. "He was a noble fellow and distressed at the prospects of the dissolution of the Union." (McPherson was later killed at the Battle of Atlanta, while Ferguson was fighting McPherson's soldiers a few miles away in Decatur.) Ferguson arrived in Charleston on May 1, 1861. [12] There he would have a part in the beginning of the Civil War. Having resigned his commission in the U.S. Army, Ferguson was made a first lieutenant in the Confederate army and an aide to General P.G.T. Beauregard, who had taken command of the Confederate forces in Charleston. "Before we opened fire on Fort Sumter, I went three or four times to that fortress with flag of truce," Wragg recalled. "An agreement was entered into between Gen. Beauregard and Maj. [Robert] Anderson, the Commander of the Fort, by which the latter was allowed to purchase one day's supply, each day, of certain articles, the intention being to avoid subjecting the Garrison to unnecessary hardship, and at the same time not to allow them to accumulate food enough to stand a siege. I knew all the officers of the Garrison, some intimately, two of them, Sneider and Mead had been class mates, so when I was sitting waiting for a reply to the communication I had taken under flag of truce, we conversed freely." Ferguson would later take cigars, brandy and whiskey to his friends at the fort. [13] From the steeple of St. Michael's Church, Ferguson watched the firing of the first shot of the war, a shell from a Confederate mortar battery. After Fort Sumter's surrender following a 33-hour bombardment, he was ordered to go out to it where he was among the officers to receive Major Anderson's surrender. Ferguson also assisted in raising the Confederate flag over the fort. Ferguson next traveled with General Beauregard to Virginia, where just before the First Battle of Bull Run on July 18, "I was under infantry fire for the first time, and I cannot say that I liked it, or ever got to like it."

In February 1862, Beauregard with his staff was transferred to Mississippi, where the war in the so-called "Western Theater" was heating up as Federal forces under General Ulysses S. Grant pushed south into Tennessee. Ferguson went with Beauregard and was made a lieutenant colonel of the 28th Mississippi Cavalry. In April 1862, Ferguson rejoined

Beauregard in Corinth, Mississippi, and took part in the Confederate attack on Grant's forces just across the Tennessee state line at the great, bloody Battle of Shiloh. Ferguson spent most of the next two years fighting Federals in Mississippi and Alabama. While in Mississippi, during a fight between his troops and a mounted Federal patrol, Ferguson shot three Federals with his pistol, including one who he shot dead in the head at point blank range. Later, Ferguson would have another adventure of a different sort in Mississippi, marrying Kate Lee, a relative of Confederate General Robert E. Lee. [14] In July 1863, Ferguson was commissioned a brigadier general of cavalry. [15] In February 1864, Ferguson's command opposed General William T. Sherman's march on Meridian, Mississippi. Ferguson was next ordered to report with his command to Confederate General Joseph Johnston in northwest Georgia, where the Confederates were massing forces to oppose the Federals' expected campaign southward from Chattanooga to capture Atlanta. There, Ferguson's command would join the large Confederate cavalry force commanded by General Joseph Wheeler.

George Knox Miller

What was it like to be one of the Confederate soldiers who fought at the Battle of Decatur? Memoirs and letters written by the men of Wheeler's Cavalry are scarce. One great exception is a collection of letters written by a young Alabamian, Knox Miller. Miller was an educated and well-read young man from a prosperous, slave-owning family in Talladega, Alabama. Born on December 30, 1836, he was an avid reader with an interest in theater who earned two diplomas from the University of Virginia in 1859 and 1860. While at the university in April 1861, Virginia seceded from the union and Miller left school to return home and enter the Confederate service. He ultimately became an officer in the 8th Confederate Cavalry, which was part of Wheeler's Cavalry. Fortunately for the historian, Miller would write (and later preserve) numerous long and detailed letters to his wife Celestine that provide wonderful eye-witness accounts of what it was like to serve in Wheeler's Cavalry. "Miller's letters ... give us many valuable insights into the life, heart, mind, and attitudes of an intelligent, educated, young, mid-nineteenth century white Southerner, his hopes, ambitions, and fears, as well as his role as a cavalry line officer in the all-important western theater," notes Richard M. McMurry, editor of a collection of Miller's letters.[16]

William L. Nugent, Ferguson's Brigade of Wheeler's Cavalry

Additional insight into the war experiences of Wheeler's Cavalry is provided by the letters written by William L. Nugent, an officer in Ferguson's Brigade, to his wife Eleanor, who was known as Nellie. Ferguson was born in Louisiana in 1832 and was well educated, graduating with honors from Centenary College in 1852. He later moved to Greenville, Mississippi, then a pioneer village, where he became a tutor to the children of a plantation owner, including a daughter, Eleanor. Nugent later began practicing law in 1854, traveling widely and practicing his profession in the slave-holding plantation economy in the Mississippi Delta region. In November 1860 he and Eleanor married. With the coming of the war, Nugent enlisted in March 1862 in a Mississippi cavalry unit which ultimately became part of the brigade of General Samuel W. Ferguson. During 1862, 1863 and early 1864 it saw service (but no major combat) in Mississippi, northern Alabama and Tennessee. Nugent was made the regiment's adjutant in August 1863. Writing to Nellie on September 7, 1863, after almost a year and a half of war and just two months after the decisive Confederate defeats at Gettysburg and Vicksburg, Nugent gave his thoughts on the conflict and its causes. Not surprisingly, his views reflect those of the class of Southerners who supported the war and the continuance of slavery. "War is fast becoming the thing natural, tho' abhorrent to my feelings. I go at it just as I used to go at law-suits. Still I am not by any manner of means fond of the profession. The idea of being continually employed in the destruction of human life is revolting in the extreme," he wrote. "...I wish Uncl. Saml. would recognize his nephew and give us peace. I do not desire a reconstruction & a hollow truce, a servile place in the family of nations and to eat the bread of dependence while I am denied all the privileges of a freeman." He then expressed his support for slavery. "I own no slaves and can freely express my notions, without being taxed with any motive of self interest. I know that this country without slave labor would be wholly worthless, a barren waste and desolate plain – We can only live & exist by this species of labor: and hence I am willing to continue the fight to the last. If we have to succumb we must do it bravely fighting for our rights; and the remnant must migrate. If the worst comes, we must go over to England or France, and become Colonies again. Never will I be content to submit to Yankee rule." [17]

General Joseph Wheeler

Who was the man who led the Confederate attack at the Battle of Decatur? "Fightin' Joe" Wheeler – who was also known by his troopers as "War Child" [18] – was a small man, just five feet, five inches tall and weighing about 125 pounds. Wheeler's small physical stature is perhaps a metaphor for his historical legacy, which is today overshadowed by more famous Confederate cavalry generals such as James Ewell Brown "Jeb" Stuart, Nathan Bedford Forrest, Wade Hampton, John S. Mosby, and John Hunt Morgan. But Wheeler built a fine combat record, and no cavalryman, Federal or Confederate, played a larger role in the Atlanta Campaign than Wheeler. Historian Albert Castel notes that, "Wheeler lacks the panache of Stuart and the genius of Forrest, but he is aggressive, possesses iron nerves and endurance."[19] Edward G. Longacre, author of a 2007 biography of Wheeler, has noted that some historians "have portrayed Wheeler as a leader who failed to inspire or discipline his troops, who was neither an adept tactician (despite authoring a wartime treatise on mounted infantry tactics) nor a skillful gatherer of enemy intelligence, and whose ambition-driven support of equally inept superiors –

especially Braxton Bragg, the army's longest-tenured commander – retarded rather than advanced Confederate fortunes in the western theater of the war. To some degree, each of these criticisms has merit; but each is also overblown. To be sure, both as an administrator and as a combat leader Joe Wheeler had his flaws and limitations...Wheeler's deficiencies as a field commander were counterbalanced by certain gifts and strengths. If he fared poorly when operating beyond the reach of his superiors, he was adept at close tactical support of the main army, a skill shared by few cavalry leaders in the West. If he sometimes failed to tap the intelligence-gathering potential of his command, he usually did a creditable job of keeping Bragg and his successors informed of enemy positions, movements, and intentions. ...Wheeler may not have made the most of his opportunities when on the offensive, but he could be counted on to defend his army's front, rear, and flanks with skill and dogged determination." [20]

Although he fought for the South, Wheeler's roots were in the North. Wheeler's father, also named Joseph, had moved from New England to Augusta, Georgia, in 1819, with the aim of making money in the Georgia cotton country. After his first wife died shortly after their arrival at Augusta, Joseph Wheeler remarried. His new wife would bear him four children, including a boy born on September 10, 1836, who they named Joseph. When his father's business in Georgia failed, the family returned to Connecticut. It was there that the young Joseph was educated. Rather than go into business like his father, the younger Joseph wanted a military career, and a family connection helped him get an appointment to the U.S. Military Academy at West Point, where he started in 1854. He graduated in 1859 without leaving a distinguished record. He was made a second lieutenant in the cavalry, and sent to New Mexico with the army. His stay in the West would be short, however, as a growing political crisis was brewing back east amid talk of seccession. Wheeler let his brother back home in Georgia know that if his services were needed by his home state, he would resign his commission in the U.S. Army and return home. In January 1861, Georgia seceded from the

Union, and Wheeler was made a lieutenant in the forces being formed by the state for the coming conflict. [21]

Wheeler rose rapidly through the Confederate ranks. While serving in Pensacola, Florida, he was promoted to colonel and given command of the 19th Alabama infantry regiment. It was with this regiment that Wheeler got his first big taste of combat at the bloody Battle of Shiloh in Tennessee in April 1862. [22] Later, Confederate General Braxton Bragg put most of the Army of Tennessee's cavalry under Wheeler's command, snubbing Confederate cavalry leader Nathan Bedford Forrest, who was much older than Wheeler and had an outstanding service record. "General Bragg did not appreciate Forrest; he did not like the man," [23] historian John Witherspoon DuBose notes in his history of Wheeler's Cavalry. Forrest apparently had expected to be placed in charge of the Army of Tennessee's cavalry. "Certainly he had a right to expect such an appointment," notes historian John P. Dyer in his 1941 biography of Wheeler. "He was the only brigadier general of cavalry. His raids and his spectacular capture of Murfreesboro [Tennessee] had marked him as an officer deserving of promotion. Moreover, at this time he was forty-one years of age, a mature and experienced man. But the cavalry was not put under him. Wheeler was allowed to retain his command and Forrest was given the remainder; and from this time on the two cavalry leaders operated under Bragg, but often in separate directions and with separate commands." [24] Wheeler saw further service with the Army of Tennessee in Tennessee and Kentucky, and General Bragg obtained a brigadier general's commission for Wheeler from Confederate President Jefferson Davis in July 1862. Wheeler was just 26 years old. He would take full command of all the cavalry of the Army of Tennessee a month later. Wheeler and his command spent the remainder of 1862 and the first half of 1863 raiding and disrupting Federal lines and communications in Tennessee. Their specialty was destroying Federal supply trains sometimes containing hundreds of wagons. When attacking a wagon train, Wheeler began to employ a successful tactic he would use repeatedly during the war (including the later Battle of Decatur) of splitting his forces up into several groups and attacking the Federals from several directions at once. Wheeler used this tactic spectacularly in December 1862 in an attack on a train of more than 300 Federal wagons at LaVergne, Tennessee, south of Nashville, destroying almost a million dollars worth of supplies and provisions. [25]

As a result of his success, the Confederate Congress in May 1863 promoted Wheeler again, to major general. [26] It was during this period that Wheeler began to earn his reputation for bold fighting. During the war he commanded in more than 200 battles, would be wounded three times and have 16 horses shot out from under him. [27] More than 50 officers who fought beside him were wounded or killed during the war. [28] Fifteen members of Wheeler's staff lost their lives in battle at the general's side. "Such statistics indicate how often Wheeler put himself and those near him in harm's way – the habit of an officer who believed in always leading from the front," [29] notes historian Edward G. Longacre. On June 27, 1863, while fighting Federal cavalry at the Duck River at Shelbyville, Tennessee, Wheeler and about 50 of his men were trapped by Federals. "Calling to his men to follow, Wheeler broke through the encircling enemy line and plunged his horse over an embankment fifteen feet into the swollen river below," [30] writes historian John P. Dyer. "He spurred his horse to the leap, lost his seat in the descent, but, clinging to the neck of the animal, guided him, swimming, to the opposite bank in safety." [31] His men followed, but only thirteen reached the other side.

So Wheeler was undoubtedly brave. But historian Albert Castel also noted that, "Unfortunately, Wheeler suffers from two weaknesses that are characteristic of cavalry generals in both armies: the inability to exercise effective control over his troopers except when personally present, and, worse, a penchant for making exaggerated claims about what he can accomplish and what he has accomplished." Castel cites an example of an occasion after the fall of Atlanta, when Wheeler provided reports to General John B. Hood that were "arrant, lying nonsense" and "false, misleading intelligence." [32] And historian Edward G. Longacre cites a grandiose statement by Wheeler after his forces destroyed a Federal cavalry raid south of Atlanta in late July 1864 that they had stopped "the most stupendous cavalry operation of the war." "Designed to win for him and his men the highest possible honors, this statement was a gross exaggeration even by Wheeler's standards," [33] Longacre notes.

Wheeler was a stickler for training. One of his cavalrymen, George Knox Miller of the 8th Confederate Cavalry, noted in a letter to his wife on April 23, 1864, that "We drill almost incessantly under the supervision of Gens. Wheeler, Kelly & Allen. Gen. Wheeler had some 'dummies,' made of old clothes stuffed with straw and stood up like infantry on a line about 100 yds long. Some 60 yards behind these he has a line of men on foot with guns loaded with blank cartridges. We charge over the 'dummies' at full speed when the footmen fire and run. Very pretty sport for the Generals but dangerous and fatiguing to the men who do the work. ...Gen. Wheeler comes around about sunrise almost every morning to see the command grooming their horses." [34] It was a good thing Wheeler was preparing his men for battle at this time, for as Miller wrote his letter to his wife, just a short distance northward the massive Federal forces under General William T. Sherman were about to come charging south out of Chattanooga.

IV

Chattanooga to the Chattahoochee

The events that led to the Battle of Decatur began to take shape as the spring of 1864 approached. After the Federal army's defeat the previous fall at the Battle of Chickamauga, it would try a second time to invade Georgia. By the beginning of March 1864, General William T. Sherman was beginning to concentrate forces in Chattanooga for the coming Atlanta Campaign. On March 10, 1864, the 35th New Jersey, the 25th Wisconsin and a number of other Federal units in Vicksburg, Mississippi, were ordered to move to Athens, Alabama, west of Huntsville, traveling by steamer up the Mississippi River to Cairo, Illinois, then up the Tennessee River. [1] The first of May 1864 found the 63rd Ohio, 25th Wisconsin and 35th New Jersey together in Decatur, Alabama, a town on the Tennessee River not far from the Alabama/Tennessee line that saw a great deal of military activity during the Civil War. The 63rd, 25th and 35th were there organizationally combined with the 43rd Ohio Volunteer Infantry to form the Second Brigade of the Fourth Division of the 16th Army Corps. The four regiments at that time totaled 2,548 men. [2] On May 1, the brigade began its journey to Chattanooga to join the swelling Union horde gathering there. The brigade left Decatur, marching east to Huntsville and then southeast to the little town of Woodville, Alabama, which is on the railroad that goes to Chattanooga. May 3 found the 25th Wisconsin "on the march again thru pine forests and over mountains enroute for Chattanooga," private Chauncey Cooke would write his mother. The unit marched 23 miles that day to the railroad, where they got into rail cars and were taken by train to Chattanooga. "Troops are coming in and swelling our force from all directions." [3]

The regiments arrived at Chattanooga at 11 a.m. on May 5. With the huge campaign starting, there was no time to rest, and the regiments marched the same day with three days' rations in their haversacks to Rossville, Georgia, arriving at 7:30 p.m. On May 6 they began marching into Georgia. The Atlanta Campaign began with the Federal army swarming south out of Chattanooga, generally following the railroad toward Atlanta, which is now paralleled by Interstate 75. The Federals faced the Confederate army of General Joseph E. Johnston that was dug in behind almost impregnable defenses on top of high and steep Rocky Face Ridge at Dalton. Sherman here made the first of his flanking maneuvers, digging in part of his army in front of the Confederates and then sending another part around behind to cut the railroad linking the Confederate army to its supply base in Atlanta. The Second Brigade was part of the flanking movement and headed south, on May 6 marching past the battlefield of Chickamauga and camping at Gordon's Mills. Here, eight months earlier in September 1863, the Federal army's first effort to invade Georgia had ended in disaster. On May 7, the brigade marched to Ship's Gap and then to the tiny town of Villanow, Georgia, and then on to Snake Creek Gap.

Early in the morning of May 9, in a foreshadowing of events two and a half months later in Decatur, the advance of the 16th Army Corps was attacked by Ferguson's brigade of Confederate cavalry. [4] The 25th Wisconsin's Chauncey Cooke was "awakened from dreams of home by the rushing cavalry horses and the grinding of artillery wagons. We soon learned that the rebel Gen. Wheeler was making a move to capture our supply trains. The wagons were being hurried to the rear and every surrounding regiment ordered to get in motion and join in the retreat." [5] After driving off Ferguson's troopers, on the 9th the brigade made a reconnaissance to near Resaca, Georgia, then returned to near Sugar Valley, just west of Resaca. It was imperative for the Confederates to hold Resaca because the railroad to Atlanta ran through the town. Writing to his girlfriend Mary in May 1864 from Kingston, Georgia, private John Brobst of the 25th Wisconsin described what it was like to be in Sherman's army. "It is very hard to be a soldier," he wrote. "No matter how bad the weather is you must go. If it rains you must stand or sleep out, with not as much as a leaf to shelter you from the storm. Perhaps have about half a meal for two days, and that the poorest kind of living... Now, I will tell you as near as I can what the load is that a soldier has to carry, and march from 15 to 25 miles a day. He has a gun that weighs 11 pounds, cartridges and cartridge box about 6 pounds, woolen blanket 3 pounds, rubber blanket 5 pounds, two shirts, two pairs of drawers about 3 pounds, canteen full of water which they oblige you to keep full all the time, which is about 6 pounds, then three or five days' rations, which will weigh about 8 pounds, and then your little trinkets that we need, perhaps 2 pounds, makes a total of about 45 or 50 pounds. That is what makes us think of our homes in these hot days." [6]

On the 13th, the Second Brigade marched with the Army of The Tennessee back toward Resaca. There, from May 13-15, 1864, the 25th Wisconsin and 35th New Jersey would get their first big baptism of fire as General Sherman tried to outflank Confederate General Joseph Johnston's defensive lines and cut the Confederates' vital railroad supply line back to Atlanta. On the afternoon of the 13th, the 35th New Jersey was part of a line of battle that went forward against the Confederate lines "advancing in line over fences and up a wooded hill and crossing ravines, coming out on a wooded plain facing the Oostenaula River about two miles north of Resaca. The regiment had but cleared the wood when two rebel regiments opened a brisk fusillade fire on us," [7] the 35th New Jersey's commander, Col. John J. Cladek, would later report. "I immediately gave the command 'commence firing,' not, however, before I had three or four men wounded." The 35th was in the front facing the Confederates, who after about 15 minutes of firing "gave way and ran." The 35th had lost one killed and 13 wounded. The 35th next moved to support some artillery batteries, "in such a position as to be under two fires, the enemy's shells bursting over us, and our own shot tearing limbs of trees to splinters above our heads, which became dangerous for my men." The 35th lost several more men wounded, with two companies – E and I – out skirmishing with the rebels.

The 25th Wisconsin's Chauncey Cooke "had several close calls as did all the boys for that matter. We have been under fire and losing men right along for three days," he wrote his parents on May 17. At one point "a shell burst directly over me, cutting a hole in my blanket and the piece [of shell fragment] making a hole in the ground within a few inches of my body." Writing more about the battle of Resaca in another letter a few days later he would note that as he and his comrades approached the Confederate lines at one point, "The rebels discovered us first and began a terrific fire on us from their cover of brush and logs. Then the order came for us to open fire. There is no use to try to tell you of the excitement, of the cries of the officers, of the whistling of bullets and shells and above all else the roar of the guns. Every fellow loaded and fired fast as he could." During fighting the next day, "I emptied my cartridge box many times during the day as did the others. I saw [Confederate] men often drop after shooting, but didn't know that it was my bullet that did the work and really hope it was not. But you know that I am a good shot." [8] On May 14, 1864, in the midst of heavy fighting for two ranges of hills, Brigadier Gen. Charles R. Woods called for reinforcements. Woods recalled that the "fortunate arrival" of Colonel Milton Montgomery with the 25th Wisconsin, and the 35th New Jersey, enabled him to relieve an Iowa regiment which was out of ammunition after hard fighting. "I sent the 25th Wisconsin immediately forward. They advanced to the crest of the second hill in the most gallant style, and poured in a fire which drove the enemy back to the crest of the next hill, about fifty yards in the rear, where they reformed, but did not venture again to advance." Hearing that General Giles A. Smith, who was on Woods' right, was hard pressed by a Confederate attack, Woods sent five companies of the 35th New Jersey to Smith's assistance as it began to get dark.

Colonel John J. Cladek, commander of the 35th New Jersey Infantry.

"After arriving on the new position assigned me, the Thirty-fifth gave three rousing cheers, tending to inspire our troops in front with fresh energy, when the rebels opened a cross-fire of shot, shell, and canister upon us as we advanced, but fortunately we escaped with one man wounded,"[9] the 35th New Jersey's Cladek reported. The New Jersians were posted behind Smith's line as a reserve but did not actively fight. The Confederates were repulsed, with the fighting not stopping until about 8:30 p.m. [10] That night the 35th threw up entrenchments, where it spent the next day, May 15, safely, "delivering a murderous fire, and repulsing every attempt made by the rebels to advance, the enemy's fire taking no effect upon us," Cladek said. That night the Confederates evacuated Resaca. The 25th Wisconsin's and 35th New Jersey's first big combat was over and the rebels were in retreat. The 25th Wisconsin lost 24 killed and wounded at Resaca. [11] General Woods sent a note on May 21 to division commander Brigadier General Grenville M. Dodge "speaking in the highest terms of the conduct and gallantry of Colonel Montgomery and his regiment" while they were under Woods' command on May 14 and 15. Woods also spoke "most approvingly" about the five companies of the 35th New Jersey that had come to his aid at Resaca. [12] During the three days of fighting at Resaca, the 35th New Jersey had lost three men killed and two officers and 20 men wounded plus one missing. [13]

With the beginning of the Atlanta Campaign, Wheeler's Cavalry had been assigned the duty of protecting the flanks of the Confederate Army, beginning a period of four months of nearly non-stop fighting and riding where any minute could, and often did, bring death or disfigurement. The command of General Samuel Wragg Ferguson had reported to General Joseph E. Johnston at Kingston, Georgia. Although technically part of Brigadier Gen. William H. Jackson's Cavalry Division, and not Wheeler's, Ferguson's Brigade fought with Wheeler and later had a major role in the Battle of Decatur. In his memoirs Ferguson later described the critical role of the Confederate cavalry. "From that day until [Confederate General John B.] Hood started on his march to Kentucky [in November 1864, following the Federals' capture of Atlanta]," Ferguson would write, "I was engaged almost every day, never out of range of bullets, day or night. Not in any great battle, but in so many affairs, that at the end of a month, the muster roll showed a greater number of men killed and wounded, than would reasonably have been the case in a severe pitched battle. Generally, when the Infantry fell back from an entrenched position, the cavalry, dismounted and with horse holders a little in the rear, occupied the trenches with an exceedingly thin line to mask the movement until the Infantry had time to fortify a new position, then fall back, defending the rear. Many were the sleepless nights." [14]

Twenty-eight-year-old George Knox Miller of the Eighth Confederate Cavalry captured what the start of the Atlanta Campaign was like in letters to his wife Celestine, also known as Cellie, sometimes writing at the exact moment fighting was occurring. Miller described the intimate violence of the combat. On May 9 his unit made a charge "under a leaden storm from the Yankee cavalry... At one time we were in five steps of the second Yankee line, shooting each other down with repeaters [Editor's note: revolvers or repeating rifles]..." Miller seems to have wanted to prepare his wife for the possibility of his own death, telling her, "But, darling, the conflict is not yet over, and I know not what an hour may bring forth. But be sure of one thing, that if I fall it will be with a full consciousness of having endeavored at least to serve my country as best as I could. If I survive, I shall always believe that the petitions of a pious wife have been heard and answered. Keep up courage my loved one & I will do likewise. I never went into battle more cheerfully than at present. There is an inward satisfaction never experienced before." [15] On May 13, just as the Federal and Confederate armies were about to clash at Resaca, Miller wrote while he was "almost in the smoke of battle with death and destruction all around." [16] [Editor's note: One wonders what fearful impact such words had on his wife.] He told his wife how he had read one of her letters to him "while in line of battle with shells & solid shot hissing & bursting overhead... Thanks to a kind Providence my life is yet spared tho' the end has not come yet. We have been fighting almost incessantly for 7 days."

A wartime photograph of Private John Brobst of the 25th Wisconsin Infantry.

The Federal Second Brigade resumed its march south on May 16, arriving at Kingston, Georgia, where it rested until May 23. Already by this time, many soldiers in the Confederate army opposing Sherman were growing weary of the Atlanta Campaign, especially as Federal columns elsewhere invaded the South and threatened their families back home, leading many Confederates to desert or surrender. Writing to Mary on Sunday morning, May 22, perhaps in a moment of Sabbath cease fire, the 25th Wisconsin's John Brobst told of the surrender of five companies of Rebels totaling 173 men including nine officers. "They say they are sick of the war and want peace on any terms," Brobst wrote, describing them as "poor miserable half-starved brutes." Brobst saw a train of railroad cars heading north with about 2,000 Confederate prisoners who had been captured the day before. "They look very hard. They say they have not half enough to eat when they are in camp and much less when they are on the march. Our men would not stay here one month if they had to live as the rebs have to live." [17] Brobst described for Mary what it was like to be near the front line, awaiting action and exhausted from marching and lack of sleep. "We had to have a little sleep, so one part of the regiment would lay down among the flying balls [bullets] and the roar of cannon and muskets and go to sleep, and sleep as sound as though he was at his quiet home. It sounds nice to hear the rattle of the cannon and muskets and shell, grape[shot], and cannister balls and everything making its peculiar noise. It certainly is music. It is not in time of action that chills the blood, but after the action when you see your comrades with arms and legs shot off and mangled in all forms. Those are the hardest sights of the battlefield." [18]

In the Chicago Board of Trade Battery, gunner John Nourse's days began early – he and his comrades were often up at 2:30 a.m. or 3:30 a.m. in the morning to make breakfast and get ready and be on the road by 5 a.m. or 6 a.m. As the Federal army began moving south out of Chattanooga toward Atlanta, the horse-drawn battery rode long distances: 30 miles one day, 15 the next, often fighting Confederate cavalry. The battery would pass near Rome, Kingston, and Cedartown, Georgia.

On May 24 it would be in big fight near Dallas, Georgia, with Nourse's section of guns firing 44 rounds. Despite life and death encounters with the Confederates, Nourse could feel empathy for them. On the 24th he recorded in his diary how the Federals he was with had captured 30 Confederate prisoners, "two of them, boys home from Lee's Army [Editor's note: from Confederate General Robert E. Lee's army in Virginia] on a furlough. Poor fellows, are within eight miles of their home, and have not seen their families for years. Now they must start for the north as prisoners." [19]

The Second Brigade was then again ordered forward and it passed through Van Wert to arrive at Dallas, Georgia, on the evening of May 26. [20] At sunrise the next morning the brigade began active skirmishing with the Confederates that continued for several days, "at times almost becoming a battle," brigade commander John W. Sprague would recall. [21] The morning of Friday May 27, 1864, found the 25th Wisconsin in line of battle behind the skirmishers up on the front line. At this time in the Atlanta Campaign, the slugfest between the Federals and Confederates in the Dallas, Georgia, area was nearly continuous, and this was the day the bloody Battle of Pickett's Mill was fought. The 25th Wisconsin's John Brobst may have been worried he would soon be killed or wounded. In a letter to his girlfriend Mary he told how three men in the regiment had been hurt before noon that day, including one in his company wounded in the hand. "Dan Hadley is sitting by my side smoking his pipe, taking comfort. Eat, drink, smoke and be merry, for tomorrow you may die. I have had your picture out and looking at it but you look as calm and collected, as though there were no prospects of a battle. The rebels are about fifty rods in front of us [Editor's note: about 250 yards]. I expect we will soon have to charge the hill and storm the castle for them. We will see what this afternoon will bring forth." [22]

The same day, the Chicago Board of Trade Battery's John Nourse came close to getting killed. Nourse's day began at 4:34 a.m. when he and his comrades were up to feed and clean the horses that pulled the battery's guns. Skirmishing with the Rebels began at 5:30. About 1 p.m.

Nourse's guns were in combat, firing 67 rounds at the Confederates, who fired back. "Soon the rebels got one piece of artillery to bear on us from the top of a hill in our front. Said gun was too high up for us to bring our gun to bear on it and a creek at the foot of the hill, with very steep sides prevented our cavalry from charging them. The first shell was in the range, but fell short. The second fell to our left in the woods; the third killed two horses belonging to King and Harvey, and only a few feet from me; the fourth struck the ground at our limber wheel, but did not explode. This was the closest call I have yet had." [23]

On Saturday May 28, Companies E and I of the 35th New Jersey at one point advanced up some high ground, but were forced by Confederate fire to pull back. Later the 35th served on the skirmish line. In total at Dallas the regiment lost four killed, eight wounded and one missing. [24] By May 28, the 25th Wisconsin's Chauncey Cooke and his comrades were also near Dallas, Georgia, west of Kennesaw Mountain, as Sherman once again was making a wide swing to the southwest to try to outflank the Confederates' defensive lines. That morning Cooke and his good friend, fellow private John W. Christian, were sent out on the picket line, which is a thin line of soldiers advanced most closely to the enemy lines and whose duty is to prevent the main line behind them from being surprised by an attack. It is lonely and dangerous duty, and Cooke and Christian risked being shot by Confederate snipers. "Our beat lay within 80 rods [Editor's note: 440 yards, or a bit more than four football fields] of the rebel breastworks on the side of Lost Mountain. Sharpshooters in the tops of the trees kept pegging away at us for four hours. We changed our position several times but they kept their eyes on us. We were in a cornfield full of rotten [tree] stumps. We got behind one of these stumps [and] put up a rubber blanket for a shade and lay down as close together as we could. They got our range and presently the bullets began to whistle past us, striking the ground but a few feet from us. I said to John, 'Let's get out of this.' 'Wait,' he said, 'until they come closer.' The next moment two shots ripped through the rubber above us, one of them grazing John's breast and tearing a hole in the ground between us. We rolled out of that in a hurry, grabbed our blanket and took a position lower down the hill. John Christian is a dandy boy. He isn't afraid of anything." At 4 o'clock that afternoon they were relieved and allowed to return to their main line to rest. [25]

The hardship of combat was just as difficult for the Confederates. Writing from near Cartersville, Georgia on May 20, Confederate cavalryman Knox Miller had noted to his wife, "Thanks to a good Providence I am spared to drop another line to my angel wife. I write all covered with dust and begrimed with powder and smoke from the field of battle. [Editor's note: the black powder ammunition used in Civil War weapons often left soldiers literally black with soot.] For the last fifteen days scarcely an hour of day-light has passed that our command has not been under fire." At this point Wheeler's Cavalry was serving as the Confederate army's rear guard as General Sherman's flanking maneuvers forced the Confederates to retreat south. The Confederate retreat distressed Miller, who wrote to Cellie that "it has sickened within me at the sight of the devastation & distress along the route. Thousands of families fleeing from happy homes – their beautiful fields & gardens laid waste. Mothers frantic with fear flying with their little ones in their arms – is a sight I never wish to behold again." Miller went on to note that "Frequently lately we have kept so close to the enemy that their batteries would shell us at night while in camp. Until last evening I had not taken the saddle off my horse for five days", adding, "I thought I had seen much of war but the last two weeks experience has been the most trying of any. I can scarcely speak above a whisper [Editor's note: He was so close to the Federal lines that loud talking would draw fire.] I have had nothing but my over coat to sleep on or under during all this time, but sleeping has been almost out of the question – fighting all day & marching during the night. I did not know my powers of endurance before. I have not had a change of clothing since yesterday two weeks." [26] The soldiers grew accustomed to constant battle. Miller wrote to his wife on May 31 while waiting in line of battle behind the skirmish line. "While I write heavy skirmishing is going on within a few hundred yards of me, and occasionally a stray bullet whistles by, but their music is all I have listened to for 24 days, & I can sleep soundly now without being disturbed by them." Getting enough to eat was always an issue for the Confederates (less so for the usually well-supplied Federals). Wheeler's troopers also often lacked food for their horses. "As for ourselves," Miller told his wife, "we have fared much better than I expected, generally having a fair supply of bacon & crackers." One of his officers received a box of food from home, and Miller was able to replenish his haversack from it. But the constant fighting often made it difficult to cook, and Miller candidly told his wife he was suffering from diarrhea. "The cause of it is, that being on the skirmish line all the time we cannot have fires even to broil our meat & have to eat it raw." Fear of being killed continued to dog Miller. "At times I feel as tho' all I ask is to be spared to enjoy life with my darling," he told Cellie. "God alone can so direct it and on him I have placed my trust, knowing that my tenure is frail and weak. I still have that abiding faith that God will spare us to meet again. I believe that it was his intention that we should be united and trust that he may yet preserve us both for some good purpose. My escape [from harm] thus far seems miraculous. It seems almost impossible for a creature to pass thro' what I and others have and still be spared. I am cheerful as to the result but am horrified at the sacrifice necessary." [27] The terrible toll that the first month of the Atlanta Campaign took on Wheeler's Cavalry is shown in the casualty count. Between May 6 and May 31, it reported 73 men killed, 341 wounded, 53 captured and 81 missing. [28]

As June 1864 began the Federal army was pushing southward closer to Atlanta. Many accounts of the Atlanta Campaign describe how the Federal and Confederate private soldiers who spent their days and nights trying to kill or maim each other would, especially as the campaign and the killing dragged on and on, occasionally call a truce and fraternize with each other. Writing home on June 1, the 25th Wisconsin's Chauncey Cooke described how this would occur as the Federal trenches pushed up close to the Confederate trenches around Lost Mountain, west of Kennesaw Mountain. "All day long we shot wherever we saw a hand, a head, or puff of smoke [from a Confederate gun firing] and the rebels did the same. Some times our side would call out to the rebs, asking them to hold up and talk things over. 'All right,' they would say, and for some time both sides would talk over things about the war, and about their girls, and about exchanging hard-tack [army crackers] for ham, and whiskey for tobacco. Then some voices would call out, 'Look out for your life!' and the shooting would begin. Several times during the day both sides would agree to a truce for ten minutes or twenty minute, and some of the more daring on both sides would meet half way and exchange tobacco for whiskey and sometimes newspapers, sometimes to shake hands merely. Soon as the first fellow got back to his barricade he would call out, 'Say pard are you ready?' If the answer came back, 'All ready!' at once a dozen guns, perhaps a hundred would answer back the challenge." [29] The Second Brigade moved to Pumpkin Vine Creek and then on June 6 to Acworth, moving on June 10 to Big Shanty. More than a week of continuous skirmishing with the Confederates followed. [30] On the skirmish line on June 14 and 15, the 35th New Jersey suffered two of its deadliest days yet, losing seven killed and eight wounded. [31]

By early June 1864, Confederate cavalryman William L. Nugent's regiment was near Lost Mountain in Cobb County. Writing to his wife Nellie on June 9, he seems to have been questioning or rationalizing his participation in the "dread reality" surrounding him. "Ah! Little do those, who live in peace provided with everything that heart could desire, know what a torrent of feeling the bowed head of a Southern Soldier indicates. Sustained alone by a patriotism that has been purified by fire, in camp he often dreams of loved ones at home and wakes to the dread reality that encompasses him with a firm trust in the God of battles and a fixed purpose to abide his holy will. On the lonely picket post, in the damp & noisome trenches, sweeping over the open plain in a charge, or covertly seeking a tree to pick off & destroy the Yankee sharp shooters who continually annoy him in a fight, he is actuated by one moving impulse continually and that is to do and dare everything for the independence of his country. A soldier's life is very tame except when on a raid or in a skirmish and then the danger of being killed by any stray bullet that comes along is not very encouraging. It is absolutely shocking to witness the horrors of war; to see the number of the dead and dying scattered all around; to inhale the sickening stench of bodies in every state of decomposition; and listen to the obscenity & blasphemies that are being continually uttered all around." [32]

On June 18th, the 35th New Jersey earned the recognition of General Grenville M. Dodge, whose corps was on the railroad at Big Shanty, modern day Kennesaw. The Federals charged and took the first line of the Confederates' rifle pits. "In this charge the Thirty-fifth New Jersey Infantry displayed great gallantry; under a heavy fire it held its position for a long time after its ammunition was exhausted and until it was relieved." [33] During the night of June 19th the Confederates fell back to Kennesaw Mountain, with the federals in pursuit. The Chicago Board of Trade Battery during this time served on picket duty (Editor's note: that is, out in front of the main line as a guard) for 60 hours without relief. The battery was in action on June 8th, 9th, 11th, 15th, 18th, 20th and 27th. [34]

In a June 21 letter written from near Marietta, Georgia, Confederate cavalryman Knox Miller told his wife Cellie about a charge by Wheeler's Cavalry on Federal cavalry in which he "was more exposed perhaps than in any fight during the campaign – men & officers were killed and wounded around and on all sides of me." [35] Reading this later, how Cellie must have worried. The campaign was just as trying for Miller's comrade, William Nugent. Writing to his wife Nellie on June 20 from near Marietta, Nugent graphically described the trials of life as a Confederate soldier. "We have had dreadful weather for the last twenty days. It has been raining nearly the entire time and the roads have become almost impassable in consequence. There is a terrible exhalation of odors from the ground near the trenches and in the vicinity of the camps; so much so, as almost to sicken a hearty man ... how I would like to be five thousand miles from here now. Mud, filth, rain; every imaginable species of vermin crawling all around you; little sleep, hard work & fed like a race horse; constantly annoyed with stray bullets, whizzing shells &

pattering grape [shot]; dirty clothes and not a change along; little or no time to wash your face and hands and very little soap when the opportunity offers..." [36] The reader may wonder about the worry that reading descriptions such as these caused Nugent's wife. This thought occurred to him five days later on June 25 when he wrote in a letter to Nellie about the filthy soldiers and camps of both armies. "I am extremely anxious, however, to get away from this big army and breathe a little fresh air. The great number of dead horses, mules and human beings, makes the air extremely offensive in the vicinity of the trenches. I am very nearly worn out under it and greatly fear I can never become accustomed to it. I forget though, that I am unnecessarily drawing an unpleasant picture; for I know that the bare recital of a reality which shocks me, is sufficient to unstring your nerves. Let me then draw the veil over the sickening theme..." [37]

The continual battles, unhealthy food, lack of sleep, exhausting marches, contaminated drinking water and exposure to rain and hot weather sickened thousands of soldiers on both sides, and by late June the health of the 25th Wisconsin's Chauncey Cooke was suffering. "I hate to own it, but I am very close to the sick list," he would write home in a June 24 letter to his parents. "I am not scared a bit, I am sure I shall be all right soon." [38] When the fighting stopped, a Confederate cavalry officer's thoughts quickly turned to more mundane issues. Knox Miller wrote his wife Cellie on June 26 describing a "little resting spell" in which he got the opportunity to have some of his clothes washed.

The Chicago Board of Trade Battery's John Nourse spent June moving with the Federal army as it closed in on Atlanta from the northwest, approaching Marietta. Food was short, as the Federal army had moved away from the railroad and heavy rains made it difficult for supply wagons to get over the horribly muddy roads to the front lines. It was intensely hot in addition to being wet. June 19th found Nourse's guns fighting in a pouring rain. By June 22nd he was near Kennesaw Mountain. "At night we plainly see the flash of the rebel guns away up there." On June 27th the Federal army would fight the great Battle of

Kennesaw Mountain, when General Sherman, exasperated with being unable to outflank Confederate General Joe Johnston, ordered a frontal attack against Confederate lines on and around the mountain. Nourse's day began at 3 a.m. and his guns were on the move at 8 a.m. Four guns of the battery were soon firing in support of Federal General George H. Thomas' attack on the Confederates. "We opened our battery on some rebel guns, and shelled each other for six hours, the longest time we have been under fire this campaign," Nourse recorded. Luckily for Nourse, "the shells from the rebel artillery flew over and around us; some fell short; and none exploded near enough to hurt anyone belonging near enough to the battery." [39]

The Second Brigade continued skirmishing and advancing its earth works around Kennesaw until July 3.[40] The brigade would remain at Kennesaw until July 3, when it marched south toward Nickajack Creek near the Chattahoochee River, where the Confederates had prepared strong earthworks to try to keep the federals from crossing the river. In a fight on July 4th, during which the Federals tried to break the Confederate line, Acting Major Charles A. Angel of the 35th New Jersey was killed in action. "The country has lost no braver or truer soldier in all the war," John W. Sprague would later write. [41]

The Federal army was now approaching the Chattahoochee River just north of Atlanta, and General Sherman began massing forces for his planned crossing of the Chattahoochee to swing around to cut the railroad east of the city. On July 3 the Chicago Board of Trade Battery moved with other Federal forces to Marietta. The next day they continued north to Roswell on the Chattahoochee River, fighting with Confederates and firing 85 rounds. [42] Writing home on July 4, perhaps as many Northerners were celebrating Independence Day with picnics and festivities, the 25th Wisconsin's Chauncey Cooke would note that "It's a fearful strain to live such a life and yet the fear of bullets don't bother me half as much as the fear of disease. But strange to think, soldiers never think of dying of disease. Just the same not ten minutes passes during our long encampments, but we hear the muffled funeral drum and the blank musket discharges, above some soldier's grave, who died a victim of southern fever." [43] Poor diet no doubt played a role in the soldiers' poor health. Cooke described his breakfast on July 8 "of sowbelly, hard-tack and black coffee, yes, and blackberries." The Federal lines were so close to the Confederate lines and the fighting so continuous that the Federal soldiers often couldn't properly cook their meals. Cooke describes how on July 4, he and his comrades lay on the ground just behind the front lines as a fierce battle raged. "While the roar of musketry went on in our front we lay flat on our bellies while we munched hard-tack and ate our raw pork, and expecting every minute an order to advance." Cooke describes the stark horror of the front line: "It was something to see the dead and wounded. Many of the boys were crying like children, running back and forth without hats or guns and cursing the rebels for killing their comrades."[44] By sometime in mid July, Cooke's poor health forced him to leave his comrades on the front line and enter a field hospital in Marietta. As a result, after two months of mud and blood, he would miss the final acts in the drama of the Atlanta Campaign. But Cooke's comrades in the 25th Wisconsin would push on. He would keep up with their marches and battles by talking to other soldiers in the hospital.

On July 5 the Chicago Board of Trade Battery was a few miles west of Roswell, and the Federal advance reached the town by July 7. Gunner John Nourse recorded seeing the town's textile mills burning. Now, after the mud and blood of the campaign from Chattanooga, he and his comrades got some much needed rest. Food became plentiful. "We got all the potatoes, apples, cucumbers, onions, etc. we could carry," he noted on July 9. That day some of the Federals forded the Chattahoochee on foot, driving away the Confederates on the south side without much fighting. "Our guns shelled the bluffs across the river but got no reply," [45] Nourse recalled. That same day the 16th Army Corps, including the four regiments of the Second Brigade, marched north to Marietta and then to Roswell, where it arrived on the 10th. The brigade forded the river to the south side and constructed defensive works. The next day the

Federals commenced building a 600- to 700-foot bridge across the river, which was completed on July 13th. [46] In a July 11 letter to his girlfriend Mary, the 25th Wisconsin's John Brobst described how the Federals got across the Chattahoochee. "On the afternoon of the tenth we came to the river, but the bridge was burned down and the rebs were on the other side of the river, and our work was to cross the river, so the cavalry went up the river several miles and crossed over and came down on the rebs with a fierce charge, and at the same time we jumped into the river and commenced swimming, wading, falling down, rolling, and yelling like wild men, and the rebs running for life again, and the result is here we are on the south side of the river building works [Editor's note: trenches] to keep the rebs back, and I think Atlanta will soon be ours." [47] Like many other Federals, Brobst took advantage of being by the river to wash his filthy clothes, "and you may believe they needed it bad enough, as we have to go a long time that we can't get a chance to wash any. I have had to go thirty days without a change of clothes, marching in the dirt and sweating, and you can well imagine how we look in such cases, and then to top off with, perhaps we will have to lay in rifle pits for a week at a time, but, Mary, there are better times coming. If I live to get out of this safe and sound, I certainly will know how to enjoy home and its comforts."

Insight into what it was like to be in Wheeler's Cavalry at this time is provided by the letters written home by Orlando Devant Chester of the 5th Georgia Cavalry. A Georgian who was obviously well educated and a close observer of events and his surroundings, Chester had enlisted in the Georgia State Guards in August 1863 but by June 1864 had joined the 5th Georgia Cavalry. [48] Sometime around July 8, 1864, Chester and his comrades were on the railroad near Marietta, under heavy artillery fire while fighting the Federals closing in on Atlanta. He describes how one man would hold the horses while others fought the Federals (these were known as led horses), and the exhaustion of near continuous fighting. "After we left that place we were not under fire anymore that day. We marched on down the Railroad to Smyrna where we turned left and marched several miles farther when we stopped and waited for our horses that had been led on by the fourth man. While waiting for the horses, I laid down and went to sleep. I dreamed of cannon firing all the time and once or twice started up hearing a canteen rattle and taking it for shell bursting. I never was so worn out in my life as I was that day. The sun poured down on my head as I laid behind the rails and drew the perspiration out in streams. On the march I wanted water so badly that I was glad to drink water out of the mud puddles on the side of the road. On the retreat to the [Chattahoochee] river we saw a better time, had no fighting to do and were on our horses. The Yanks shelled us as we crossed the river on the Pontoon bridge but did no damage although they threw their shells close." Chester writes of enjoying his rations of cold cornbread and bacon, and the luxury of finding a creek near one camp where he could bathe, "which is quite a luxury. If I could get my clothes washed I would be very well satisfied." [49]

Chester's comrade, George Knox Miller of the 8th Confederate Cavalry, similarly described crossing the Chattahoochee in a July 5 letter to his wife. "Yesterday we had a somewhat quiet day on our part of the lines. This morning at 3 o'clock we again began the retreat and I have just crossed the river under a terrible shelling. I have just passed several of our gallant cavalry-men stretched on the amputating table. No casualties in my Regt." [50] Miller's brigade was on the south bank of the Chattahoochee, trying to prevent the Federals' crossing. Writing again on July 12, Miller described the fraternization that was common among the private soldiers of the two armies. "The river at Pace's Ferry is but little more than 100 yards wide and our pickets and the Yankees had agreed upon a truce. Both parties would leave their rifle-pits and sit on the banks and converse. Some would go in swimming, and the Yankees being hard run for tobacco would propose trades – knives, canteens, money – almost any thing was offered for the 'obnoxious weed.' Some of our men would take a plug in the teeth and swim out to the middle of the river where a Yankee would meet him with a knife and a trade was the result. After sundown the Yanks assembled on the bank and began to sing songs – national, humorous, sentimental. There were some fine singers among them, and it sounded beautiful on the still summer air. Squads of Confederates would return the compliment, and each would praise the performance of the other. It was one of the most impressive scenes I ever witnessed." [51]

In a July 14th, 1864, letter home, the 5th Georgia's Chester described camp life in Wheeler's Cavalry. "The life here is very monotonous. When I am in camp (which is about every other day) when I get up the first thing I do is to get my haversack and take out a pone of corn bread, split it open and take a piece of bacon and hold it over the fire by means of a stick until the grease runs out of it, then let it drip on the bread, by the time the meat gets done, the bread is pretty well greased over, I then put the bread on a stick and hold it over the blaze until it gets a little brown, my breakfast is then cooked. Dinner [editor's note: lunch] and supper are the same, except when I am marching, when I have to eat the bacon raw, and the bread cold. It is astonishing to me how well I like the fare, I am always hungry and eat all I draw with the greatest relish. We have been expecting to draw vegetables for some time but have not done so yet." [52]

The relaxation that Chester was enjoying was about to end. Up in Roswell, where the 16th Army Corps had arrived on July 10, it was joined on July 12th by the 15th Army Corps, which also crossed over to the south side of the Chattahoochee. The 17th Army Corps arrived next on the morning of July 17th and also crossed the river. [53] With the three corps massed on the south side of the river, that day General Sherman launched the movement that would bring the Federal army to Decatur, sending the 15th, 16th and 17th Corps on a big swing around the east side of Atlanta to cut the railroad coming into the city through Stone Mountain, while the 23rd Army Corps descended directly on Decatur. The remainder of the Federal horde began crossing the Chattahoochee at various points, pushing south through Buckhead to the northern edge of Atlanta. The same day, with the impending loss of one of the Confederacy's most strategic cities, Confederate President Jefferson Davis relieved General

Joseph E. Johnston of command of the Confederate army opposing Sherman, and replaced Johnston with General John B. Hood. Hood immediately attacked the Federals to try to stop their advance, first at the Battle of Peachtree Creek on July 20. After this initial bloody assault failed, Hood launched a second desperate attack on July 22. This epic contest would become known as the Battle of Atlanta, and includes the Battle of Decatur.

V

The Civil War Comes To Decatur

Two related events combined to cause the Battle of Decatur.

The first cause is that by early July 1864, the Federal army led by General William T. Sherman had pushed the Confederate army commanded by General Joseph E. Johnston to Atlanta's doorstep, with the Federals on the north bank of the Chattahoochee River and the Confederates on the south bank. Sherman is worried that as his army approaches Atlanta, the Confederates defending the city will be reinforced by General Robert E. Lee in Virginia, who could send additional soldiers to Atlanta via the railroad coming into the city from the east through Augusta. Lee had done this before just eight months earlier in September 1863, reinforcing the Confederate army outside Chattanooga with troops sent from Virginia, helping to win a decisive Confederate victory at the Battle of Chickamauga and delaying the Federal invasion of Georgia. So, in his Special Field Orders No. 36, Sherman orders the Federal corps commanded by General James McPherson (the 15th, 16th and 17th Corps), together with General Kenner Garrard's cavalry, to advance from Roswell and march southeast through DeKalb County to reach the railroad between Stone Mountain and Decatur. They are to destroy the tracks thoroughly for miles, and then move westward toward Atlanta. Nearby, just to the west of McPherson's forces, General John M. Schofield's 23rd Corps advances southward toward Decatur on other roads through Cross Keys (now known as Brookhaven). This brings the

Federals to Decatur on July 19. [1] Simultaneously with these two movements, the forces of General George Thomas are pushing south toward Atlanta from the Buckhead area.

The second event that ultimately caused the Battle of Decatur is that Confederate General Johnston, who had battled the Federal army all the way from Chattanooga -- preserving his army largely intact but failing to stop the Federals' advance to the vital railway and manufacturing hub of Atlanta -- is relieved of command by Confederate President Jefferson Davis on July 17, the same day the Federals cross the Chattahoochee. Davis is desperate to stop Atlanta from being captured and has watched with growing frustration as the Federal forces moved closer and closer to the city. In Johnston's place, Davis puts General John B. Hood, a Texan who is famous for his aggressive fighting. Immediately upon taking command, Hood launches a bold attack to stop the Federals from capturing Atlanta. First, he attacks at the Battle of Peachtree Creek on July 20 to try to throw back the Federal forces advancing on the city from the north. This bloody attack fails. Meanwhile, as this battle is being waged, McPherson's and Schofield's corps have reached Decatur and Stone Mountain, cutting the rail line running through the towns. They are now advancing on Atlanta from that direction and threatening Atlanta's last remaining lifeline, the railroad entering the city from the south. Mustering almost superhuman effort from his exhausted and battle-weary troops, Hood then launches a second bold attack against these Federals. This will become known as the now-famous Battle of Atlanta and the all-but-forgotten Battle of Decatur.

Sherman first mentions a possible movement in the direction of Decatur on July 10, in a note to General McPherson. Sherman had just sent the Federal cavalry commanded by General George Stoneman down the Chattahoochee River to the southwest of Atlanta toward Newnan, Georgia, to mislead the Confederates about where the Federals were going to cross the river. Writing from the north bank of the Chattahoochee River, Sherman told McPherson, "I have pretty much made up my mind as to the next move, but would be glad to hear any suggestion from you... When General Stoneman is back, I will give you the word to shift rapidly to Roswell and cross [the Chattahoochee to the south bank]... At the right time I will leave Generals Stoneman and [the cavalry under General Edward M.] McCook to cover the front, and cross all the balance of the army and advance its right on or near Peach Tree Creek, and the left (you) swing toward Stone Mountain..." [2] Two days later on July 12, Sherman telegraphs his boss in Virginia, General Ulysses Grant, about his plans, telling him, "As soon as I hear from Stoneman I will shift all of McPherson['s three army corps] to Roswell and cross [the army corps commanded by General George H.] Thomas about three miles above the railroad bridge and move against Atlanta, my left well to the east, to get possession of the Augusta [rail] road about Decatur or Stone Mountain. I think all will be ready in three days. I will have nearly 100,000 men." Sherman ended his note to Grant – who was then slugging it out with Robert E. Lee in a bloody war of attrition around Richmond -- with this flourish: "Let us persevere and trust to the fortunes of war, leaving statesmen to work out the solution." [3] Sherman's plan is communicated to his field commanders on July 14 in Special Field Orders No. 35, which notes, "A week's work after crossing the Chattahoochee should determine the first object aimed at, viz, the possession of the Atlanta and Augusta [rail]road east of Decatur, or of Atlanta itself." [4] Six hundred miles away in Washington, D.C., Sherman's bosses discuss possible moves by the Confederates. In a July 15 note to Major General H.W. Halleck, the U.S. Army's chief of staff in Washington, Grant says he believes that either Confederate troops will be sent by rail from Virginia to re-enforce Atlanta; or if Atlanta is captured by Sherman, the Confederates will "bring most of Johnston's army here with the expectation of driving us out [of Virginia and away from Richmond], and then unite against Sherman. They will fail if they attempt this programme. My greatest fear is of their sending troops to Johnston first." [5] Back near Atlanta, Sherman is well aware of the perceived threat. On July 15, Sherman sends a short note to McPherson, whose troops have now marched north to Roswell and crossed the

Chattahoochee, digging in a beachhead on the south bank. Sherman emphasizes the importance of his orders, telling McPherson to "make all preparations to move out toward the Stone Mountain the day after to-morrow. ... That Augusta [rail]road must be destroyed and occupied between Decatur and Stone Mountain by you and [Federal cavalry commander] General [Kenner] Garrard." [6]

In case Sherman needed any more encouragement to rapidly break the railroad leading through Decatur, on July 16 he receives two telegraph dispatches from Virginia and Washington. First, Grant sent Sherman a note at 10 a.m. warning him of the possibility that Johnston's forces could be reinforced with 25,000 Confederate soldiers from Virginia. "It is not improbable, therefore, that you will find in the next fortnight re-enforcements in your front to the number indicated above," Grant wrote. "I advise, therefore, that if you get to Atlanta you set about destroying the railroads as far to the east and south of you as possible..." [7] Then at 4:30 p.m. that afternoon, Halleck sends Sherman a short note from Washington, which says, "General Grant wishes me to call your attention to the possibility of Johnston's being re-enforced from Richmond, and the importance of your having prepared a good line of defense against such increase of rebel force..." [8] At 11 p.m. that night from his headquarters at Powers Ferry, Sherman replies to Halleck with a copy to Grant, acknowledging receipt of their notes earlier that day, and telling them he is confident and well prepared. "I do not fear Johnston with re-enforcements of 20,000 if he will take the offensive," Sherman wrote. "But I recognize the danger arising from my long line and the superiority of the enemy's cavalry in numbers and audacity. I move to-morrow from the Chattahoochee toward Decatur and Stone Mountain, east of Atlanta. All well." [9] On the morning of the 17th, Sherman makes his move. The three Federal army corps of General James McPherson at Roswell move out from their entrenched beachhead on the south bank and start marching toward Decatur and Stone Mountain. The army corp of General John Schofield begins to march toward Decatur. Other Federal forces simultaneously begin moving toward Atlanta from the north. Aware that his superiors in Washington are watching, Sherman telegraphs General Halleck that night at 10 p.m. to tell him "we have moved out from the Chattahoochee..." [10] Among the forces joining the march are the 63rd Ohio, 25th Wisconsin and 35th New Jersey. The other regiment in their brigade, the 43rd Ohio, remains behind in Roswell to guard the bridge over the Chattahoochee River and wagon trains loaded with precious supplies.

The Federals follow several routes to Decatur and Stone Mountain. The 23rd Army Corps crosses Nancy's Creek and Peachtree Road near what's now Chamblee, camps on the north fork of Peachtree Creek on the night of Monday, July 18, and then on Tuesday, July 19 continues marching to what is now North Druid Hills Road and Clairmont Road and then on into Decatur. McPherson's three corps take the "Shallowford Trail," a former Native American trail that leads from the "shallow ford" crossing of the Chattahoochee at Roswell toward Decatur. Part of this road is still known today as Shallowford Road, while other parts are now called Briarcliff Road, Oak Grove Road and Clairmont Road. The 15th Army Corps and Garrard's Cavalry turn off on to what's now Chamblee-Tucker Road to reach Browning's Court House, now the town of Tucker, and they then push south on what's now Idlewood Road to strike the railroad. On July 18, 1864, the 16th and 17th Army corps reached the north fork of Peachtree Creek where Shallowford Road now crosses Interstate 85. They camp that night on the large flat fields along the creek, now occupied by apartment complexes and a shopping center. The next day, July 19, the 17th Corps marched up the hill and then turned off on what's now Briarcliff Road to reach Montreal Road and then march to the railroad, reaching it at a point between Decatur and Stone Mountain. The 16th Army Corps, meanwhile, continues south on Briarcliff Road, past what's now Lakeside High School, then up the hill on to Oak Grove Road to Lavista Road at Oak Grove. The 16th Corps had not gone far on what's now Lavista Road before its lead scouts encountered the infantry of the 23rd Corps, which had come down what's now North Druid Hills Road to where it intersects Clairmont Road. With the road into Decatur (now Clairmont Road) thus occupied by other Federal troops, General Grenville Dodge of the 16th Corps orders his pioneers to cut a parallel road heading south into Decatur. [Editor's note: The mystery of how a Federal infantry corps with thousands of soldiers, supply wagons, artillery caissons and ambulances could move cross country without a road is solved by a close study of Civil War maps made by the Federal army. The author calls the reader's attention to one of these contained in the Official Atlas of the Official Records, Plate LXXXVIII. This shows that when the 16th Army Corps turned south off what is now LaVista Road and headed cross county, it would have had to cross Burnt Fork Creek, which is small and shallow. But then the Federals would have encountered a dirt road running east from Mason's Mill all the way to Decatur. (Traces of this road are still visible today in Mason Mill Park.) Turning left on this road, the 16th Corps would have shortly crossed the South Fork of Peachtree Creek, and then followed the road directly south until it ran into Church Street and into Decatur. Today the section of this road south of the south fork of Peachtree Creek is known as Medlock Road.]

Let us now turn to numerous accounts of the Federal advance on Decatur.

A newspaper correspondent writing under the nom de plume "Quartus" [Editor's note: His true identity is unknown to the author but he was certainly an officer in the Federal army, most likely the 63rd Ohio] described the Federal advance toward Decatur in an account published a week later on July 30 by the Cincinnati Daily Commercial newspaper. [11] The account is so vivid it is worth repeating at length:

"On Sunday morning the 15th and 16th Corps moved from their camp on the south bank of the Chattahoochee River. We marched on the road leading from the Roswell Factories to Decatur, the county seat of DeKalb County, on the railroad, seven miles east of Atlanta. We had not proceeded far when the 15th Corps took a road to the left leading to Stone Mountain, while we advanced on the road passing through Cross Keys. The intention was to make a short march, and we marched leisurely.

"The 9th Illinois Mounted Infantry were in the advance, again under the command of Lieutenant Colonel Phillips. This gallant officer has already returned to the field, although the wound he received at Resaca is not fully healed. The regiment, under his leadership, were full of spirit, and soon began to drive the rebel pickets. As we approached Nancy's Creek, they opened upon us with a ten-pounder Parrot [artillery piece] and a mountain howitzer, but did no damage. It was understood that we had a brigade of rebel cavalry along our front, but this did not intimidate our smaller force. They soon drove them again, and we occupied the ground north of the creek where we intended to camp. The 9th Illinois lost but one man, the Orderly Sergeant of Company H being killed by a musket ball.

"I have never seen elsewhere such an abundance of blackberries as are produced in this part of Georgia. They grow in profusion along nearly all the fences and creeks, and for a week past our men have gathered large quantities of them, very much to the benefit of their health. But on this march we came upon abandoned plantations, on which had sprung up a rapid growth of pine and persimmon trees and blackberry vines. They covered acres of ground, were as large and more luscious than your best Lawtons [Editor's note: a type of grape], and in such quantities that we could pick a pint cup full without changing position. Some of the vines are so tall that I could not reach the topmost berries even from my saddle. To describe the manner in which the men 'go' for them is something beyond my powers, and I leave it entirely to your imagination. ....when we marched on Monday morning ...There was a small force of rebel cavalry on our front, who gave some annoyance to our cavalry, but when they stood for a moment in an advantageous position, a few well-directed shots sent them scampering off. Soon after midday we camped north of Peachtree Creek. From a hill nearby we had a fine view of Stone Mountain.

"Tuesday morning, July 19, found us moving early, and with more interest than on the former days, for we knew that we would get possession of the railroad without the rebels developed enough forces to check our advance. It began to be apparent that the rebels had increased their cavalry force, and were making more resistance than on the day before. When we were within three miles of Decatur our corps came upon the 23rd, which were slightly in our advance and had the right of way. General Dodge opened a road to the left, hoping thereby to get the position on the front which our men coveted. But the attempt failed, and we heard the advance of the 23rd driving the enemy from the town. General Haskell's division was in the advance and gained possession of the town, losing one man killed, and five or six wounded. We followed closely, and in half an hour the 4th Division of our corps had marched into the town.

"Decatur is one of the oldest towns in Northern Georgia, and is a very pleasant Southern village. Many of the houses have marks of considerable antiquity, but others have signs of elegance and comfort. They all lack carpets, for these have been taken through out the Confederacy to make blankets for the soldiers. In the square is a very good courthouse. On the south side is a new well built jail, and there are several good tasteful churches. In the town and vicinity the Confederacy has a number of workshops in which they manufactured army wagons and cavalry equipments. You will remember that it was at this point General John Morgan re-organized his band of marauders after his escape from Ohio. The stock and tools of these establishments have been removed to Greensboro, [Georgia,] about eighty miles east, on the Atlanta and Augusta Railroad.

"The rebels had fired the [Decatur railroad] depot before we came into the town, and burned it with a large number of wagons. There were a number of new and repaired wagons burnt in another part of town. I saw a quantity of nose-bags for cavalry horses, and five boxes of pikes, which our men appropriated and made quite a display of the weapons. They would be excellent for men in earth-works resisting an assault, but worthless elsewhere...The 16th Corps was ordered to pass through the town and occupy the line of the railroad. As we were marching out, the 64th Illinois, of the 1st Brigade, 4th Division, at the head of the column, preceded by General Fuller and staff, and Colonel Morrill commanding the brigade, and the brigade band playing lively strains, we were very unexpectedly saluted by the sound of a cannon, then the bursting of a shell which came screaming from our right. It struck Dr. J.T. Stewart, senior surgeon of the 64th Illinois, acting Division Surgeon, on the hip, knocking him from his horse, and inflicting a severe wound, for it is thought that the bones are broken at the point of articulation. Fortunately, the piece of shell had struck the ground, else he would have been torn to pieces.

"Now the shells began to fall thick, the rebels having the exact range of the road on which were marching out. Sergeant Watson, of Company G, was killed, and Orderly Sergeant Theodore Gaylord, Company A, of the same regiment, was badly wounded on the right arm and on the abdomen. General Fuller at once got his men in line of battle, and sent out a strong line of skirmishers. The 14th Ohio Battery was placed in position and a few shots so well satisfied the Johnnies that they fired but one more shot, and that evidently on the retreat. The troops were soon posted for the night, and we had no other disturbance. During the night our men destroyed some considerable portions of the railroad east of the town, burning the ties and bending the rails."

Federal General John Schofield recalled the advance of his 23rd Army Corps (also known as the Army of the Ohio) toward Decatur this way. "The operations against Atlanta and the Augusta railroad commenced on the 18th of July. The Army of the Ohio, being the center of the movement, marched via Cross Keys upon Decatur. No serious opposition was encountered until we reached Peach Tree Creek, about two miles from Decatur. From this point our advance was contested by a heavy force of dismounted cavalry. [Brigadier General Milo S.] Hascall, having the advance, entered Decatur about 3 p.m. on the 19th, broke the telegraph line, and destroyed a mile of railroad. The depot, containing a large amount of army stores, also some wagons and other property, were fired by the enemy before they abandoned the town." [12]

Wheeler's Confederate cavalry troopers were experts at delaying and slowing advancing Federals such as the soldiers of the 23rd Army

Corps approaching Decatur from the north. They had been employing the same tactics since the Atlanta Campaign began two and a half months before. "Every half-mile or so they make a stand behind a log barricade erected across the road," historian Albert Castel has noted. "The only way ...[the Federals] can drive them from these barriers is to deploy into a heavy line of skirmishers, part of which engages them in front while other parts work around their flanks – a difficult, time-consuming process." [13]

General Milo S. Hascall described the 23rd Army Corp's advance this way. "Early on the 19th the division crossed Peach Tree Creek and advanced in the direction of Decatur. The enemy's cavalry offered stubborn resistance, and my artillery was freely used. They finally took refuge in the town, but were shelled out by Captain Shields with Nineteenth Ohio Battery, and Colonel Swaine with his brigade was moved forward to take the town. A train of wagons and the depot, said to contain a large amount of tobacco, was burned." [14]

Here is how the advance was described by one regimental commander, Colonel Peter T. Swaine of the 99th Ohio Infantry. "On the 19th my brigade moved in advance of the division, the 99th Ohio in advance, followed by the 123rd, 129th and 130th Indiana Volunteers. After crossing Peach Tree Creek [Editor's note: heading south on Clairmont Road where the Veterans Administration hospital is today] the enemy offered an obstinate resistance to our advance, the 99th Ohio being all deployed as skirmishers, and the other regiments following in line of battle. The resistance to our advance being very stubborn, I found it necessary to re-enforce the skirmish line by detachments from the 123rd Indiana. Lieutenant-Colonel Cummins, 99th Ohio Volunteer Infantry, by repeated charges and heavy firing, kept our command advancing slowly until within sight of Decatur, when he and his men being quite worn out and out of ammunition, I relieved the whole line with the 129th Indiana Volunteers, [commanded by] Colonel Zollinger. Everything being ready, and the rebels evidently in readiness for us, Captain Shields opened with two pieces of artillery, and I then ordered Colonel Zollinger to charge at once on the town, the other regiments following in supporting distance. The rebels were completely routed, though they attempted to hold their rail works [Editor's note: Barricades made of wooden fence rails piled up to stop bullets], and afterward occupied the houses for defense. They could not, however, check the swift and steady advance of our troops and fled from the town, burning the railroad depot, and some trains of wagons. With the town well protected by skirmishers, I posted my other troops, under the direction of the brigadier-general commanding, and then ordered the 123rd Indiana Volunteers to destroy the railroad, which was effectually done, and ably supervised by Colonel McQuiston and Lieutenant-Colonel Walters, of that regiment, about a mile of the road being destroyed and the rails twisted." Eight soldiers from the 99th Ohio were wounded in the fighting from the south fork of Peachtree Creek into Decatur. [15]

As the 99th Ohio pushed southward on what's now Clairmont Road toward Decatur, the 129th Indiana was behind it on the right of the road, that is, the west side of Clairmont Road. The 129th Indiana relieved the 99th Ohio about 1 p.m. "I advanced the skirmish line, charged the enemy, drove them through the town and across the railroad; halted and took position on a high ridge and built barricades; remained there until relieved by General Dodge's command, 16th Army Corps, at 6 p.m.; then moved back and rejoined the brigade; moved to the right [Editor's note: toward Atlanta] about two miles, and encamped in an open field," [16] recalled Colonel C.A. Zollinger of the 129th Indiana.

On July 19 as the Federals battled Wheeler's Cavalry to get into Decatur, the 19th Ohio Battery "put two pieces on the skirmish line and shelled the enemy and drove them into the town, when we again shelled them and the town and drove them from the place...," [17] Captain J.C. Shields reported. The major leading the 80th Indiana Volunteer Infantry also reported on the 19th meeting "a heavy rebel force; attacked and drove them beyond Decatur, losing a few men wounded. Here I wish to speak of the efficient, brave, and gallant conduct of First Lieut. Isum Gwin, Company D, who had charge of the skirmish line of my regiment.

He drove the rebels, having to advance through a field under a galling fire, yet with that courage rare and only belonging to the brave, led forward his men, being present at all times where most needed; steadily driving the enemy, killing and wounding many, proving himself on this occasion, as on every other, worthy of a better position." [18] Gwin himself did not describe the day quite so dramatically in his diary. "Marched early. My day for the skirmish line. In 1 ½ miles of Decatur met the Reb skirmishers. Deployed and marched on the right, had a sharp skirmish near Decatur. We were less than 1/8 of a mile of it when were ordered to join our brigade. Joined the brigade, rested until near night, went back on a road and camped." [19]

Colonel Jeremiah M. Rusk of the 25th Wisconsin heard the skirmishing as the Federals pushed southward on what's now Clairmont Road into Decatur. "Considerable firing when we neared the town," [20] he wrote later. The 25th Wisconsin did not get into Decatur until 4 p.m. "Entering the town from the north, we found our batteries shelling the timber into which the enemy had been driven by our advance," wrote one member of the 25th under the pen name "U.S.S." to a newspaper back home in Wisconsin. "The Rebel batteries replied, doing but little harm. The night of the 19th found our Regiment camped on the south side of the town near the rail road, our pickets out, and everything quiet." [21]

The Federals came pouring into Decatur. From her home just north of the courthouse in Decatur, Mary Gay had heard the oncoming Federal army as its advance was opposed by Confederate troopers of Wheeler's Cavalry. "Distant roar of cannon and sharp report of musketry spoke in language unmistakable the approach of the enemy, and the rapidity of that approach was becoming fearfully alarming." [22] The Federals soon occupied the town. Gay describes their entry: "Advance guards, composed of every species of criminals ever incarcerated in the prisons of the Northern States of America, swooped down upon us, and every species of deviltry followed in their footsteps. My poor mother, frightened and trembling, and myself, having locked the doors of the house, took our stand with the servants in the yard, and witnessed the grand entre of the menagerie. One of the beasts got down on his all-fours and pawed up the dust and bellowed like an infuriated bull. And another asked me if I did not expect to see them with hoofs and horns. I told him, 'No, I had expected to see some gentlemen among them, and was sorry I should be so disappointed.' " [23] Federal soldiers ransacked the Gays' house and killed and ate all of her livestock, "every chicken and other fowl upon the place, except one setting hen. A fine cow, and two calves, and twelve hogs shared a similar fate," Gay wrote.

Along with the Federals entering Decatur came more than 1,000 wagons loaded with supplies. On July 19th General McPherson ordered all of his corps' supply wagons to be left "in the vicinity and to the north of Decatur, until the result of our advance is determined." McPherson ordered General Kenner Garrard's cavalry to protect the Federal wagon trains in Decatur "from any cavalry dash" [24] by the Confederates. "Soon, what appeared to us to be an immense army train of wagons commenced rolling in," [25] Mary Gay reported. Garrard's cavalry placed its headquarters in Decatur, choosing Mary Gay's home and lot, so she was surrounded by the enemy she so despised. "Men in groups were playing cards on tables of every size and shape; and whisky and profanity held high carnival," she wrote.

Unknown to Gay, one of the Northern devils she despised most – General Sherman – was just a mile or so north of her. (Gay called Sherman "the Nero of the nineteenth century."[26]) Sherman, who was accompanying General John M. Schofield's 23rd Army Corps as it advanced on Decatur, set up his headquarters for the night of July 19 at the house of J. Oliver Powell, which was on the west side of Clairmont Road a short distance north of the intersection with North Decatur Road. It is interesting that Sherman did not establish his headquarters in Decatur itself, perhaps because the town was considered too far forward and susceptible to Confederate attack. It is on July 19th that Sherman learns that Joseph Johnston had been relieved of command of the Confederate army and John B. Hood put in his place. Schofield and Sherman know this likely means they are going to be attacked very soon. [27]

As the Federals had moved south out of Roswell and converged on Decatur, Confederate cavalry officer General Samuel Wragg Ferguson also receives news that General Johnston has been relieved of command of the Confederate forces defending Atlanta, and Hood placed in overall command. "For the first time in the War, my heart failed me and I doubted of our ultimate success," Ferguson later recalled. "I had known Hood in the Corps of Cadets [at West Point], and I did not believe him capable of filling the place. I believed Gen. J.E. Johnston one of the greatest of soldiers, and think so today." [28] Let us here leave Ferguson. We will meet up again with him again on July 22, 1864.

While at the Powell house, Sherman issues his controversial Special Field Orders No. 39, which tells his commanders that "Each army commander will accept battle on anything like fair terms but if the army reach within cannon-range of the city without receiving artillery or musketry fire he will halt, form a strong line, with batteries in position, and await orders. If fired on from the forts or buildings of Atlanta no consideration must be paid to the fact that they are occupied by families, but the place must be cannonaded without the formality of a demand." [29] Perhaps also because of its protected position well behind the front line, the Powell house where Sherman has his headquarters is also used as a hospital by Dr. Edward Shippen, medical director of the 23rd Army Corps. [30] Harper's Weekly, one of the nation's most widely read publications, later published a sketch of Sherman's headquarters by artist Theodore R. Davis, who was traveling with Sherman's army and making illustrations of incidents during the Atlanta Campaign. Davis's sketch shows the operating table set up by surgeons behind the house and wounded soldiers being carried in on litters. These are likely the soldiers wounded as the Federal advance pushed into Decatur. [31]

As previously described in the account of newspaper correspondent "Quartus," the first Federal soldiers would die in Decatur in the evening of the 19th. As a column of soldiers was marching through town and had reached its outer edge, the Confederates began shelling the town from a battery about 300 yards west of town, killing and wounding four soldiers of the 64th Illinois. Among those severely wounded was Surgeon J.T. Stewart. [32] After spending the night of July 19 in Decatur, on Wednesday July 20 the 63rd Ohio, 25th Wisconsin and 35th New Jersey moved westward toward Atlanta along with other Federal units that had arrived at Decatur. Late that afternoon they might have heard the sounds of a terrible battle being fought by their comrades some miles to the west – Confederate General John B. Hood, wasting no time to attack the approaching Federals, had launched the Battle of Peachtree Creek. At midnight on July 20th, General Sherman (who was clearly working a very long day as reports came in from the Peachtree Creek battlefield) took a step that would have a big impact in Decatur two days later. Remember the apprehension by Generals Grant and Halleck that Confederate re-enforcements would be sent from Virginia to Atlanta via the railroad coming into Atlanta from the east. The Federals now occupied the Decatur area with tens of thousands of soldiers, and had torn up miles of the railroad between Decatur and Stone Mountain. But clearly Sherman, perhaps recalling Halleck's warnings, wanted to be doubly sure his rear was safe. So late that night of Wednesday July 20, Sherman ordered General Garrard's cavalry to ride to Covington 30 miles east of Decatur, destroying the railroad between there and Lithonia, "especially the Yellow River

GENERAL SHERMAN'S CAMPAIGN—SHERMAN'S HEAD-QUARTERS, NEAR DECATUR, July 19, 1864.—Sketched by T. R. Davis.—[See next Page.]

An illustration published in Harper's magazine shows the Powell house north of Decatur which was General William T. Sherman's headquarters on July 19, 1864. The house was also used as a field hospital for wounded Federal soldiers, as shown in the illustration.

bridge this side of Covington" along with the railroad and road bridges east of Covington. Sherman, who had been disappointed in the past with the results of other Federal cavalry raids, made his orders to Garrard explicit and pointed. "I want you to put your whole strength at this, and do it quick and well. I know it can be done," Sherman told Garrard, later adding, "The importance of it will justify the loss of [a] quarter of your command." Sherman left no room for loose interpretation of what he wanted done. Writing as if Garrard did not know how to destroy a railroad, Sherman told him in explicit detail. "Be prepared with axes, hatchets, and bars to tear up sections of track and make bonfires. When the rails are red hot they must be twisted. Burning will do for bridges and culverts, but not for ordinary track. Let the work be well done. The whole thing should be done in two days, including to-morrow." Sherman's order sent away the cavalry's protective eyes and ears from the Federals holding Decatur. The very last line of Sherman's order was prescient: "I will notify General McPherson that he may look out for his rear and [wagon] trains" parked in Decatur. [33]

Sherman must have indeed warned McPherson, who on the next day ordered General Grenville Dodge to send troops to guard Decatur. "Brigadier General Garrard's cavalry is ordered on an expedition by Major General Sherman which will occupy them at least two days. This will leave Decatur defenseless, and the way open for a small body of the enemy's cavalry to dash into our rear. You will therefore send one brigade of Fuller's division to occupy the place, and to picket strongly the roads to the south and east until the return of the cavalry." [34] The three regiments that General Dodge sent were the 63rd Ohio, 25th Wisconsin and 35th New Jersey. The three regiments marched back to Decatur, arriving at noon on Thursday July 21. Complying with McPherson's orders, strong pickets were posted on the roads leading south and east of town. [35] Companies H and C of the 25th Wisconsin were sent out on picket duty to guard the town. [36] Meanwhile, two sections (a total of four cannons) of the Chicago Board of Trade Battery were ordered to report to Colonel Sprague at Decatur. The battery went into camp just south of the courthouse on the top of the hill facing south toward the railroad. [37] A member of the 25th Wisconsin reported an interesting incident on July 21 after the regiment had returned to Decatur. "In the evening the cavalry which we relieved from the picket duty around town started out on a raid. Near two hundred rebel prisoners and one hundred negroes have just passed our camp under guard, having been captured by said cavalry." [38]

Meanwhile, Wheeler's troopers had spent July 20 with other Confederate forces trying to stop or slow the Federals' approach to Atlanta from the east. The fighting had been vicious, with Wheeler's troops fighting as infantry behind breastworks. At one point, Wheeler recalled the Georgia brigade "repulsing a desperate assault and killing the enemy in hand-to-hand conflicts." At one point the Georgia and Alabama brigades were forced out of their trenches by an overwhelming attack by Federals, but they rallied, charged the federals and retook the breastworks. [39] It is important to understand this context because it puts into perspective how the Confederate soldiers would have viewed their attack on Decatur the following day, that is, just another day of fighting and killing. Unfortunately for the historian, a letter written by the 8th Confederate's Miller to his wife in late July near Decatur has been lost. [40] And the 5th Georgia's Chester did not leave a detailed account of the Battle of Decatur. But in a letter to his father written from Wesley Chapel in DeKalb County on July 26 (four days after the Battle of Decatur), Chester told about riding long distances and not having enough to eat. The letter provides great detail about the everyday life of Wheeler's Cavalry around the time of the Battle of Decatur, so it is worth quoting at length. "I am most of the time in the saddle, more than ever since we crossed the Chattahoochee," Chester wrote. ".... I have started at daybreak or sooner and ridden till after midnight without stopping long enough to unsaddle and then lying down with all my things on and without unrolling my blanket or un-saddling my horse and slept with my gun for a pillow. We have been separated from our [supply] wagons for some time and consequently have been very much in need of food.

There are so many of us that the Citizens cannot supply us all [with food], though they do a great deal. Our wagons came up today and we got a supply of hard tack [Editor's note: flat, dry army crackers that were a staple of both Federal and Confederate soldiers during the Civil War that could be eaten as is, fried, or crumbled up into stews] and bacon so for the time we are doing finely... I enjoy starving and hard riding a great deal better than I expected..." [41]

It was here, after the Confederates' defeat at the Battle of Peachtree Creek and with the Federals threatening Atlanta from the east, that Confederate General John B. Hood launched his bold plan to save Atlanta and win the war for the Confederacy. Hood describes how the Battles of Atlanta and Decatur came to be. "The position and demonstration of McPherson's army on the right threatening my communications made it necessary to abandon Atlanta or check his movements. Unwilling to abandon, the following instructions were given on the morning of the 21st ... [Confederate General William J.] Hardee was ordered to move with his corps during the night of the 21st south on the McDonough road, crossing Intrenchment Creek at Cobb's Mills, and to completely turn the left of McPherson's army. This he was to do, even should it be necessary to go to or beyond Decatur. Wheeler, with his cavalry, was ordered to move on Hardee's right, both to attack at daylight, or as soon thereafter as possible. ..." [42] If things had happened as originally envisioned by Hood, Decatur might have been the scene of the beginning of the Battle of Atlanta, rather than a side show to the great battle. "On the 21st of July General Hood decided to attempt on the following day to turn the enemy's left flank," wrote Lieutenant General W.J. Hardee in a report nine months after the Battle of Atlanta and Battle of Decatur. "The original plan was to send my corps by detour to Decatur to turn the enemy's position, but my troops had been marching, fighting, and working the night and day previous, had had little rest for thirty-six hours, and it was deemed impracticable to make so long a march in time to attack on the following day. This plan was therefore abandoned, and General Hood decided to strike the enemy in flank." [43]

Thus, if the original plan had been followed and Hardee's corps had reached Decatur, the Battle of Decatur might have been a much more historically significant affair. Or it might not have been fought at all, as Wheeler sent a dispatch to Hood proposing that he pursue Garrard's Federal cavalry troopers that Sherman had sent to Covington, rather than attack Decatur. Hood refused. [44] Late in the day on the 21st, Wheeler was ordered to pull his troops out of the Confederate line, and their spot was filled by other Confederate infantry. On the night of the 21st Hood ordered Wheeler to take his men and ride around the Federals' rear to attack in conjunction with Lieutenant General Hardee. "My orders from General Hardee were to attack Decatur at 1 p.m., which was the enemy's extreme left, and owing to the curvature of his line, was far in his rear," Wheeler would recall.

So rather than "a small body of the enemy's cavalry" that General McPherson had warned could ride into Decatur, on the way were maybe 3,000 tough, battle-hardened veterans. Unknown to the Federal soldiers in Decatur and their comrades moving westward toward Atlanta, one of the most momentous days of their lives was at hand.

VI

The Battle of Decatur

The predawn skies over Atlanta on Friday July 22, 1864, were brightly lit by a waning but nearly full moon. The morning dawned with Decatur occupied by approximately 1,000 soldiers [1] of the 25th Wisconsin, the 35th New Jersey and the 63rd Ohio. The three regiments were all units of the Second Brigade of the Fourth Division of the 16th Army Corps, commanded by Colonel John W. Sprague. The brigade included one other regiment, the 43rd Ohio, which was to the north in Roswell preparing to accompany a wagon train full of supplies, which was going to travel to Decatur later that day. The 43rd would play a part in the last moments of the coming battle, as we shall see.

Colonel John W. Sprague, commander of the three
Federal army regiments in Decatur.

On arriving in Decatur the afternoon before, Colonel Sprague had sent strong detachments of soldiers to guard the roads leading south and east of town, the directions danger was most likely to come from. Six companies were posted covering all the approaches, and the three regiments and artillery were put in position to defend and hold the town. Thus, if the Confederates attacked, it would not be a surprise. Sprague was somewhat in the dark about whether the enemy was nearby because he had no cavalry out in front of him to be his eyes and ears. The day before, General Sherman had sent Garrard's Cavalry to ride to Covington, east of Decatur, to burn two strategic railroad bridges and further disrupt any chances of Confederate reinforcements coming from that direction. [2] The three regiments posted south of Decatur by Sprague were supported by the fire power of two cannons of Battery C of the First Michigan Artillery and would soon be joined by four guns of the Chicago Board of Trade Battery.

At Garrard's Cavalry headquarters at Mary Gay's house, "The day passed without any immediate adventure," Gay later wrote. "Great activity prevailed in the army ranks. The coming and going of cavalry; the clatter of sabre and spur; the constant booming of cannon and the report of musketry, all convinced us that the surrender of Atlanta by the Confederates was quite a matter of time." [3] Gay was likely hearing the fighting several miles to the west as the Federals pushed closer toward the city of Atlanta. "Quartus," a correspondent for the Cincinnati Daily Commercial who was probably an officer in the 63rd Ohio, reported that, "Early on Friday morning it was discovered that the rebels had strengthened their pickets. Some of our men who went out to pick blackberries were fired upon, and they reported when they came in that the enemy were in strong masses, and gave evidence of making an attack. The firing of pickets became stronger, but did not approach a skirmish. We were not, however, alarmed." [4] Colonel John J. Cladek's 35th New Jersey was camped southeast of the courthouse between it and the railroad. After arriving back in Decatur the day before, "we occupied the remaining portion of the day in arranging our camp and building sheds [Editor's note: Probably sun shelters to provide shade during the heat of the day], thinking to have a few days' rest, but the morning of the 22nd dispelled our calculations," one member of the 35th would later recall. [5] Significantly, two of the regiment's companies were sent out on the picket line on the south and southwest edge of Decatur. About 11 a.m. the men of the 35th could hear the sound of distant artillery, but they thought nothing of it until it began to get nearer and nearer. [6] Men of the Chicago Board of Trade Battery were enjoying a lazy day. "This morning each one lay in his bed as long as he chose," gunner John Nourse said. "There is no feed for the horses, besides that, all are tired. We did some washing and got ready for moving – We have to improve every half chance we get or suffer by neglect." [7]

Around noon Confederates were reported in heavy force south of town. [8] "It was rumoured through camp that the rebels were advancing, news brought in by stragglers," Nourse recounted. "The brigade of infantry and a section of the 3rd Michigan Battery [Editor's note: actually the First Michigan Battery] that were here to train guard got out into line and position, but before they were fairly in position the 'Johnnies' opened on them. We had not received the order to harness, but our own knowledge told us to be up and wide awake. So we harnessed and hitched up the moment the skirmishing commenced." Another artilleryman, Lieutenant Henry Shier of the First Michigan Light Artillery, described the beginning of the battle from his perspective. "About 10 a.m., observing the enemy's cavalry in the skirt of woods, about 1,500 yards in our front, I ordered the gun teams harnessed; about 12 [noon] I received orders from Col. J.W. Sprague, commanding Second Brigade, Fourth Division, to take a position a little to the right of the road, so as to have a greater range for our guns. Shortly after our skirmishers began to fall back before the greatly superior force of the enemy. About the same time the enemy opened with batteries from their right and left; we replied to the left battery. I received in return a cross-fire from both batteries. I still continued firing, but on account of the position of the enemy's guns could not tell the effect of our shots, their guns being hid behind the crest of a hill. Our infantry having all been driven in I ordered the section limbered." [9]

Colonel Sprague described how the battle began. [10] "In the forenoon of the 22nd instant, the enemy's cavalry made some demonstrations along our front, particularly on the road over which the Seventeenth Corps had just passed." Sprague is referring to the road leading southwest from Decatur toward Atlanta, the old Fayetteville Road.[11] Sprague continues, "I ordered four companies of the 63rd Ohio, all under Lieutenant-Colonel Rusk, to make a reconnaissance, and ascertain, if possible, the force of the enemy. Colonel Montgomery, commanding 25th Wisconsin, asked permission to go, and I consented." Montgomery did not yet know that by volunteering to go with the reconnaissance party he had just made one of the most momentous decisions of his life. Companies D and G of the 25th Wisconsin under command of Captain M.E. Leonard were the farthest south of Decatur, about a mile, on picket duty. The Federals ordered out on reconnaissance by Sprague were Companies B, E, F and I of the 25th Wisconsin along with four companies of the 63rd. [12] The four companies of the 63rd -- Company A under Captain Frank T. Gilmore, Company F under First Lieutenant Louis Schmidt, Company D under Captain William Cornell, and Company G under Captain George Wightman – reported to Colonel Montgomery of the 25th Wisconsin at Hoyle's House, where they joined a detachment of Montgomery's soldiers. The group moved half a mile down the road and formed a line of battle facing west. Company G deployed as skirmishers. Sprague's report continues: "Colonel Montgomery had proceeded with the eight companies but a short distance before the enemy was developed in considerable force."

A member of the 25th Wisconsin writing under the name "U.S.S" described the prelude to the battle. "Friday the 22d, Co. D and G went into the picket line south of town. Up to 10 o'clock A.M. some rebel cavalry had been seen lurking around but no attack had been made. At that hour Capt. Leonard with 12 men – including myself in charge of Lieut. Farnham started for a hill on our right, on which he proposed forming a picket post. Leaving Lt. Farnham and 9 men in suitable place for reserve, the Capt. Moved forward with the remaining three men, in order to post them in such a manner as to watch a belt of timber in which the enemy was concealed. Gaining the crest of the hill, a squad of rebel cavalry was seen coming towards them at a distance of only ten rods [Editor's note: about 165 feet]. Our men fired on them, and the rebs returned the fire, doing no harm, then retreated into the woods. The men were posted, and all was again quiet until noon." [13] Back in the town itself, soon after the four companies departed, Second Lieutenant Trumbull D. Griffin, with four guns of the Chicago Board of Trade Battery, reported to Colonel Sprague, and he assigned Griffin a position on the hill north of the jail and near the road and facing the railroad. Griffin described the beginning of battle. "About 1 p.m. my attention was called to the fact that [Federal] infantry and artillery were moving across the road in front, evidently for the purpose of forming line of battle. I immediately proceeded to the front to ascertain the cause and there found Colonel Sprague. Upon inquiry the colonel informed me he thought the enemy not in any considerable force, nothing more than a few cavalry, but that he was then endeavoring to find out what there was. I then returned to the battery, and, hearing an occasional shot, as a matter of precaution ordered the horses harnessed and hitched up to be ready for any emergency that might occur. Before the battery was fairly hitched up the enemy opened with artillery, and his shells fell in the road just to the left of our camp." [14]

At about 1 p.m., the 35th New Jersey got a wakeup call when a shell flew over their camp in town and exploded. The 35th was ordered to form a line of battle and moved up to the railroad. Corporal D.S. Brittin of Company B of the 35th New Jersey, the so called "Yellow Hammers," recalled the beginning of the battle this way. "On the morning of the 22nd two companies of our regiment were ordered out on picket. About 11 a.m. there was distant artillery firing in our front, but we thought nothing of it until it began to get nearer and nearer. About 1 p.m. a shell came bursting over our camp. Our brigade was ordered into line of battle, and advanced to the railroad cut. When we got to the opposite bank of the cut we were met by a volley from the Confederate line of battle, which proved to be a division of Wheeler's cavalry." [15] John Nourse of the Chicago Board of Trade Battery recalled that "before we got hitched up the shell came right into camp lighting up all around us." [16] This battery was supported by three companies of the 63rd Ohio Infantry. The two remaining companies of the 63rd were on the right of the line near Doctor Hoyle's house on the hill south of the railroad. On their left were the two guns of Battery C, First Michigan Artillery; next the remaining companies of the 25th Wisconsin; farther on the left, and covering the roads from the southeast, the 35th New Jersey was posted.

Major John W. Fouts of the 63rd Ohio recalled it this way: "Enemy opened fire from wood[s] about 400 yards in front and at 2 p.m. opened with one piece of artillery upon the picket line on the McDonough road." So the Confederate attack was now coming up the two roads, from the southwest and south of Decatur. Fouts' vivid description of what happened next continues. "Under orders from Colonel Sprague, the command was moved by the left flank to take position in support of the line. During this movement, while passing a deep ravine in single file, the enemy opened upon the command with two batteries, one in front and the other on the left flank. At the same time [the Federals] charged from same points, when they reformed, faced to the rear, and, after a sharp fight, fell back to join [the] main line on the ridge south and west of town, near Hoyle's house. Company E, Lieut. Thomas J. McCord commanding, and Company K, Capt. Daniel T. Thorne commanding, were on the grand guard line. At 1:30 p.m. their outposts were attacked, Company E's by cavalry and Company K's by artillery. The attack made by cavalry was repulsed. The enemy then advanced with two lines of skirmishers and a line of battle, when, under orders from Lieutenant-Colonel Henry, Thirty-fifth New Jersey Infantry, commanding guard line, it fell back fighting until it reached the railroad." [17]

Confederate General Joseph Wheeler was just 28 years
old at the time of the Battle of Decatur.

Let us now turn to the recollections of Confederate General Joseph
Wheeler, who had been ordered to attack Decatur at 1 p.m. Wheeler was
just 28 years old, 19 years younger than Colonel Sprague, the Federal
commander who opposed him. "Wheeler, Lieutenant General John Bell
Hood's Chief of Cavalry and a native Georgian, was a restless, energetic man, known to be fearless," [18] notes historian Ben Fuller Fordney.
Wheeler and his soldiers arrived south of town, where they got a big
surprise. "General Hardee supposed the place to be occupied only by
cavalry, but on reconnoitering the position in person about 12 o'clock
I found that a division of infantry, strongly intrenched, occupied the
town." [19] Wheeler is mistaken in stating that the town was occupied by
a division of Federals, as it was only a brigade of three regiments. He is
also mistaken that the Federals were entrenched. The many detailed
accounts of the Federals' occupation of Decatur are unequivocal that

while some of the Federals had erected rail barricades when they first entered the town, they quickly moved westward toward Atlanta and did not entrench. The Battle of Decatur would be an open ground, running battle, just as was the far larger Battle of Atlanta being fought several miles to the west.

Wheeler dismounted his soldiers and attacked the Federals in Decatur "at the appointed hour." The attack would be what historian Edward G. Longacre has descriptively termed one of Wheeler's "patented multidirectional assaults."[20] Wheeler continues his account of the battle: "Just as I was moving my line the enemy commenced to throw out two regiments of infantry to meet my approach. These were overthrown, a number of prisoners captured, and the remainder driven in confusion into the enemy's works, from which we received a most galling fire from both infantry and artillery. Seeing the strength of the position in front, I threw a force upon his right flank and rear and formed my main line so as to bear obliquely upon the enemy's right, with the right of my line covering and engaging the enemy's front. From these positions simultaneous charges were made upon the enemy, the troops bearing upon the enemy's right being somewhat the most advanced." Wheeler described what it was like to be on the receiving end of the Federals' terrific storm of lead and iron. "At first the galling fire made the most exposed portion of my line waver, but, quickly rallying, the onset was renewed, and with a triumphant shout the entire line of works was carried." [21] Wheeler's reference to "line of works" almost certainly refers to the fence rail barricades the Federals had erected when they entered Decatur.

Let us pick back up the attack as seen from the Federal side. Colonel Sprague's account continues: "Our skirmishers being sharply engaged, and discovering the enemy moving in force to the left of Colonel Montgomery, with the evident design of cutting him off, I ordered him to move to the left and rear so as to be in supporting distance of the main line. He had hardly executed the movement before the enemy advanced in strong force in my front, and at the same time pretty large masses were seen moving to my rear, both on my right and left." [22] General

Sherman, who at mid-day on July 22nd was a few miles to the west of Decatur with General John Schofield examining the Confederate lines between Atlanta and Decatur, heard the beginning of the battle in Decatur. He described the start of the dramatic battle that would make July 22 famous in Civil War history. "I heard the sound of musketry to our left rear, at first mere pattering shots, but soon they grew in volume, accompanied with artillery, and about the same time the sound of guns was heard in the direction of Decatur. No doubt could longer be entertained of the enemy's plan of action." [23] Back in Decatur, here occurred a dramatic moment in the battle, as described by Colonel Sprague. "Colonel Montgomery's battalion got somewhat entangled in a swamp, which was found in the rear, when he attempted to rejoin the main line, and, being heavily pressed by the enemy, the command came in with the organization somewhat broken. Before all could extricate themselves from the swamp some were surrounded and captured by the enemy." [24]

Lieutenant Colonel Jeremiah M. Rusk of the 25th Wisconsin described his unit's experiences in the battle, writing, "Companies D and G were on picket, under command of Capt. M.E. Leonard, about one mile south of Decatur; at 12 [noon] Companies B, E, F and I, with four companies from the 63rd Ohio Infantry, under the command of Col. Milton Montgomery and myself, were ordered out on the road leading south to ascertain what the strength and position of the enemy was (it having been reported that the enemy was in overwhelming force). We moved forward, deploying two companies about half a mile, when we discovered the enemy in strong force. At this moment we were informed that the enemy was coming in our left, when Col. M. Montgomery moved rapidly to the left with six companies, leaving me in charge of the right. At this moment I discovered a line of battle on my right flank advancing rapidly, also a heavy force was coming in on our left. We were obliged to fall back to the line of battle, composed of one section of the Chicago [Board of Trade] battery and Companies C, H, and K of our regiment [which] were under command of Maj. W. H. Joslin. Here we attempted to make a stand." This would have been along the railroad. [25]

Colonel Milton Montgomery, commander of the 25th Wisconsin Infantry, was shot and captured by Confederates during the Battle of Decatur. Confederate surgeons amputated his wounded arm. He survived prison and was later exchanged and returned to his regiment to finish the war.

A later account described what next happened to Rusk and Montgomery. "The enemy advancing in strong force, Colonel Montgomery moved the reserve by the left flank, and in attempting to cross the ditch to reach the battery in the rear, his horse sank in the miry ground, and he was shot by the enemy and captured. Lieut. Col. Rusk, with the skirmishers, held the enemy in check for a short time on the road, but were soon obliged to retire. In attempting to do this, Lieutenant Colonel Rusk [who was on horseback] was surrounded by six or eight rebels who came at him with bayonets at a charge. One of them made a dash at the Lieutenant Colonel and grabbed his sword, which hung in its scabbard by his side, the squad crying out for the 'Yankee' to surrender. The Colonel made a characteristic reply [Editor's note: it was obviously too profane for publication!], and very coolly pressed his revolver to the side of the head of the rebel, and gave him its contents. In falling, the fellow still held to the Colonel's sword which broke from its fastening. Putting spurs to his horse, the Colonel dashed down the road, under the fire of the rebels, to which he replied with his revolver and succeeded in rejoining the regiment near the battery in the rear, not, however, until he had his horse shot from under him." [26] A very large man, Rusk's escape uninjured was miraculous. [27]

A newspaper correspondent writing under the name "U.S.S." later described what was happening. "At this time our regiment was getting in a tight place, being in a ravine near the timber, with unprotected flanks. They did not observe the enemy until, with a wild yell they came down on their right, threatening to surround and capture the whole regiment. The men delivered their fire, but were forced to fall back. At the same time fighting the enemy pressing us closely we were ordered to fall back; this we did, rallying at times and pouring into the enemies [sic] ranks a deadly volley. Retreating back to the rail road, what was our astonishment at finding the 'Grey Backs' there before us – it was even so – they had come around our flanks, formed a line on the rail road, thinking to easily capture us on our retreat; but we could not see the point. The horrors of incarceration in the rebel prisons came to our minds vividly; and with one thought – go through or die – in our minds, we rushed forward and cut through their lines. 'Twas a bold attempt, but death by the bullet or bayonet was preferable to imprisonment; which would surely be our doom if captured." [28]

Colonel Sprague continues his account of the battle. "The two companies on the right of the battery being joined by one or two companies of the reconnoitering party, a line was at once formed nearly perpendicular to the original line to meet the enemy on my right, and Colonel Cladek, with the 35th New Jersey, was doing the same on the left. There was little difficulty in checking the advance of the enemy in front at any time during the action, but [as] the masses passing to my rear on the right and left would endanger the trains in town and on the road from

Roswell, I fell back to the hill at the south line of town. The line was soon formed with six guns in position, and the fight continued until the town was very nearly enveloped by the superior numbers of the enemy." [29]

The 35th New Jersey reached the railroad and "Hardly had I reached that point and formed line of battle when I became hotly engaged with the enemy, the regiment on my right having been driven across the railroad, thus leaving my right flank exposed to the enemy, which was immediately taken advantage of by them," [30] commander Colonel John J. Cladek wrote. "At the same time, cavalry and infantry of the enemy got between our picket-line and the left flank of my regiment. Seeing that I would shortly be cut off, and not receiving orders, although checking the enemy for the time being in my immediate front, I retreated up the hill about 50 yards, and immediately faced about and commenced firing." When the Confederates got between the 35th New Jersey's pickets and main line, the 35th's two companies that were out on the picket line, Company I led by Captain Augustus Dusenberry, and Company D led by Second Lieutenant David Oliphant, were cut off and were nearly all captured. [31] Only nine men escaped from the two companies.

The nature of the combat south of the railroad was described by Confederate General Samuel W. Ferguson, whose brigade led the attack with other Confederate cavalry brigades joining in. He describes the battle in his memoirs, beginning with an amusing anecdote. While riding on horseback through the woods toward the Federals, an unexpected encounter with a hornets' nest caused Ferguson's horse to momentarily ride between the Federal and Confederate lines, putting Ferguson in a dangerous spot. His account begins with the battle beginning southwest of town, south of the railroad. "I made the direct attack, fighting on foot and through thick woods of black oak," Ferguson wrote. "The resistance was stubborn, we were driving the enemy back slowly, when I rode into a hornets' nest. My horse dashed off, almost scraping me off through the thickets. My hat was knocked off and the hornets stuck on my head and neck. I was between two fires and altogether in a very hot place. As soon as an opening was reached, I threw myself from my horse, landing on my heels and jerked the horse down. The hornets had been distanced, and for a moment or two I did not know which way to go, for I had not taken notes of directions in my little excursion. However, a glance at the sun and my habits as a hunter enabled me to take the way back to my command. The first man I met had my hat in his hand." [32] "In a few minutes more we had driven the enemy from the woods and then advanced rapidly to the railroad cut. Here my horse was shot under me," Ferguson recalled.

The Confederates pressed down upon the Federals by the railroad "with very superior force and with such vigor as to cause the companies and men to separate in squads," the 63rd Ohio's Major John W. Fouts said. "Company B, Lieut. L.G. Matheny commanding, and Company C, Capt. Winslow L. Bay commanding, were ordered to support section of Company C, First Regiment [Michigan] Light Artillery. They had been in position but a few moments when the enemy opened upon them with artillery and charged with so much superior force in front and upon their right flank as to cause them to fall back." [33] The Federals were driven over the railroad. Sprague ordered the Federals to fall back into the court-house square, fighting from three sides (east, south and west) of it. Finding the Confederates were closing in on both flanks, "we fell back to town," Colonel Rusk of the 25th Wisconsin said. "Here we successfully checked the enemy, holding our position until ordered to fall back farther. In falling back we had a swamp and deep ditch to cross. Colonel Montgomery got his horse down and had to abandon him. He took his revolvers from the holders, and I am told fired several shots at the enemy. He was shot in the arm, breaking it between the wrist and elbow, and was captured." [34] A newspaper correspondent in Decatur at the time described Montgomery's capture. "Colonel Montgomery was badly wounded in the arm, and had to give up from exhaustion. No braver man fell into the hands of the enemy that day; for in this campaign, from the charge of Resaca down, he showed the courage of a lion," [35] wrote "Quartus," the Cincinnati Daily Commercial's correspondent. "Quartus" continues to describe the fight. "South of the railroad a line of battle was formed, and our men were very resolute.

The two guns of the 3d [sic 1st] Michigan Battery were advanced and did good service. But bravery could not compete with numbers, and after a short resistance, our men were ordered to fall back, and a new line was formed at the jail." [36] "Our guns opened fire (from where they stood) on the rebels who were coming up at a brisk walk across the hill," wrote the Chicago Board of Trade Battery's John Nourse, no doubt describing the Confederates coming across the railroad as viewed from his position near the courthouse. "Our caissions got out into the road, ready for retreat or advance." [37]

Lieutenant Henry Shier of the First Michigan Light Artillery received orders from Colonel Sprague "to take a position on a hill near the jail in town, but finding it occupied by the Chicago Board of Trade Battery I moved a little to the left of them and commenced firing at the enemy's left battery; but wishing to embarrass them as much as possible we moved to the right and rear about fifty yards and commenced [firing] again on their skirmishers, who were advancing on our left. We caused them to fall back for a short time. Perceiving the enemy endeavoring to gain our right and rear we moved still farther to the right and again checked their advance and kept them from gaining the road on which the [wagon] train was passing. [Editor's note: This is now Clairmont Road, leading north out of Decatur.] We then fell back 150 yards and took another position, using a few rounds of canister on the enemy with good effect. We held this position with one company of the 25th Wisconsin until all our troops had left town and passed us; we then fell back and fell in line with the Chicago Board of Trade Battery by order of Col. J.W. Sprague." Remarkably, none of the gunners of the First Michigan Light Artillery were injured, Shier reported. The two guns of Battery C of the First Michigan Light Artillery fired 59 rounds during the battle. [38]

While the battle had raged along the railroad, the hundreds of wagons holding the Federal army's precious supplies that were parked in and near the cemetery began getting out of town as fast as they could, heading north up what's now Clairmont Road toward what's now North Decatur Road. "There was scarcely any confusion, but the mules were urged by shouting and whipping to their utmost speed. The rebels threw shells along the line of the road, and some of the last teams on the road were fairly riddled by bullets. Yet there was but one teamster hit, and only a few mules wounded; not more than three wagons were lost," [39] noted newspaper correspondent "Quartus". "The wagon trains of the 15th, 17th and 23rd army corps were here, but they got to the rear without the loss of a single wagon," wrote Nourse of the Chicago Board of Trade Battery. "It was wonderful to see the men drive, and they can thank their stars the road was wide and all the fences down – They drove at a tearing gallop three and four abreast, no stop for any obstruction." [40]

In the ranks of the 63rd Ohio, private Isaiah R. Rose saw his younger brother Thompson, who was also a member of Company K, fall mortally wounded and was assisting him when he (Isaiah) was taken prisoner. Thompson was severely wounded in the chest and would shortly die. [41]

On the southeastern side of town the 35th New Jersey was fighting bravely. "Knowing that it depended upon my regiment to cover the left of the brigade," commander John Cladek continued, "I sent a company to the left between the houses and the field this side of my camp. At this time the regiment on my right again fell back, with the exception of Captain Gilmore, 63rd Ohio Volunteers, with a number of his men, who kept upon my immediate right flank. Captain Sine, Company E, whom I sent to the left to cover my flank, at once became hotly engaged, being forced again to fall back step by step, and contesting sharply with the enemy for every foot of ground lost. The men of my regiment cheered lustily, which had the effect to cause the enemy to feel their way more cautiously into town." [42]

Confederate General Sam Ferguson's account of this part of the battle is notable for his description. "The town was on the other side of the railroad and had to be taken house by house." [43] Ferguson's description is supported by the account of newspaper correspondent "Quartus." The battle now intensified on the east side of Decatur toward the cemetery. In the 35th New Jersey, Colonel Cladek wrote that "At this time I changed front to the rear to resist an attack upon my left about being made, but seeing our battery and infantry falling back more rapidly than I expected, I immediately worked my way up to the public square to cover the artillery. At this time the ammunition of my regiment became exhausted… In fact, the officers and men of my regiment showed no signs of giving up the contest without making the enemy pay dearly." [44] "Quartus" described it this way: "The rebels now pressed the left heavily, also sweeping away two whole companies of the 35th New Jersey, who nevertheless made a bold fight, as they have ever done. The line again fell back, and were reformed in the public square, near the Court-House. The 63rd Ohio had raised the national flag here, and it floated proudly where only the rebel bars had been seen for nearly three years. Company I, 63rd Ohio, was here on provost duty. They fell into line, having taken down the flag. The stand here was brief, for the enemy poured in through all the streets, by the back door of the houses, and fired on the men from the front." [45] When during the battle the 63rd's banner bearer, Corporal William J. Harris of Company C, was shot dead in the courthouse square, the regiment's flag was picked up by private Alonzo J. Shuman of Company D who "waved it above his head, and called upon the men to stand by him for he would die before our banner should fall into rebel hands," [46] the 63rd Ohio's Major Fouts recalled.

As the Confederates were moving around the western edge of town to try to surround the Federals, an infantry lieutenant colonel told Lieutenant Trumbull Griffin of the Chicago Board of Trade Battery it was best for the guns to retreat. [47] Griffin limbered up one section of guns (two guns) and moved to the rear, leaving the other section in the command of Lieutenant Henry Bennett at the courthouse. Bennett's guns now started getting shelled by the Confederates, but he silenced them "by a few well-directed shots." Bennett's work was noticed by newspaper correspondent "Quartus", who later wrote, "The section of the Michigan Battery joined the section of the Chicago Board of Trade Batteries [sic], and the rebels did not seem to be eager to advance into range of the guns. Lieutenant Bennett, who was a stranger to us, won our admiration for his cool, energetic bravery and will always obtain a hearty greeting from Colonel Sprague's brigade." [48]

As Wheeler's Confederates pressed the federals around the court-house, the 63rd Ohio's Lieutenant Colonel Charles E. Brown was in the thick of the fighting. Major Fouts' account continues. "Company I, Lieut. James A. Gilmore commanding, was on provost duty in Decatur, formed in the public square, and met the enemy, fell back fighting and in good order to the ridge north of town, where, deploying as skirmishers in front and on the left flank, protected the disarranged parts of the brigade, which were being rallied on the ridge. Company H, Lieut. Charles M. Harrison commanding, was the only company left in camp. This company and the camp guard took position to the right of section of Chicago Board of Trade Battery. The enemy advanced in greatly superior force and it became necessary for the battery to retire. While retiring the battery became entangled in a heap of old iron and was in danger of being captured. In order to save the battery Company G, which had formed on the left of the battery, and Company H fixed bayonets and made a determined charge on the advancing line of the enemy, causing it to fall back to the railroad and giving the battery time to get off, and giving a large wagon train of the Fifteenth Army Corps time to leave the field, which, but for this charge, would have fallen into the hands of the enemy. These companies, under command of Lieut. Col. Charles E. Brown, then fell back in good order to court [house] square. Adjt. Howard Forrer was killed during this movement. The other companies of the regiment coming in at this time were rallied and formed on south side of court [house] square with part of the 25th Wisconsin Infantry, and held the ground until completely flanked on right and left, when we were ordered to fall back to [the] ridge north of the town. In rallying the regiment at this point Lieut. Col. Charles E. Brown was severely wounded and carried from the field. The enemy continuing the attack with a much superior force in front and on both flanks obliged us to fall back to the cover of the woods, and we took position with the balance of the brigade." [49] Brown would have been taken, probably in a horse-drawn ambulance, to a field hospital north of town – possibly at the Powell house. Newspaper correspondent "Quartus" described what had just happened: "The rebels began to pour in in crowds on the right. Col. Brown, Major Fouts and Adjutant Forrer, of the the 63rd Ohio, took Company H, the only one at liberty, and a few men who were falling back, and made so bold a charge on them that they fell back into the woods. In a moment they emerged again in increased numbers, and the company had to fall back. As they did so, a ball [Editor's note: bullet] struck Adjutant H. Forrer and he fell dead. He was one of those noble-hearted, brave, conscientious young men, justly the pride of his family, whose death makes us feel how sad and savage a thing war is." [50] With the 63rd Ohio's Colonel Brown now hors de combat, command of the 63rd Ohio was passed to Major John W. Fouts. Colonel Sprague later recalled that, "On the fall of Colonel Brown, I rode up to Major Fouts and told him he must hold his position until I relieved him. His eyes sparkled as he replied, 'We will hold until the last man falls.' Such troops, commanded by such officers, could be killed, but they could not be conquered." [51]

Private Marcellus S. Roach of the 63rd Ohio Infantry was among the Federals captured by Confederates during the Battle of Decatur.

Joining in to help the hard-pressed Federal infantry were some of Garrard's cavalry. They had been left behind in Decatur to watch over Garrard's pack mule train when the main force of the cavalry rode off on the morning of July 22 to destroy the railroad near Covington. And unlike most of the Federal infantry (who were armed with single-shot muzzle loading rifles), the cavalry had seven-shot, repeating Spencer rifles. As the Confederates charged into Decatur, "our boys with the pack mules were used to moving quick, and so gathered up and got out of the way without loss, but they were terribly scared, and said they did wish our brigade had been there," notes the regimental history of the 72nd Indiana Volunteer Infantry, which was among Garrard's forces. "The infantry rallied, and as soon as our boys got the pack mules out of the way, all that could be spared rushed to the rescue, and by their help the infantry were enabled to drive the rebels back through the town; but they were in turn reinforced by such numbers as to drive our men back again; but they fell back slowly, and by this time the [wagon]trains were all hitched up and moved rapidly to the west. This fight, for the numbers engaged, was just as desperate as on any part of the lines, and there is not the least bit of doubt that but for the boys of our brigade the rebels would have gobbled the whole outfit. Sergt. Stewart, of Company A, speaks thus of Henry Heiney, private of the same company, which simply illustrates what was done by numbers of others: 'He went through the whole engagement, firing nearly 100 rounds of ammunition. His Spencer rifle was a great curiosity to the infantry regiment he fell in with; he knew they were hard pressed and needed his help, and as he had plenty of ammunition and there were plenty of rebels to shoot, he entirely satisfied their curiosity.'" [52]

In her later book, Mary Gay describes the part of the battle that would have occurred as the Federals retreated north out of the town and the Confederates occupied the ground where her house was. Gay says (Editor's note: remember that what Gay wrote should not be accepted uncritically) a Confederate officer wearing a gray uniform "came dashing up and said: 'Go in your cellar and lie down; the Federals are forming a line of battle, and we, too, will form one that will reach across your grounds, and your house will be between the two lines. Go at once.'" Gay writes that her mother and two of their slaves took shelter in a neighbor's cellar, while Gay says she stayed in her house. "Shot and shell flew in every direction, and the shingles on the roof were following suit, and the leaves, and the limbs, and the bark of the trees were descending in showers so heavy as almost to obscure the view of the contending forces. The roaring of cannon and the sound of musketry blended in harmony so full and grand, and the scene was so absorbing, that I thought not of potential danger, and more than once found myself outside of the portals ready to rush into the conflict – for was I not a soldier, enlisted for the war?" [53]

As the Federal infantry retreated north out of town, the cannons of the Chicago Board of Trade Battery stood their ground and fought on, leaving the gunners alone and exposed to death or capture. "The rebels came on by the thousands, and the infantry and Michigan Battery fled before them," gunner John Nourse later wrote bitterly. "Away to the rear they went without looking at our boys – while we gave the rebels cannister, fearfully, which checked the rebels and allowed the Michigan Battery to bring off two guns, but they lost their battery and baggage wagons. Then the rebels came on again – we stopped them, but it was no use for we had no (infantry) support, and they stretched their wings, and so flanked us on both sides. We drew back one hundred yards to a cross street, and so placed the guns as to rake both streets. Here we did good work with cannister, but having no support (all the infantry having gone to the rear) the rebels came up on both sides of us, through lots, behind fences, houses etc., and shot our men like dogs, dropping them all around the guns, with not a soldier to help us, and not a shot from the Michigan Battery, which had gone to the rear. We stood it for about three minutes, then moved back one mile, where we found the infantry and Michigan Battery had halted, and were in line. To sum up, there were eight men wounded out of thirty two, and all this occurred in less than thirty minutes' time. But we stopped the rebels long enough to allow all the ammunition and commissary trains for three army corps to get safely to the rear. The rebels did not get a single supply wagon. ... We are thankful their artillery firing was so poor or they might have killed us all." The battery's wounded were all taken away with it as it retreated north. [54]

Colonel Sprague did indeed see the work of the cannoneers. "Here again the artillery opened with effect," he later remembered. "The trains of the Fifteenth Corps, which were in town when the fight commenced, had all withdrawn and were safe. I had no doubt about my ability to hold the courthouse square and the town, but this would not prevent the enemy from attacking the trains of our army coming up from Roswell, so I withdrew from the town on the Roswell road..." [55] Major Fouts, now in command of the 63rd Ohio, would later write about this stage of the battle, "The enemy attacked on all sides with a very superior force, and after two hours' hard fighting, we were finally driven out of the town." [56] But the Federals then discovered that in the confusion of battle the Second Brigade's flag had been left flying from the top of the courthouse, in the center of the public square, which had been occupied by the Confederates. Sprague called on the 63rd Ohio and part of the 25th Wisconsin to charge the enemy and rescue the flag. The Federal soldiers went forward "double quick" "with cheers that still ring in my ears," and drove the Confederates away and saved the flag, Sprague recalled almost 30 years later in 1892. [57] As the Federals retreated out of Decatur, they made a short stand on the northern edge of the town "to beat off the enemy who were approaching from the west," Sprague said. They then moved further north to the intersection of the Roswell and Pace's Ferry roads (now Clairmont and North Decatur roads). It was then and there that the first reinforcements arrived just in time to help Sprague's forces. The 43rd Ohio and five companies of the Ninth Illinois Mounted Infantry and one section of Battery C of the First Michigan Artillery had left Roswell the morning of July 22nd, escorting a train of 400 wagons headed for Decatur. As the column approached, they could hear the Confederate cannons and learned the Confederates had captured the town. The 43rd's commander, Colonel Wager Swayne, urged the wagon train to move down what's now North Decatur Road toward what's now Emory University. He then gathered up the troops that had been distributed throughout the wagons and placed them in defensive positions, except for three companies of the 9th Illinois under Major John Kuhn who went to assist Sprague's soldiers then retreating northward out of Decatur. [58] The soldiers of the Ninth Illinois "threw out a strong line of skirmishers to the west of the road mentioned," Sprague said. "He had just come up with the [wagon] train from Roswell, which some time before I had ordered turned to the right toward the rear of the Twenty-third Corps. After the artillery had all passed, I moved along the Roswell road leisurely to the junction of the Pace's Ferry Road, and took a strong position and threw up some rude but strong defenses. This point is about one mile northward from Decatur. Here Col. Wager Swayne, commanding [officer of the 43rd Ohio Infantry], came up and joined me. The [wagon] trains which were passing in my rear toward the Twenty-third Corps were hastened forward and soon all were known to be safe, but the enemy did not see fit to follow and continue the fight. My skirmishers were advanced and remained during the night in sight of the town..." [59]

The Federals received additional reinforcements from the nearby 23rd Army Corps, who moved into position along Pea Vine Creek near what is now the Emory University campus. Major General John M. Schofield noted in a report that, "Shortly before noon, the enemy having commenced a heavy attack upon the Army of the Tennessee [Editor's note: this was the main Battle of Atlanta], three brigades of Cox's division and one of Hascall's were put in reserve, ready to act when the general-in-chief [Editor's note: General Sherman], who was present, might direct. About noon Reilly's brigade was sent to Pea Vine Creek, to protect our rear against a force which had turned our left through Decatur, and was reported to be threatening our trains. [Editor's note: Colonel James W. Reilly commanded the First Brigade of the Third Division of the 23rd Army Corps, which included the 112th Illinois, 16th

Kentucky, 100th Ohio, 104th Ohio, and 8th Tennessee regiments.] About 1 p. m. General Cox was sent with two brigades to a point on the railroad about a mile from Decatur, to cover the immediate left rear of the Army of the Tennessee. These dispositions proved ample, and the enemy was deterred from making further attempts to strike our rear." [60] Two regiments from the 23rd's First Brigade, the 8th Tennessee Infantry and 16th Kentucky Veteran Infantry, moved to a position near the intersection of North Decatur and Clairmont roads to support Sprague's soldiers. The move was helpful but unnecessary, as the Federals were not attacked by Wheeler's troops. [61] Sprague did not know it, but the Confederates had already called off their attack and were heading back to Atlanta. As the Federals had retreated north out of Decatur, Confederate General Wheeler received ordered to halt his attack because his help was needed by the main Confederate army then fighting the Battle of Atlanta six miles westward. That Confederate attack was failing in the face of determined Federal resistance. "Just as I was pursuing the enemy beyond the town," Wheeler recounted, "three of General Hardee's staff officers came to me in rapid succession, directing that I should re-enforce General Hardee as quickly as possible. The pursuit was stopped and all my available troops moved at a gallop to General Hardee's position." [62]

But there was still time for some of Wheeler's hungry and exhausted men to grab some goodies. When they had overrun Decatur, some of the Federal soldiers lost the knapsacks they taken off so they could fight unencumbered. The 25th Wisconsin's John F. Brobst lost his knapsack, which held his precious photo of Mary Englesby, his girlfriend back home. [63] Newspaper correspondent "Quartus" noted that as the Confederates "began to see that their victory was over; they would not advance further, but began their usual stealing." The Confederates' need for clothing is shown by this: when the Federals later re-entered Decatur and recovered the body of the 63rd Ohio's Howard Forrer, he "was found stripped of all but his underclothes." [64]

Three decades after the battle, one Confederate participant, Captain W. A. Campbell, recalled this incident involving a soldier of the

63rd Ohio "just at the edge of Decatur." "As my command (Muldrow's Mississippi Cavalry) went into Decatur I saw a wounded Federal in the hot sun, and I halted and asked him if I could do anything for him. He said, 'Yes, please give me water and get me out of the sun.' I unslung my canteen and gave him half of his own canteen and carried him to the shade. He then pointed to one of our men and said, 'That man took my money and knife.' I ordered the man to return them to him, which he did, and I said to the Federal that as soon as the battle was over I would have him carried to the field hospital. After the fight was over I went back to see about him, but he had been taken away, and I do not know anything more of him. He was shot through the right lung, and may have died." [65]

William L. Nugent of Ferguson's Brigade described the battle in a letter written to his wife Nellie on July 26, just four days afterward, including important details about the Confederate attack. "We attacked Decatur on the 22nd and took the town driving out a Brigade of Infantry and a good deal of Dismounted Cavalry. Our Brigade really took the town, tho' it was supported on both flanks by a Brigade of Cavalry dismounted. The fight lasted about two hours and was very hot for awhile. The Yankees had the hills and houses on us and fought very well for a time... We captured over a hundred prisoners and killed and wounded about one hundred and fifty." [66] Another one of Wheeler's Confederate cavalrymen, Orlando Devant Chester of the 5th Georgia Cavalry, wrote briefly about the battle in a July 26 letter to his father. His description includes an additional important detail – that while the main Confederate attack went in on foot, others of Wheeler's Cavalry were apparently held back waiting on horseback, and then launched a mounted attack once the Federals began to retreat through the town. "If it were not so late I would give you a long account of our dash into Decatur. We were held back until the Yankees commenced to run when we charged after them at a break neck gallop, capturing some prisoners and considerable plunder. I myself made no captures except in the eating line. I went into a little shop where some officers had been cooking and pounced upon a pot of beef that was just done and very nice. I had had nothing [to eat] for some time. I tried some coffee I found on the table but it was too much shaken up." [67]

Another Confederate soldier, O.P. Hargis of the 1st Georgia Cavalry, recounts a fascinating scene that occurred during this part of the battle, also involving food rather than fighting, "when we made that famous charge into the town of Decatur. When we got into the public square three women ran out in the street and cheered us on, when General Allen saw them he ordered them to be taken into the cellar out of danger. I ran into the back yard of the hotel to get some water and while there, I saw two big pones of egg bread on a stove in the kitchen, and I ran in and grabbed them out, took them on my arm, and carried them on to my company. We drove the Federals out of Decatur and we captured a good many prisoners that was hid in the town during that time." [68] Recall Decatur resident Mary Gay describing how during the battle she "more than once found myself outside of the portals ready to rush into the conflict" and that as the Federals retreated "the women and children, until now panic-stricken and silent as death, joined in the rejoicing." [69] One can't help but wonder if she was one of the women who Hargis saw out in the street. Even if Gay was not one of them, the event demonstrates the spirit of Southern women like Gay in towns like Decatur.

Newspaper correspondent "U.S.S." described the scene in Decatur toward the end of the day. "After carrying off their dead and wounded, plundering the town and the knapsacks which our men, to facilitate their retreat, had thrown away, the rebels left and returned to their old position. About sun-set our cavalry went back to the town and found our wounded men, I am most happy to state, in private houses, receiving the best care and attention that circumstances would admit of. They had been conveyed from where they fell by the soldiers and citizens." [70] A newspaper account by correspondent "Quartus" published in Cincinnati about a week afterward noted that, "As night drew near Colonel Sprague selected a position north of the town and threw up rail fortifications.

Here they were reinforced by the 43rd Ohio, which had just come forward from Roswell on guard duty with the supply trains. The rebels only remained in town long enough to gather what booty they could find, and then fell back south of the railroad. Our cavalry returned to the town and remained there during the night. Let it be noted to the credit of those [Editor's note: Decatur residents] who professed Unionism, that by their care of our wounded men, and other services which we need not mention [Editor's note: burying the dead], they proved their devotion to our cause. If it were wise I would like to mention the names of these, but it would probably be for their injury." [71]

In his later after-action report about the battle, Colonel Sprague called out his soldiers for their gallantry. "The gallant Thirty-fifth New Jersey was commanded by Col. John J. Cladek, and from first to last was handled with rare skill and bravery," Sprague said. Sprague also called out the artillery, saying the guns of the Chicago Board of Trade Battery and First Michigan Artillery were "served and worked with admirable skill and rapidity during the action. Many daring deeds were done by line officers and non-commissioned officers and privates, and some brilliant charges were made, in which the bayonet was freely used with effect upon the enemy," Sprague added. [72] This note about the bayonet being "freely used" is interesting, as by most accounts the bayonet was seldom actually used in Civil War combat. But if Sprague's report is accurate (and there is no reason to doubt it), it speaks to the house to house, close-in fighting that day.

Major John W. Fouts likewise praised the soldiers of the 63rd Ohio, saying they "displayed unusual gallantry and courage in their behavior." Lieutenant Henry Shier of the First Michigan Light Artillery praised his men for serving their two cannons under heavy fire of artillery and musketry, calling out for special praise First Sergeant Gregg, Sergeants White and Cheney, and First Lieutenant William W. Hyzer.[73] In his account published in Cincinnati on August 2, newspaper correspondent "Quartus" lamented the death of one brave Federal in particular. "Our losses were considerable; but how could it be otherwise, when nearly the whole of Wheeler's force opposed three medium regiments and four guns. The men proved their pluck again. There were many instances of bravery, but I cannot report them in the haste in which I write; yet I can not pass over the regimental color bearer, Corporal [William J.] Harris, Company C, who fell in the town square. His boldness during the day attracted the attention of his comrades, and they cherish his memory." [74]

Conclusion

Who won the Battle of Decatur? The gallant defense by Colonel Sprague's outnumbered infantry, the artillery and Garrard's cavalry prevented the life-supporting wagon trains of the Federal army from falling into the hands of the Confederates. If the Federals had been routed, not only could the wagon trains in Decatur have been lost, but so too could have been all the wagons coming down the road from Roswell under escort of the 43rd Ohio. Although Wheeler's Confederates drove the Federals out of the town and could have prosecuted the attack northward, they would have quickly run into the defensive line formed by Colonel Sprague which had been reinforced by four additional Federal regiments. The Confederates would certainly have been stopped without capturing the Federal wagon trains or getting into the rear of Sherman's left wing. In his 2003 pamphlet on the Battle of Decatur, Albert Rauber wryly observes that, "Had Wheeler continued his pursuit he would have found himself in the predicament of the dog that chased a skunk, and caught him." [75] This is exactly right. General Sherman recognized Sprague's performance a week after the battle by promoting him to brigadier general. So the victory was clearly Colonel Sprague's and the Federals'. Colonel Sprague's corps commander at the time of the battle, Major General Grenville M. Dodge, praised Sprague's performance in a report written several weeks later, noting that Sprague had "by determined, unyielding fighting, held the enemy in check and gained a position north of the town, which he was able to hold. By so doing he saved the trains of the Fifteenth, Sixteenth, and Seventeenth Army Corps, then on the road from Roswell to the commands. Great credit is due Colonel (now General) Sprague and his brigade for their conduct on this occasion. We were, no doubt, saved a serious disaster by his cool judgment and excellent dispositions." [76] Years later, Dodge again declared the fight a Federal victory, noting that at Decatur, "Sprague's Brigade of the Sixteenth Army Corps met and defeated Wheeler's Cavalry." [77] The Confederates accomplished nothing in their attack on Decatur, just as they accomplished nothing in the far larger and far bloodier Battle of Atlanta.

But what if the Confederates had routed the Federals at Decatur and captured all the wagon trains? Might it have changed the course of the Atlanta Campaign? Historian David Evans, author of the magisterial study "Sherman's Horsemen," speculated that it could have. Writing in Civil War Times in 1988 about the Battle of Decatur, Evans noted that although Wheeler "made much of driving Sprague from the field, he had failed in his larger objective, to capture Sherman's trains." Evans went on to say that while the "appalling bloodletting" at the main Battle of Atlanta was front-page news in the North, "Sprague's fight for the wagons was scarcely mentioned. But the defeat [of the Confederates] at Decatur was just as important to Sherman as his victory at [the Battle of] Atlanta. Were it not for Sprague's gallant stand, Wheeler might well have captured the ordnance and supply trains of the XV, XVI, XVII and XXIII Corps. Without these wagons, half of Sherman's army would have been virtually immobilized for want of transportation to carry food and ammunition. This would have made it difficult, if not impossible, for him to shift his Army of [The] Tennessee from his left flank to the extreme right to threaten Hood's communications as he did on July 27. [Editor's note: After besieging Atlanta unsuccessfully during August 1864, and under immense pressure from Washington to capture Atlanta for political reasons, Sherman shifted his army around to the west and southwest side of the city in an ultimately successful effort to cut the last rail line to Macon, finally forcing its surrender.] Of course, Sherman would have eventually recouped his losses, but replacing perhaps as many as 1,600 wagons and teams would have taken time. Instead of capturing Atlanta on September 2, it might have been October or even November before he brought the city to its knees. With Grant bogged down in front of Richmond, and Rebels raiding in Pennsylvania and Maryland, such a setback might have had a profound effect on that Autumn's presidential elections in the war-weary North. Without the early Autumn [Editor's note: Actually late summer] capture of Atlanta to buoy their spirits, Yankee voters might have instead chosen Democratic peace candidate George McClellan, not Republican incumbent Abraham Lincoln. Sherman fully appreciated the significance of what Sprague had done, and at his urging the War Department promoted the officer to the rank of brigadier general of volunteers on July 30, 1864." [78] While it is a stretch to suggest the Battle of Decatur could have affected Lincoln's re-election, it is certainly true that a Confederate victory at Decatur would have been a setback for Sherman's effort to capture Atlanta.

But the battle was now over. For many of the soldiers on both sides who fought at Decatur and survived unscathed, it was probably quickly forgotten as the bloody contest for Atlanta continued for another six weeks. Many would go on to be killed or wounded in other battles as the war dragged on for another eight months. For the dead at Decatur, the war was over, their families and loved ones left to grieve and rebuild their lives once news of their loved one's death reached them at home. For the wounded of both sides, and the hundred Federal soldiers who had been captured, their lives had taken a very bad turn for the worse. Let us now look at the immediate aftermath of the battle.

VII

Aftermath, Part 1

With the Federals driven out of Decatur, followed by the departure of Wheeler's Cavalry, Decatur was very briefly unoccupied by either Federals or Confederates. On Saturday July 23, Mary Gay got up at dawn. "The morning after the hurried evacuation of Decatur by the Federal troops, I arose, as was my custom, as day was dawning, and, as soon as I thought I could distinguish objects, I opened the front door and stepped out on the portico" where she "stood looking upon the ruin and devastation of my war-stricken home." [1] A short time later Gay heard horses, and saw they were Confederate scouts looking to see if the town was occupied by Federals. The Yankees she hated were gone, but not for long. The Federals, who had spent the night behind their defensive line just north of Decatur, soon re-entered the town. Beginning at 6.am., the Federals left the breastworks they had quickly erected the day before a half mile north of town and moved back into Decatur, encountering no resistance from Confederates. Details were sent to find the Federal dead and wounded, who were buried or cared for "as far as our limited means would allow," the 25th Wisconsin's Lieutenant Colonel Rusk recalled. After a two-hour halt, the Federals proceeded west on the road to Atlanta, marching about two miles, where they stopped and entrenched. [2] Newspaper correspondent "U.S.S." described events on Saturday morning. "Reinforcements were received, and at 8 A.M. Saturday morning, we advanced on the town a strong skirmish line in front, the enemy was seen south of town, but no fighting took place. After caring for our wounded and arranging matters in general, we moved out towards the main army two miles..." [3]

Lieutenant Colonel Jeremiah Rusk of the 25th Wisconsin Infantry took command of the regiment when Colonel Milton Montgomery was captured by Confederates during the Battle of Decatur. Rusk is shown here in a post-war photograph when he was a member of the U.S. Congress. He would go on to become governor of Wisconsin and the first-ever U.S. Secretary of Agriculture.

In a testament to the ferocity of the Battle of Decatur, the casualties included the commanding officers of two of the three Federal regiments engaged. With the commander of the 63rd Ohio – Colonel Charles E. Brown -- in the hospital missing a leg, and the commander of the 25th Wisconsin – Colonel Milton Montgomery -- wounded and captured by Confederates (and he had lost an arm), new commanders had to be named. For the 63rd Ohio, Major John W. Fouts had been named commander. For the 25th Wisconsin, command went to Lieutenant Colonel Jeremiah M. Rusk. Colonel John W. Sprague reported his loss in the battle as 242 killed, wounded and missing. [4] In the 63rd Ohio, one commissioned officer, Howard Forrer, had been killed and four were wounded, and one wounded and taken prisoner (Captain Daniel Thorne), for a total of six officers as casualties. Among the enlisted men were 87 total casualties, including 10 killed, 44 wounded, and 31 missing, for a total loss to the 63rd of 91. [5]

The 25th Wisconsin's casualties totaled 100, including 15 killed in action. Lieutenant Colonel Jeremiah Rusk wrote to Wisconsin Governor James T. Lewis the day after the battle that the losses among commissioned officers were one wounded and taken prisoner; one wounded and supposed taken prisoner, five wounded and one killed. Among enlisted men, 14 were dead, 39 were wounded, 10 were wounded and missing, 25 were missing, three were "sunstruck"; and one was taken prisoner. [6] The 35th New Jersey's loss in the battle was 1 killed, 16 wounded; and 2 officers and 37 men missing. [7] The Chicago Board of Trade Battery had suffered terribly, losing eight men in half an hour. The battery's Lieutenant Trumbull D. Griffin praised the conduct of Lieutenant Henry Bennett and the other gunners for their "more than ordinary coolness and courage" during the fighting. "Each and every man, non-commissioned officer and private, of the battery discharged their duty nobly and manfully, and appeared to vie with each other in their exhibition of coolness and bravery." Griffin went to the field hospital to visit private Thomas McClelland, who had lost his left arm. McClelland "manifested an enthusiasm and bravery that was truly surprising in a young lad of nineteen," Griffin recalled several days after the battle. "When spoken to in regard to the loss of his arm he replied that his only regrets were that our forces were obliged to fall back." [8] Gunner John Nourse was bitter about so many of his comrades being shot down when the Chicago Board of Trade Battery was left without infantry support toward the end of the battle. "This morning we went back through Decatur – no rebels in town. We passed through the place and joined the left wing of the army. At nine o'clock Col. Sprague told us we could go – so we left him, after saving his brigade and artillery, and all the trains placed under his care, and losing eight of our men. For all this, he did not so much as thank us, or express the least regret at our loss. Shall we ever receive any credit for yesterday's work? I doubt it." [9]

The Atlanta campaign and Battle of Decatur took a terrible toll on the Federal regiments that fought at Decatur. In a September 3, 1864, report, newly promoted Brigadier General Sprague tallied up the losses of four months of fighting between May 1 and Sept. 3, 1864:

Regiment	Killed Officers	Killed Men	Wounded Officers	Wounded Men	Missing Officers	Missing Men	Aggregate
25th Wisconsin	2	29	9	114	1	25	180
35th New Jersey	1	18	4	76	2	30	140
63rd Ohio	1	22	5	88	0	38	154
Total	4	69	18	278	2	93	474

Another chart in Sprague's report showed the strength of the regiments at the beginning of the Atlanta Campaign on May 1, 1864, and how much they had been reduced by September 3, 1864:

Regiment	May 1, 1864			September 3, 1864			Loss from all causes	Percent of loss
	Officers	Men	Aggregate	Officers	Men	Aggregate		
25th Wisconsin	21	519	540	18	260	278	262	48%
35th New Jersey	17	419	466	13	198	211	255	55%
63rd Ohio	27	711	738	21	399	420	318	41%
Total	65	1,649	1,744	52	857	909	835	48%

These statistics are shocking. From an aggregate strength of 1,744 officers and men on May 1, 1864, the three regiments were reduced to 909 by September 3, a reduction of 48 percent. [10]

Casualties on the Union side

In the 63rd Ohio, those killed in action at Decatur included Adjutant Howard Forrer; Sergeant Hiram R. Williams; Corporal William J. Harris, the 63rd Ohio's color bearer; private Amos Partlow; private Gallatin S. Marquis; Corporal Aaron Hendershott; private Thomson Rose; private John M. Swickard; private Christian Bowman; Corporal Weston Ray; and private George Milligan. The 63rd Ohio's wounded included Lieutenant Colonel Charles E. Brown, who lost his left leg; Sergeant Abraham Doll; Sergeant James W. Warstler; Corporal David Weaver (who would die from his wounds two days after the battle on July 24); Captain George Wightman, who would leave the Army in October because he was disabled; private John F. Dill, private Solomon Spitler (who would die from his wounds about two weeks after the battle, on August 8) and private Lyman S. Sells (who would die from his wounds in a field hospital on August 3.) [11]

Sprague's Brigade's fight at Decatur made front-page news in the Cincinnati Daily Commercial on August 2, 1864, which ran a detailed account of the battle and the following casualty list from the 63rd Ohio: [12]

Lieutenant Colonel Charles E. Brown, left leg amputated.

Adjutant Howard Forrer, killed.

Company A

Sergeant William H. King, head, severe.

Corporal Jacob Ebel, leg, slight.

Ezra Perry, leg, severe.

Jacob Britenstein, hip, flesh.

Joseph Wright, hand, slight.

Sergeant Hiram Williams, wounded and missing.

Wallace Picket, wounded and missing.

William Barnes, wounded and missing.

Alonzo Courtney, captured.

John Courtney, missing.

Jacob Krumm, captured.

Andrew Larrison, missing.

Ammon Perry, missing

Company B

Sergeant Abraham Doll, wounded, left hand, severe

Corporal David Weaver, wounded in abdomen, killed in action.

Corporal James W. Warstler, wounded, hip, severe.

Corporal David A. Speakman, wounded, throat, severe.

George Shiers, wounded, left arm.

Sergeant William R. Oliver, captured.

Duncan Ross, captured.

Amos Ross, captured.

Company C

Second Lieutenant M A Stewart, wounded, right leg, severe.

Corporal William J. Harris, killed.

Amos Partlow, killed.

George W. Rike, wounded, arm.

Corporal Joseph Fitch, wounded, shoulder, severe.

John W. Wandling, wounded, hand.

Vachel B. Boring, wounded, head, slight.

Samuel Karch, wounded, head, slight.

Corporal Presley S. Brown, missing.

Horatio N. Warren, missing.

Dunmore Wilson, missing.

Company D

Second Lieutenant August McDonald, wounded, arm, flesh.

Gallatin S. Marquis, killed in action.

First Sergeant O P Hill, wounded, foot, slight.

Franklin Ross, wounded, leg, flesh.

Lyman S. Sells, wounded, breast, severe.

William Clayton, wounded, shoulder, severe.

Edward Blakely, wounded, arm severe.

Simon Johnson, wounded in the thigh, flesh, and captured.

Samuel Hoon, left leg amputated.

James Johnson, wounded, leg, flesh.

Samuel Coffee, missing.

Matthew Gilpin, captured.

Company E

Joshua Francisco, wounded, hand.

Henry Stuhlman, wounded, arm, flesh.

William Grove, wounded, knee, slight.

Collin Mourhouse, missing.

Company F

Corporal Aaron Hendershott, killed in action.

John M. Swickard, killed in action.

Sergeant Abraham Rhoades, wounded, shoulder, slight.

Adis Linn, wounded, leg, slight.

Benjamin Dyer, wounded, thigh, severe.

Thomson Rose, killed in action.

Alexander Richie, wounded, shoulder, slight.

Sergeant Benjamin A. Tilton, missing.

Corporal Marcellus S. Roach, wounded and captured.

Austin A. Bridgeman, captured.

William Hendershott, missing.

Frederick Harmon, missing.

James W. Lang, missing.

Horace E. Weaver, captured.

Benjamin Winans, captured.

Isaiah Rose, captured.

John Olinger, captured.

Thomas Wolf, captured.

Company G

Captain George Wightman, wounded, head, severe. (Wightman would be discharged from the army on October 19, 1864, because of his disability.)

John Byers, wounded, leg, slight.

James L. Wills, leg, slight. [Editor's note: He is on the Cincinnati Daily Commercial's list of casualties, but not on the regiment's official roster]

Sergeant Levi Wible, wounded and captured.

Corporal Theodore Swartzel, killed in action.

John Dill, wounded and captured.

Christian Bowman, killed in action.

Company H

Corporal Weston Ray, killed in action.

George Milligan, killed in action. (also listed as George Mulligan)

Solomon Spitler, wounded, arm.

Edward Duffy, wounded, leg, flesh.

David Ingmire, wounded, arm, flesh.

Martin Drowan, wounded, leg, slight.

John Connor, wounded, leg, slight. (apparently reported incorrectly as John Bonnor in the Cincinnati Daily Commercial of August 2, 1864)

James E. Pratt, wounded, hand.

Company I

Isaac O'Brien, missing.

Company K

Captain Daniel T. Thorne, wounded and captured.

Sergeant David E. Hisey, wounded, ankle, severe.

Sergeant Frank Chatsey, wounded, side, slight.

Corporal Henry J. Arnold, wounded, head, slight.

Francis M. Randall, wounded, neck, slight.

William A. Roseboom, wounded, leg, severe.

Abijah H. Simms, wounded, neck, severe.

Sergeant David H. Reynolds, missing. (He was captured and exchanged in April 1865.)

Francis B. Dunnington, missing. He was later paroled.

The Cincinnati Daily Commercial's August 2 article noted that the 63rd Ohio's total loss at Decatur was 92. The paper did not provide a casualty list for the 25th Wisconsin or 35th New Jersey. It does report that the 25th Wisconsin's loss was "Killed, 9; wounded, 51; missing, 45; of whom a number are known to be wounded. Total, 105." For the 35th New Jersey, the paper reported, "Killed, 1; wounded, 17; missing, 30; total 57. Total for brigade, 254." As this was a newspaper account, it may not be completely accurate. The Cincinnati Daily Commercial's report is very close to the numbers later reported by Colonel Sprague and Colonel Henry in their official reports.

For the 25th Wisconsin, Lieutenant Colonel Jeremiah Rusk would write in his after-action report "our loss in this action was severe, but we have reason to believe the enemy received a greater loss". [13] There are conflicting tallies of the regiment's casualties at Decatur. Rusk, who had just taken command of the regiment after Colonel Milton Montgomery was shot and captured, does not provide casualty counts in his official reports. [14] However, as noted above, in a letter to Wisconsin Governor James T. Lewis written the day after the battle, Rusk reported a total of 100 casualties. [15] Newspaper correspondent "U.S.S.", writing home three days after the battle on July 25, gave the same figures as Rusk: One commissioned officer killed, five officers wounded, one wounded and missing, one wounded and supposed taken prisoner, and one missing, for a total of nine officers. U.S.S. lists 14 enlisted men killed, 39 wounded, 10 wounded and missing, three "sun struck" and 25 missing, for a grand total of 91. So both Rusk and "U.S.S." say 15 were killed outright. [16]

E.B. Quiner, in his authoritative Military History of Wisconsin, lists the 25th Wisconsin's casualties at the Battle of Decatur as 20 dead and died from wounds, 44 wounded and 25 missing. [17] The discrepancy between Rusk's and "U.S.S.'s" figures and Quiner's likely is due to deaths that occurred among the 25th's wounded in the days following the battle after the initial reports were sent back to Wisconsin. Assuming Quiner's tally is accurate, just how terrible a toll the battle took on the 25th Wisconsin can be seen by comparing these numbers to the total mortality figures for the regiment for the entire war: The regiment reported 27 killed in action, 16 died of wound, 376 died of disease and five died in accidents, for a total of 424 deaths. Thus, if Quiner's numbers are accurate, with the regiment suffering 20 of its wartime total of 27 killed in action at Decatur – then 74 percent of its battlefield deaths were suffered at Decatur. (The total tally of 376 dying from disease also illustrates graphically that the greatest killer in the Civil War was not big slugs of lead and fragments of iron, but tiny disease-causing microbes.]

Colonel Milton Montgomery, senior commander of the 25th Wisconsin, was now a prisoner of the Confederates, whose surgeons would amputate his right arm. [18] Montgomery's wounded arm had been dressed by a citizen of Decatur, who reported his capture to the Federals. [19]

The 25th Wisconsin's other casualties included: [20]

Company B

Captain William H. Bennett, wounded in the heel and taken prisoner, his leg was amputated three times. He died in the Confederate prison camp at Macon, Georgia, on August 10, 1864.

Minor [also reporter as Miner] Bennett, wounded in right arm, severe, discharged December 8, 1864, because of his wounds. He had enlisted in the regiment on February 20, 1864.

James A. Blair, wounded in hand, severe. He was also a new recruit, enlisting in the 25th on February 2, 1864.

Simon S. Blake, wounded in breast, severe, discharged March 20, 1865, because of his wounds. He had served with the 25th since August 1862.

Corporal William S. Breese, killed in action. He had also served with the 25th since August 1862.

Robert F. Carver, wounded in right thigh, slight.

Darius P. David, taken prisoner, he died March 8, 1865, at Andersonville. He had only enlisted in the 25th in January 1864. His brother Marquis was also a member of the 25th, and would survive the war.

James Lewis, wounded. He had enlisted in the 25th just five months before, in February 1864.

Timothy Manning, wounded in hip and ankle, severe. Another February 1864 enlistee, he was discharged February 9, 1865, because of his wounds.

Ira A. Merrill, wounded in right arm, severe.

Robert J. Nimocks [also reported as Nimock], wounded in ankle and taken prisoner, his right leg was amputated.

William R. Peckham, wounded in arm, slight.

William W. Rasy [also reported as Racy], killed in action. He had been wounded, apparently slightly, on June 16, 1864. His luck ran out at Decatur. He had only enlisted in the 25th in January 1864.

Edwin B. Waggoner, taken prisoner.

Company C

Charles C. Coates, wounded in hip, severe.

Charles Croft, wounded in arm and side. He had enlisted in the 25th at the end of 1863.

Newton M. Doty, wounded in leg, severe.

Charles O. Jones, wounded in arm, slight.

Henry Julius, wounded in arm.

Isaac C. Murray, wounded in hip, severe.

Sergeant Zachariah Thomas, wounded in arm, severe.

Warren D. Worden, wounded in breast and taken prisoner.

Company D

Captain Mortimer E. Leonard, wounded in foot [also reported as wounded in leg], slight.

1st Lieutenant Charles S. Farnham, wounded in ankle, slight.

John Birdsill, wounded in wrist, severe.

Sergeant David B. Bon, wounded in both legs, severe.

Peter Boyle, wounded in the arm and taken prisoner. He died September 4, 1864, at Andersonville.

Leroy Bunn, wounded.

Daniel H. Cleveland, wounded in leg, slight.

Henry W. Cressy, wounded in bowels. He died from his wounds in the hospital in Decatur.

Samuel N. Darwin [also listed as Dorwin], wounded in both legs, severe.

Corporal J.P. Demmon, wounded in hip, slight.

Robert B. Dunlap, wounded in neck, slight.

Thomas Dunlevy, wounded. He died July 23, the day after the battle in Decatur, from his wounds.

Corporal Anson T. Foster, wounded in hip, severe, and in hand, slight.

Amos J. Hollenbeck [also listed as Hollinbeck], taken prisoner. He died August 4, 1864, at Andersonville.

Philemon P. House, wounded in ankle, severe. He died August 7, 1864, from his wounds.

Jabez L. [also listed as Jabez S.] Huntley, killed in action.

John Randles, taken prisoner. He died at Andersonville on November 4, 1864.

William N. Wilcox, right thumb shot off.

Company E

Second Lieutenant William H. Gribble, killed in action.

Corporal William H. Bailey, wounded in thigh and taken prisoner, he died at Andersonville on August 13, 1864.

Sergeant Benjamin F. Bailey, wounded in arm, severe.

Ransom J. Bartle, killed in action. After originally enlisting in August 1862, he had been discharged due to disability a year later in August 1863. He then re-enlisted in January 1864, only to get killed at Decatur.

Frederick T. Batchelor, taken prisoner. He must have been paroled by the Confederates, because he later died of disease in Atlanta on September 23, 1864.

Isaac N. [also reported at J.N.] Clifton, wounded in leg, slight.

Thomas C. Daugherty [also listed as Dougherty], killed in action.

Corporal George M. Douglas, wounded in leg, slight.

Benjamin C. Durley, wounded in thigh, flesh, slight.

Jacob Eiseman [also reported as Eiserman], wounded in leg, slight.

John Grover, killed in action.

Marion Heigh [also reported as High], wounded in shoulder and taken prisoner. Died at Andersonville, September 12, 1864.

George LaFollette, killed in action.

Frederick Libert, taken prisoner.

Uriah T. Long, wounded in thigh, slight.

Orlando McQuestion, taken prisoner.

James Overton, wounded and taken prisoner.

Charles Richie [also listed as Richey in some documents], killed in action.

Joseph M. Rose, wounded in leg, slight.

Sylvester Simpkins, taken prisoner.

Frederick Stanover, wounded in arm and thigh, slight.

Albert R. Taylor, taken prisoner, he died August 1, 1864, at Andersonville.

George M. Thomas, wounded in shoulder, slight.

Charles Weittenhiller [appears as Weitenhiller in some records], taken prisoner.

Elias Worley, wounded in arm, flesh, slight.

Company F

Captain George G. Symes, wounded in back and side, severe.

Julius Hensel, wounded.

Milton Janes, wounded. He died September 21, 1864, in Rome, Ga., from his wounds.

Edward Lamere, taken prisoner.

Ezra M. Lockman, wounded in neck, severe.

Darius Loper, wounded.

John C. Nichols, killed in action.

Darious Seper, wounded in leg

Albert N. Sutton, missing in action.

Company G

Ozro B. Allen, wounded.

Sylvester [also reported as Sylvanus] Bearss, wounded in leg, slight.

John W. Christian, killed in action.

Israel Taylor, wounded.

Company H

1st Lieutenant Robert H. Kendrick, taken prisoner.

James L. Clarke, taken prisoner.

Robert Crouch, wounded in arm and taken prisoner.

Howard Finley, killed in action.

William A. Kaump, taken prisoner.

Louis Polander, taken prisoner.

Bartholomew Stoll [also reported as Stell], wounded in hand, slight.

Company I

1st Lieutenant John T. [also reported as John P.] Richards, flesh wound in arm, slight.

Peter Finnegan, taken prisoner.

Patrick Keys [also reported as Kees], wounded and taken prisoner. His left arm was amputated.

Sylvester Moody, wounded in wrist, severe.

Simon P. Muffley, wounded in right arm and head, severe.

Bernard Vonderryt, wounded and taken prisoner. His left arm was amputated.

Company K

2d Lieutenant Lewis F. [also reported as Lewis P.] Grow, wounded in leg, severe, and leg amputated. He would die in Decatur from his wounds on July 26, 1864.

Sergeant Charles H. Anderson, wounded in thigh, severe.

Martin Diegle, killed in action.

Henry Finch, wounded in right leg, severe.

Corporal Simon C. Reistad, killed in action.

John Salt, wounded in arm and hip, severe. He would die in Marietta, Georgia, on August 23, 1864, from his wounds.

Back in the army hospital in Marietta where the 25th Wisconsin's Chauncey Cooke was still convalescing from his illness, the news would not reach him for 12 days that his best friend John W. Christian was dead. In an August 4 letter to his father, Cooke would write, "Last night I heard such news that I could not sleep, and with the flap of my tent thrown back so my three companions who lay near me could see we watched the flashes of light from our besieging cannon around Atlanta that lit up the darkened sky until after midnight before we went to sleep. The news that came to me last night made me shed bitter tears. My chum and my next roll companion, and always my next beat comrade, both on picket and guard duty, was killed in the fight at Decatur. He was shot and killed instantly by a volley of rebel shots from the far side of the street during the surprise and retreat of our forces... John was one of the best and bravest boys that ever lived. I thought that I had inherited your courage, father, all that any man should have, not to be foolhardy, but

John Christian went beyond me. I wrote to you of his daring at Kenesaw [sic] Mountain. Poor fellow he did not need to die there [in Decatur], he might have retreated, but he would not and a Minnie ball went rushing through his brain." In his letter Cooke provided some more details he had been told about the fight at Decatur, some of which was erroneous and sometimes confusing events there with events at the larger battle fought simultaneously several miles to the west. "The fighting around Atlanta, if we can believe unofficial reports, is of the fiercest kind. And it seems my regiment is in the midst of it rough and tumble. Today we are getting reports of heavy losses. Our Colonel was badly wounded and Lieutenant Colonel taken prisoner. We hear that Colonel Rusk killed two of his captors before surrendering [Editor's note: Colonel Milton Montgomery was wounded and captured. Lieutenant Colonel Jeremiah Rusk did shoot at least one Confederate as he escaped but was not captured.] Several other officers of the 25th were killed and made prisoners, so the report is, but there is nothing as yet official. It seems our brigade repulsed every rebel charge. Our batteries were taken and again retaken. [Editor's note: None of the Federal artillery was captured at the Battle of Decatur, but some guns were captured at the Battle of Atlanta.] The rebel soldiers it seems were crazed with gunpowder and whiskey given them to make them brave. They drew their caps down over their eyes and rushed upon our batteries to be mowed down with grape and cannister." [21]

In the 35th New Jersey, casualties totaled one killed, 16 wounded, and two officers and 37 men missing (captured.) [22] Two companies, Company I under Captain Augustus Dusenberry and Company D under Second Lieutenant David S. Oliphant, were in an advanced position on picket duty when Wheeler attacked and were nearly all captured when the Federal lines fell back. All but nine men of the two companies became prisoners. [23] For Dusenberry it was the second time in Confederate captivity. Prior to joining the 35th New Jersey in September 1863, he had been sergeant major of the 9th New York Infantry, also known as Hawkins' Zouaves, where he was captured during the bloody Battle of

Antietam in Maryland on September 17, 1862, and briefly imprisoned in Richmond, Virginia, before being exchanged. Casualties included William Saums, Company B, killed in action; Simon Harris, Company C, wounded; John Leddy, Company K, missing in action and presumed dead; and August Phillipe, Company C, wounded. [24]

In the Chicago Board of Trade Battery, eight men were wounded: [25] Corporal Andrew J. Close, wounded

Thomas A. McClelland, wounded in the arm (it would be amputated four days after the battle on July 26. The men of the battery pitched in more than $700 for him.)

John D. Toomey, wounded

Charles Holyland, wounded

William H. Tinsley, wounded

James B. Appleton, wounded

George Gackenheimer, wounded

Edward C. Field, wounded

Edward C. Field would die near Atlanta on August 1, 1864. John Nourse recorded the scene. The army was on the move that day, and the hospital had to move with it. "The surgeon knew that Edward could not be moved in an ambulance, so he detailed four men to carry him. They bore him as easily as possible, but he died while on the way to the new hospital just as he was on the stretcher. He is buried near the railroad track three miles from Atlanta. Everything that could be done was done for him. So they go, one after another. Good boys all." [26]

Losses on the Confederate side

Estimates about Confederate losses in the Battle of Decatur are much harder to determine than for those on the Federal side. The Confederates' record keeping was much looser than the analytical Federals, who usually kept detailed rosters and records which were later published. The author has been unable to find a Confederate casualty count of the Battle of Decatur in official records. One of the first books about General Joseph Wheeler, a hagiography published in 1899 and based on material provided by him, contains a short account of the Battle of Decatur that is marred by errors. It states that "Our loss was less than a hundred killed and wounded." [27] William L. Nugent of Ferguson's Brigade provides some corroboration for Wheeler's estimate. Writing to his wife about the battle just four days afterward on July 26, 1864, he said, "Our loss about seventy killed and wounded." [28] Historian Albert Castel believed a "generous estimate" of Wheeler's losses to be 150 casualties. [29] The 1899 book about Wheeler previously mentioned lists the names of officers who were wounded or killed while in action by his side during the war. The list includes five for July 22, 1864. These may have occurred at Decatur, or they may have occurred later in the day when Wheeler's command returned to the Battle of Atlanta to help General Hardee. The list includes: [30]

Lieutenant Colonel Wadkins, killed July 22, 1864

Lieutenant Colonel J.W. Dawson, shot in face July 22, 1864

Major Pope, shot in breast July 22, 1864

Captain W.H. Sparks, killed July 22, 1864

Lieutenant I.C. Stafford, shot in hip July 22, 1864

On Saturday, July 23, Sprague's Brigade left Decatur and moved westward toward Atlanta, once again leaving Decatur temporarily unoccupied by either army. But Confederates apparently soon returned. On Sunday July 24, shortly after noon, Garrard's cavalry division, which had been sent two days before on the raid eastward to tear up railroad, came riding back into Decatur. "We had left our pack train here and nearly the whole of McPherson's wagon train; but what was our surprise on approaching the town to find it occupied by rebels," notes the regimental history of the 72nd Indiana Volunteer Infantry, which was part of Garrard's force. "There were evidences of a terrible battle having been fought here, and for aught we knew our army had been driven back across the Chattahoochee. There was not a single Union soldier, team or mule, to be seen, and in the direction of Atlanta everything was quiet. Our scouts drove the [Confederate] pickets in and our brigade dismounted and moved in line of battle to the center of the town, where we halted and sent forward skirmishers, who soon developed the fact that the rebels were in force not far away. While lying there in line of battle, close to the Court-house, Gen Garrard and his staff, and Col. Miller, came and sat down on the Court-house steps, and the General made out his report of our expedition." Late in the evening Garrard's forces got orders to abandon Decatur, which they did, going into camp two miles northwest of the town. [31]

Colonel John W. Sprague's star would rise, literally, just six days after the Battle of Decatur. He was notified by wire on July 28, 1864, that he had won his star as a brigade commander. "For his uniform good conduct during the [Atlanta] campaign, and especially his gallant services in this action, he was immediately promoted to brigadier general," said his commanding officer, Major General Grenville M. Dodge. [32] He was later promoted to major general in 1865. Dodge would later praise Sprague for "stubbornly" holding Decatur, "knowing that if he failed the trains massed there and en route from Roswell would be captured. His fight was a gallant and sometimes seemingly almost hopeless one..." [33]

Press accounts of the Battle of Decatur

The Battle of Decatur was very quickly reported in the Southern press as a Confederate victory (as was the larger Battle of Atlanta). In the Confederate capitol of Richmond, Virginia, the Daily Enquirer on July 25, 1864, trumpeted "Glorious News From Georgia," including a July 23 dispatch datelined Atlanta and reporting, "Gen. Wheeler, last evening, attacked the enemy's left, in the neighborhood of Decatur, and drove them back, capturing five hundred wagons, with supplies, and a large number of prisoners. He is still pursuing." The erroneous account was completely wrong about the wagons, but accurate about the prisoners. This account was picked up by many other Southern newspapers, such as Charleston, South Carolina's, The Charleston Mercury on July 25, 1864.

The North's major publications had closely followed and reported on Sherman's campaign in Georgia. Correspondents, sketch artists and at least one photographer accompanied the Federal columns (often to the chagrin of General Sherman). Because of the difficulty in transmitting information from the front, stories about battles and other events were often published days or even weeks afterward. One of the first Northern press accounts of the Battle of Decatur appeared in the Cincinnati Daily Commercial on Saturday morning, July 30, in a lengthy front-page story about the Battle of Atlanta that contained details of the fight and casualty lists. [34] The newspaper followed up on Tuesday morning August 2 in another front-page story with a very lengthy account of the Battle of Decatur from a correspondent who was one of its participants. Included in the story is a list of the 63rd Ohio's casualties in the battle. On August 5, 1864, the Philadelphia Inquirer published a long story on Page 8 entitled "Wheeler's Repulse at Decatur, Ga.," which it obtained from the Cincinnati Commercial. The New York Times in early August had published an erroneous account of the Battle of Decatur taken from a Richmond, Virginia, newspaper which had wrongly reported that Wheeler had captured 500 Federal wagons at Decatur. On August 6, the Times set the record straight by republishing the Cincinnati Daily Commercial's highly accurate account, noting that it "does not sustain the assertion of the Confederates." On August 9, the Cincinnati Daily Commercial published an account taken from The Dayton Journal of the death at Decatur of the 63rd Ohio's Howard Forrer. Meanwhile, in New Jersey, the Newark Daily Advertiser on August 16 published a Page 2 account that had been sent in from a member of the 35th New Jersey which describes the Battle of Decatur and other events of the Atlanta Campaign.

Frank Leslie's Illustrated Newspaper published an illustration on August 13, 1864, of the 16th Army Corps wading the Chattahoochee on July 10. [35] And in New York, Harper's Weekly ("A Journal of Civilization"), which during June and July 1864 carried numerous accounts of Sherman's advance into Georgia, on August 27 published a sketch of the Powell house north of Decatur used as Sherman's headquarters on July 19. [36]

The fate of the Federal prisoners: Andersonville and other Confederate prisons

The Federals did not capture any Confederates at Decatur. But the Confederates captured many Federals, for most of whom a living hell awaited. At the beginning of 1864, the Confederate government had opened a new prison camp in remote southwest Georgia, known officially as Camp Sumter but more infamously known as Andersonville. The prison was 26 acres of open ground surrounded by a wall of pine logs, with a small stream running through it that served as both the water source and latrine for the prisoners. The first prisoners would arrive in February 1864, and hundreds would arrive daily. By June, just a month before the Battle of Decatur, the prison held 26,000 and by August, just weeks after the Battle of Decatur, the number would reach 33,000. Thus, the Federals captured at Decatur arrived at the prison at its most crowded time. During its 14 months of operation an astonishing 12,000 prisoners would die from disease, exposure, poor sanitation, and starvation. The prison's commandant, Henry Wirz, was hung for war crimes in November 1865. [37]

Alonzo Courtney of the 63rd Ohio was captured by
Confederates at the Battle of Decatur.

Among the 63rd Ohio taken prisoner were Corporal Presley S. Brown (he was imprisoned at Andersonville but fortunately exchanged in Atlanta just two months later on September 19); Alonzo Courtney; Jacob Krumm (Krumm was imprisoned in Andersonville but fortunately for him his stay in the camp was short as he was exchanged on September 22, 1864, and would finish out the war.); John F. Dill (wounded when captured, he would die at Andersonville on September 10, 1864); William R. Oliver (listed as both a private and sergeant in the 63rd's roster, he had been promoted to sergeant on June 1; he was imprisoned in Andersonville); Amos Ross (he would be paroled but died on June 16, 1865, in Annapolis, Md.); Duncan Ross (he was imprisoned in Andersonville); Matthew Gilpin (he was imprisoned in Andersonville and died there); Simon Johnson (he was imprisoned in Andersonville); Corporal Marcellus S. Roach; private Austin A. Bridgeman (he was imprisoned in Andersonville and survived to the end of the war only to die on the trip home when the steamship Sultana exploded near Memphis, Tennessee, on April 27, 1865); private John Olinger (he died in Andersonville and is buried in grave 12429); Corporal Horatio N. Warren (he was imprisoned at Andersonville but fortunately exchanged on September 19, 1864); private Horace E. Weaver; private Thomas Wolf; Captain Daniel T. Thorne; Benjamin Winans of Company F (he would survive captivity and be exchanged on March 1, 1865, in Wilmington, North Carolina); Sergeant David H. Reynolds of Company K (he would survive captivity and be exchanged in April 1865); and Levi Wible (he would survive captivity only to perish on the voyage home when the steamer Sultana exploded). Private Andrew Larrison, who was captured at Decatur, died at Andersonville on August 14, 1864. Although the author was unable to find a report of him having been wounded, this is likely the case since he died such a short time after reaching the prison camp.

For private Isaiah R. Rose of the 63rd Ohio, the horror of seeing his 19-year-old brother Thompson shot dead on the battlefield at Decatur (Thompson received a severe wound in the chest) gave way to the horrors of prison in Andersonville, where he was imprisoned for seven months. "When it rained, we didn't get anything to eat. I've gone without a bite for three days because it was raining; those fellows [the Confederate prison guards] didn't want to get their feet muddy and dirty or get wet bringing us anything. I've sat on the ground and killed 500 vermin [lice] along the seams of my trousers in one hour. I've leaned over a little puddle of water and brushed my hair with my hands and seen vermin drop in the water by the dozens," he told a Columbus, Ohio, newspaper years later. Rose and other prisoners were later transferred to other Confederate prisons. "On his third attempt, Isaiah escaped from one on December 26, 1864," Ohio historian Betty K. Rose wrote in a 2010 article about Isaiah Rose. "He slept in the day and traveled by night through the Carolina swamps along with a Confederate straggler. For thirty days and nights they subsisted on acorns and similar fare. Isaiah induced his companion to throw away his gun, after which he told him his identity. The Southerner was promised good treatment if he'd go with him and he accepted. As they neared the Union lines, Isaiah walked in advance. Without any warning, he was shot in the left leg by a Union sentry. When Isaiah's identity was established, he was sent to a field hospital without proper facilities for treating his wounds and gangrene developed. In this condition, he was sent to Washington, where for months, he hovered near death. In the meantime, however, he had made good his promise to the Confederate straggler; the colonel of his regiment had seen to it that his former comrade was given a place as an ambulance driver. It developed that Isaiah had been shot by a member of the 33rd Indiana Infantry who had been obeying new orders to fire without a challenge." [38]

Captain Augustus Dusenberry of the 35th New Jersey also had an adventure after being captured at Decatur. He wound up in a Confederate prison in Charleston, S.C. In a letter sent home to friends on August 14, 1864, he wrote, "You have doubtless heard before this that I, with 38 others, was captured by the Confederates (Wheeler's cavalry) at Decatur, Ga., on the 22d of July. I was taken to Macon, Ga., and there continued until the 11th of August, at which time we were moved by rail to this place, arriving here on the morning of the 13th. Nearly my entire company was captured with me and sent to Andersonville, Ga. We are very comfortably situated here in the city workhouse, and hope soon to be exchanged. My health is good." [39] But Dusenberry would not long remain "comfortably situated." In November 1864 Dusenberry and some other Federal prisoners, including a Lieutenant Harry Welsh of the 87th Pennsylvania Infantry, found an opportunity to escape. It's not clear where in South Carolina they were, as the Confederates at this time were moving prisoners around to keep them from being liberated as General Sherman's columns pushed south into Georgia during the March to The Sea. Civil War historian Scott Mingus, author of a history column for the York Daily Record in Pennsylvania, pieced together the dramatic escape story of Dusenberry and Welsh taken from the *Reading Eagle* newspaper of July 30, 1907: [40]

"On Nov. 9, 1864, Lieutenant Welsh and eight other prisoners arranged to bribe a guard by agreeing to give him $1,800 in Confederate money. They rolled $400 around a thick wad of brown paper, and handed it to the guard at 3 a.m. as they passed through the guard line. Then they skipped away in the dark as rapidly as possible. The trick was discovered, however, when they were about 100 yards away, when the whole guard line fired a volley after them. They all dropped as if shot, but a few minutes later disappeared in the darkness. The following day they covered each other with leaves in the woods. The last man had to cover himself as best as he could. They remained in the woods, thus concealed, until evening came again; then traveled all night.

"They kept up this manner of escape for a month, until they reached the mountain region of North Carolina. In the mean time they lived on fruit, raw pumpkins and grains of corn, occasionally obtaining food from negroes, whom they could always trust. While still in South Carolina, they were discovered one night by a squad of confederates, when all were captured except Lieutenant Welsh, Captains Wilson and Skelton, of Ohio, and Captain [Augustus] Dusenberry, of Newark, N.

J. [Dusenberry commanded Company I of the 35th New Jersey Infantry).
After getting into the mountain district, they travelled during the day
and slept at night. Upon reaching Table Rock Mountain, one of the
ridges of the Alleghenies, John Masters, a union man, furnished them
with corn bread and pork and concealed them about his home four days.
After leaving him, on going down the mountain side in Transylvania
county, North Carolina, two white men and a colored man came along,
behind them. The leader of the party was John Aiken, who said: 'I am
sorry to tell you, boys, but you are in danger of being captured. There
is a squad of men after you. Go with me and I will conceal you till the
chase is over.' He took them to his own log cabin and kept them seven
days. He then directed them to a secluded spot in the mountain, called
Little Bear Wallow, where they built a small log cabin and lived in it
three weeks. While here, they made the acquaintance of 19 deserters from
the Confederate army. The party of 31 persons started on a tramp for
Buchtown [sic Bucktown], in the mountains of eastern Tennessee. After
three nights of marching they were attacked by a troop of cavalry, when
all were killed or taken prisoners, except Captain Dusenberry, of New
Jersey; Lieutenant Welsh, and Samuel Tinsley, a Confederate deserter
from South Carolina.

"Three days later they were captured by a Confederate Lieutenant
and 12 men, near Knottly [sic Nottley] river, and were taken to an old
farm house, where during the night Tinsley escaped. The following evening, Captain Dusenberry and Lieutenant Welsh got away also. They
were now free again, and started together for Cleveland, Tennessee,
where they arrived after many exciting experiences and long marches,
on January 25, 1865. Then they went to Chattanooga, Tennessee, and
got an order from General [George "Pap"] Thomas in command at that
place, to report at Washington, D. C. Lieutenant Welsh was mustered
out of service Feb. 10, 1865, three years and six months from the time of
his enlistment. He brought his friend Tinsley to York with him. The latter
remained in the North several months, and then returned to his plantation in South Carolina."

Just as Augustus Dusenberry was captured by Confederates for the second time at Decatur, so too was Second Lieutenant David S. Oliphant of Company D of the 35th New Jersey captured for the second time (he previously had been captured at the Second Battle of Bull Run in Virginia before he joined the 35th). And also like Dusenberry, Oliphant was in for an adventure similar to Dusenberry's. Oliphant was transferred to various Confederate prisons at Macon, Georgia, and Charleston and Columbia, South Carolina. At Columbia he escaped with three other officers and "by concealing themselves in the day time and traveling nights, they arrived after a perilous journey to the Federal lines at Knoxville, Tennessee, January 17, 1865," a later biography notes. [41] Oliphant's arrival in Knoxville along with numerous other escapees was reported in The New York Times on January 17. [42]

The 25th Wisconsin's Milton Montgomery was held as a prisoner of the Confederates for six weeks in prison camps at Macon, Georgia [probably Camp Oglethorpe, a prison camp on the Ocmulgee River in Macon], and at Charleston, South Carolina, probably Castle Pinkney. Given that he was still healing from the recent amputation of his arm, this may have saved Montgomery's life because Castle Pinkney was more sanitary and offered better medical care and food. [43] Montgomery was then exchanged and returned North. When he recovered from his wounds, the army wanted him to return to Wisconsin to recruit new volunteers, but he wanted to rejoin the 25th Wisconsin, which by that time had completed the March to the Sea and then marched north into the Carolinas. Back on the battlefield as the war neared its end, Montgomery received a field promotion to brigadier general. After the war ended in April, Montgomery and his soldiers marched to Washington, D.C., where they took park in the Grand Review of the armies, marching down Pennsylvania Avenue.

Captain Daniel T. Thorne of the 63rd Ohio wasn't as fortunate as Dusenberry or Montgomery. Thorne had "received a gunshot wound which entirely disabled him, and he was captured by the enemy," according to The History Fuller's Brigade. "He was kept a prisoner, his arm was amputated, and he was finally confined in prison in Savannah,

Ga., where he died from the effects of his wound and the amputation October 5th, 1864." When he had gone off to war, Thorne left behind his wife of 10 years, the former Hannah S. Murphy, whom he had married in January 1852, along their two children, 9-year-old Alonzo, who had born on Christmas Eve in 1852, and 7-year-old Adelbert, who had been born on November 8, 1854. A later pension claim filed by Thorne's widow describes his wounding differently, saying that "his wound was in the ankle, his leg was amputated by the rebels into whose power he fell." [44] In either event, Thorne was dead.

Some of the men from the 25th Wisconsin who had been captured by the Confederates during the Atlanta Campaign were exchanged in September 1864 and came back to the regiment. Some had been imprisoned in Andersonville. "They look very bad," John F. Brobst noted in a September 27 letter to his girlfriend Mary. "They had hard treatment. Not half enough to eat, scarcely any fire to cook what scanty meals they did get, no blankets to keep them warm or any shelter to keep them dry, not even a shade to sit under, but had to lay out in the hot sun and burn." [45]

The Sultana disaster

As if the horrors of Andersonville and other Confederate prison camps weren't enough, more horror awaited a few unlucky members of the 63rd Ohio who had been captured at Decatur. They were to be part of the worst maritime disaster in American history, a tragedy that would claim more lives than the sinking of The Titanic.

With the end of the war, the hellish prison camps of Andersonville, Georgia, and Cahaba, Alabama, were liberated. Many of the thousands of freed Federal soldiers were starving and sick and the Federal government was unprepared to care for them, so efforts were made to get them home to the North as fast as possible. Many of the Federals freed from Andersonville and Cahaba were transported to Vicksburg, Mississippi, there to be loaded onto steamboats operated by private contractors, who were eager to get fat Federal contracts for transporting the former prisoners northward up the Mississippi and Ohio rivers to their home states. Regulations limiting the number of passengers the steamers could carry were being routinely ignored. [46]

The steamer Sultana regularly sailed between St. Louis and New Orleans, and with the end of the war its owners got in on the lucrative business of transporting prisoners. The boat left New Orleans on April 21, 1865, and steamed north to Vicksburg, docking on April 23 and there took on board 1,965 Federal soldiers and officers just released from Cahaba and Andersonville. In addition to these passengers the boat carried two companies of infantry, for a total of about 2,300 people on board. The boat then traveled upstream to Helena, Arkansas, and then on to Memphis on April 26. After stopping there and receiving a load of coal, in the middle of the night the boat started up the river to its destination, Cairo, Illinois. In 1892, the Rev. Chester D. Berry published a book describing the horrors of what happened next. Let us quote from it. "All was quiet and peaceful, many of the soldiers, no doubt, after their long, unwilling fast in southern prisons, were dreaming of home

The sidewheel steamer Sultana was taking more than 2,000 Federal soldiers who had been freed from Confederate prisons back to their homes when it exploded on the Mississippi River in April 1865, killing some 1,800. Three soldiers from the 63rd Ohio who had been captured at the Battle of Decatur were on board, only one of whom survived.

and the good things in store for them there, but alas! Those beautiful visions were dissipated by a terrific explosion, for, about two o'clock in the morning of the 27th, as the boat was passing through a group of islands known as the 'Old Hen and Chickens,' and while about opposite Tagleman's Landing had burst one of her boilers and almost immediately caught fire, for the fragments of the boiler had cut the cabin and hurricane deck in two and the splintered pieces had fallen, many of them, back on the burning coal fires that were now left exposed. The light, dry wood of the cabins burned like tinder and it was but a short time ere the boat was wrapped in flames, burning to the water's edge and sinking. Hundreds were forced into the water and drowned in huge squads, those that could swim being unable to get away from those who could not and consequently perishing with them." [47]

Approximately 1,800 died on the Sultana. [48] Only about 400 of those on board would survive. Among them was William Barnes. The 22-year-old had been born in West Virginia in 1842 and later joined the 63rd Ohio. During the Battle of Decatur he was captured by Confederates and sent to Andersonville. When the war ended he was freed with other prisoners and sent to Vicksburg, where he boarded the Sultana for the trip home. "At the time the Sultana blew up I was thrown from the boiler deck and very badly hurt, but was fortunate enough, with three unknown comrades, to get hold of a bale of hay, upon which we floated till nearly opposite the city of Memphis, where we were picked up by a boat," he recalled years later. Barnes was then working as a miner in Nelsonville, Ohio. The historian regrets he did not leave a fuller account of his war experiences and remarkable survival at Andersonville and on the Sultana. [49] Two other previously imprisoned members of the 63rd Ohio, Austin A. Bridgeman and Sergeant Levi Wible, perished when the Sultana blew up. [50]

Since the sinking of the Sultana coincided with the end of the war and the assassination of Abraham Lincoln, it never got the national media attention it should have and largely passed unnoticed. Today the incident is all but forgotten. "The average American is astonished at nothing he sees or hears. He looks for large things. Things ordinary are too tame," Rev. Berry wrote in the introduction to his book on the Sultana disaster published in 1892. "This, and the exciting events of April, 1865, perhaps account for the fact that the loss of the steamer 'Sultana' and over 1,700 passengers, mostly exchanged prisoners of war, finds no place in American history. The idea that the most appalling marine disaster that ever occurred in the history of the world should pass by unnoticed is strange, but still such is the fact, and the majority of the American people today [Editor's note: this was written in 1892] do not know that there ever was such a vessel as the 'Sultana.'" Forty seven years later to the month, another great maritime disaster, the April 1912 sinking of the Titanic, would become world famous. Whereas some 1,800 were lost on the Sultana, 1,517 were lost on the Titanic.

Now in the next three chapters we will explore more deeply the experiences of three young soldiers who were in the Battle of Decatur, only one of whom lived to tell about it.

VIII

Young, Lovely, Brave and True: The Life and Death of Howard Forrer

By Lisa Rickey

> *"My nephew, H. G. Affleck, who left home so full of patriotic*
> *fire and so hopeful, was wounded at the battle of Shiloh on*
> *the sixth of April... After his return I visited Sister [Mary]*
> *and was there for a few days before his death... While witness-*
> *ing these sad scenes, I rejoice in the thought that my only and*
> *beloved son Howard, was not in the army. He had wished*
> *to go, but I was so unwilling that he gave it up... Since the*
> *reverses of our army we cannot hold him longer..."[1]*

- SARAH FORRER'S DIARY, [2 SEPT. 1862]

History is nothing more or less than the sum of the actions and experiences of all the individuals involved in it. The history of the Civil War is no different. This chapter tells the story of one of the thousands of men who fought on the battlefield at Decatur, Georgia, in 1864: Howard Forrer, a 23-year-old former teacher from Dayton, Ohio. Howard Forrer was born on November 11, 1841, in Dayton, the youngest child and only surviving son of Samuel Forrer and Sarah (Howard) Forrer. Samuel was a prominent member of the Dayton community, a civil engineer who, in

Howard Forrer, a 23-year-old former teacher from Dayton, Ohio, who enlisted in the 63rd Ohio, was shot in the neck and killed at the Battle of Decatur.

his younger days, had been in charge of the Miami-Erie Canal project that connected Cincinnati to Lake Erie. The Forrers also had three surviving daughters: Elizabeth, Augusta, and Mary.[2]

Howard graduated in 1858 from Dayton's Central High School, where he had been an excellent student, beloved by his teachers. After graduation, he became a teacher himself, accepting a position at the Second District School near his parents' home in downtown Dayton. If the notes he saved from school children and parents are any indication, he was popular as a teacher as well.[3]

After the Civil War broke out, Howard was inspired to join the cause, most likely due simply to the *rage militaire* that swept through so many men both young and old at the time. However, due to his mother Sarah's strong objections to her only son joining the army (especially after watching her nephew suffer and die from the sounds he sustained at Shiloh), Howard initially deferred to her wishes and remained safe at home in Dayton, teaching school.

But by the summer of 1862, Howard Forrer's desire to enter the army could be contained no longer. He became involved in recruiting for a new regiment, which was advertised in the *Dayton Journal* on August 17, 1862. The *Dayton Journal* (the city's Republican newspaper) printed many other such advertisements at that time, to promote Union recruitment efforts, which were then ramped up into overdrive.

According to the 1889 *History of Dayton*: "During the entire year 1862, recruitment was continually going on in Dayton. It was the great year of doubt and anxiety as to the success of the national cause... The summer and fall of 1862 witnessed great activity in recruiting men for the war..." (Dayton's famous 93rd Ohio Volunteer Infantry was formed, under the command of Charles Anderson, in July 1862.)[4]

However, while several regiments (such as the 93rd) succeeded, Howard's regiment apparently failed to fill up, as Howard's father Samuel wrote on August 24:

"Howard's company did not succeed. It was not fully officered until 4 or 5 day[s] before recruiting for new regiments was suspended. He will now not probably have any command or in any manner enter the army. He cannot even be drafted because our ward and indeed the city has furnished its full quota of the active force of the army called for to their time. Howard chafes under failure to get into the army and the more because William Howard has succeeded..."[5] (Howard's cousin William, with whom he had no doubt grown up since they were the same age and both lived in Dayton, had recently aided in the formation of the 17th Ohio Battery.)

The draft comment most likely refers to the Militia Act of July 1862. The Enrollment Act of 1863 constituted the first Union Army draft at the *national* level. However, under the Militia Act of July 1862, the federal government required governors (such as Ohio's governor David Tod) to administer their own drafts as necessary in order to meet their manpower quotas. Thus, if there were not enough volunteers, "little" drafts were held on the local level.[6]

Preparations for the first such draft in Montgomery County had begun on August 19, 1862. Formal notice was given on August 22 that drafting would begin on September 3.[7] There were many ads in the Dayton's Republican *Journal* newspaper encouraging men to volunteer before they were drafted.

Due to unforeseen events, the draft would be pushed back to September 15 and then again to October 1, and by then, the city wards of Dayton had indeed fulfilled its quota. Only 666 men from the townships were drafted. And even so, these draftees were given the option to enlist "voluntarily," receive bonuses, and choose their own company.[8]

Howard's mother Sarah was relieved by the failure of Howard's regiment and the fact that he could not be drafted. She speculated that one day Howard would be thankful for it as well: "It is a great disappointment to him now but I think he will live to see the day that he will be glad it happened to him..."[9]

However, Sarah's relief was to be only temporary, as there were still plenty of other opportunities, and Howard was not giving up.

One such opportunity came a few days later in the form of a letter from Howard's brother-in-law Luther Bruen, who was with the 12th U.S. Infantry stationed at Fort Hamilton (New York), to Howard's father Samuel Forrer on August 27:

"I have never been disposed to do any thing to get Howard into the army, because I supposed neither you nor mother approved of it. Had it been otherwise I might have got him a second lieutenancy ere this. As it is, if you are willing he should go & will send him on here to enlist, & get John Howard [a local lawyer and Howard's uncle] and other influential friends to write to the Secretary of War, I can get him a lieutenancy very soon. He will be very high upon the list too for we have very few second lieutenants. I can give you the assurance too that I can keep him by me, as I am now in command of the regiment & can make him my adjutant or Quarter Master, as soon as my battalion is organized. Now if you are willing Howard should go into the army, send him on at once & as soon as he has enlisted, let John Howard and all the other influential friends you can command, write to the Secy. of War urging his appointment as a second lieutenant and I think I can get for him very soon – in a short time any how..."[10]

Research revealed neither a response to this letter nor any other reference to it, but in short, for whatever reason, Howard Forrer did not enlist in the regular army with his brother-in-law. One might wonder how Howard's fate could have been different if Luther had been able to keep Howard by his side.

On Monday, September 1, "Howard went back to school...with extreme reluctance, he hopes only for a very short time..."[11]

As it happened, Howard's wish was to be granted in a very short time indeed, for on that very day that Howard returned to school teaching, a portion of Confederate General Kirby Smith's army was advancing through northern Kentucky, threatening an attack on Cincinnati, just 50 miles away.

"...in these stirring times I suppose it would be too much to ask of a young man of spirit to sit in the house teaching...while most of his companions are in the field..."[12]

-SARAH FORRER TO HER DAUGHTER MARY, 3 SEPT. 1862

On September 1, 1862—the same day that Howard Forrer reluctantly returned to teaching a classroom full of students at the Second District School after his efforts to join the army had so far failed—a meeting was called at Dayton's Armory Hall to discuss the city's defense needs, in light of recent intelligence that a portion of Kirby Smith's army under Brigadier General Henry Heth was advancing through northern Kentucky to threaten Ohio, following a victory at Richmond, Kentucky.[13]

As a result of the September 1 meeting, it was resolved that "in view of the impending danger of invasion of the State, all able-bodied men should enroll themselves for military discipline and drill, and hold themselves in readiness to go to the front at the call of the governor..."[14]

The call of the governor did indeed come, the very next day. On September 2, Ohio Governor David Tod issued the following call for men to defend Ohio's borders:

"Our southern border is threatened with invasion. I have therefore to recommend that all the loyal men of your counties at once form themselves into military companies and regiments to beat back the enemy at any and all points he may attempt to invade our State. Gather up all the arms in the country, and furnish yourselves with ammunition for the same. The service will be but a few days. The soil of Ohio must not be invaded by the enemies of our glorious government."[15]

H. Eugene Parrott, a 23-year-old bachelor who would later marry into the Forrer/Peirce family, wrote of the excitement in his diary on September 2:

"Our city has been a state of excitem't today on account of the proximity of the rebel army in Ky. Our forces were compelled to evacuate Lexington by Gen. Kirby Smith with 20 men, & there apparently nothing to prevent him from advancing to Covington & into Ohio. Cincinnati is under martial law & in a great panic. At a meeting of citizens this eve'g, "to prepare for the defense of the Miami Valley," it was resolved that all able bodied men should hereafter close their places of business at 4 P.M. & spend 2 hours in drilling. We are to meet at the polls of the several wards tomorrow & organize into companies & regiments..."[16]

On the evening of September 2, Howard Forrer informed his parents that he would be answering the governor's call. His mother Sarah wrote:

"[Howard] told me this evening that he has the place of Post Adjutant at Camp Dayton. Since he will go, I suppose it is best he should have some place..."[17]

The next morning, Howard's cousin William Howard departed for Cincinnati with the 17th Ohio Battery, and Howard himself reported to Camp Dayton. Howard's mother Sarah wrote to her daughter that morning:

"Howard goes to Camp Dayton this morning to take the place of Adjutant. I do not know whether it is anything that will last long, but he is resolved at all [illegible] to go from the school... Howard goes to Columbus tonight with a recommendation from Col. [Tr.?] to the Gov, for the place of Post Adjutant. He may not [receive?] it, and may not keep it long if he does. It is uncertain whether there will be a Military Post there long. But Howard thinks it would be a stepping stone to something else perhaps the Adjutancy of the 112th."[18]

In her diary entry for the same day, Sarah wrote:

"...it is very hard for me to feel willing to give up my only son, even for the defence [sic] of the country... He feels so injured by my continual opposition to his wishes that I must be silent... I suppose it is too much to ask of a young man of spirit to sit in the house and teach, in these stirring times, when most of his friends are in the field."[19]

According to Eugene Parrott, the men who turned up for the defense of Dayton on September 3 constituted "a disorganized mess," as he wrote later that day:

"Our city has been in a state of great excitement today. All the stores were closed at 4 P.M. & every body turned out to form ward companies & drill, a disorganized mess that would be little value as soldiers I think for a long time but it was encouraging to see the willing spirit manifested by such a wholesale turn-out. The news is better this eve'g; it is even said that Kirby Smith is south of the Ky river, & the story of his advance on Cin was only invented in order to have the city entrenched & fortified as it ought to be."[20]

On September 4, 1862, an address imploring men to volunteer to defend Dayton and indeed the state from Confederate invaders, appeared in the *Dayton Daily Journal*:

The result of the governor's call, the "Enemy at Our Door" article, and similar efforts throughout the state, was that "from all parts of the State, men came to the front with all kinds of arms, shot-guns, rifles, pistols, anything that came handy, and dressed in any kind of attire that happened to suit the occasion. So variously were they dressed, and so variously were they armed, that they received the name of 'Squirrel Hunters'..."[21]

On the afternoon of the September 4, there was quite a bit of excitement, as Sarah Forrer wrote in her diary on the day afterward:

"Yesterday there was an alarm. All the bells in the city rang violently. I was writing. On going out I learned all who were able were expected to go to Cincinnati. The rebels are said to be coming in force. The city is all excitement. In a few minutes a very fine-looking young man gave me a note from Brother John [Howard] saying, "Give this man, Mr. J___, your rifle." Mr. J___ said Mr. Forrer would be at home soon and would mould some bullets. I gave him the Rifle and he left, saying he would return. Husband [Samuel Forrer] came and began to mould bullets, and I to mend the old shot pouch to carry them in, and some other things, as patches, bullet moulds, etc. Husband quit his work, saying there was enough. I thought not and moulded more. Then Betty came and moulded till Mr. F. insisted she should stop. We put the old rifle in good condition. After an hour Mr. J___ came and said he did not need it, that Mr. Howard would lend him an army gun. I saw him afterwards with his outfit. The old rifle is in my chamber. It came very near seeing two wars. It was in the war of 1812..."[22]

Howard Forrer was still in Columbus when the alarm was sounded on September 4. However, he had seen similar excitement during his time in Columbus. "You ought to have seen the men going with [their] squirrel guns[,] old long rifles," he told his mother upon his return to Dayton on the 5th. She replied, "Oh, I said, I brushed up one myself today." He asked, "Were you frightened here too?"[23]

In recounting her answer to Howard in a letter to her daughters, Sarah added a few more details than what she had written in her journal:

"I said while I sat writing, about three o'clock the all bells in the City rang violently, and on inquiry I found there was a dispatch from the Gov. telling us to send everybody down that we could arm, and all were to assemble at the Court House to make arrangements. I heard the door bell ring, and on going to the door was met by a good honest working young man, with a note from Brother John, saying give this man your Rifle. I went immediately gave it to him, but told him, there were no bullets. He said he would be back in a minute or two and Mr. Howard said Mr. Forrer would come soon and <u>mould</u> bullets. In a moment Father [Samuel Forrer] came with some lead. As soon as he opened the door, he asked was not that my Rifle. I met out here, I told him, yes, I supposed thee told John to send the men here for it. He said to me, I told him Howard and I would want it. I said Howard would not use the Old Rifle if he was here, and thee <u>can't go</u>, there is no use in talking about it; it is better the young man go, let him have it, so he went to moulding bullets…"[24]

(Samuel Forrer was then 69 years old, so it was perhaps well that his wife forbade him to join the Squirrel Hunters.)

After the alarm on September 4, Eugene Parrott resolved that he too must answer the call to arms, despite his father's wishes that he remain at home. (Eugene's older brother, Edwin A. Parrott was already gone with the First Ohio Volunteer Infantry, and his father wished his youngest son to stay at home and help with the business.) Eugene wrote of the day's excitement and his decision:

"The enemy is reported today 16 miles fr Cinti & nearly every young man in town went down tonight with a gun. I have this afternoon endured agony in <u>yieldg</u> to my father's entreats, but I cannot stay, my country calls, tomorrow I go."[25]

Sarah wrote in her diary September 5 that many troops had departed for Cincinnati:

"Yesterday [Sept. 4] and today [Sept. 5] the troops and farmers, mostly the latter, pass by carloads, and many thousands have gone down. Part of a regiment in Camp Dayton left. Howard went as adjutant. I scarce allowed myself to think he was going, but made ready for him with as little delay as possible. After he was gone and evening came on I was quite exhausted. All were out and gone home, and I sat alone on the little back porch to rest my weary self. But I dared not think of Howard."[26]

She wrote of Howard's departure in slightly more detail in a letter to her daughters on September 7:

"Howard had the Post Adjutancy here 'till further orders.' And he was detailed with Hunter Odlin as Capt. To take 500 troops to Cin[cinnati]. They went Friday evening [Sept. 5]. Some think they will not be needed, and will be sent back, as they are raw troops, to drill here in Camp Dayton. I hope so...

"I was prepared to see Howard go when he returned from Colum[bus]. And I think he was very much relieved to find me composed, and manifesting no great excitement...

"I feel as great dislike to his going as ever I did, and to his being connected with the Army in any way, but there seemed a necessity, just now, and I could not prevent him if I would. I think too he felt better that I bade him fare well quietly and without manifesting much emosion [sic]. Nothing else would serve him, I hope and trust I shall soon see him again for they are quite green, and if they can be spared I think they will be sent home to prepare themselves better for service. I try not to think much about it. And I want you to do the same. It is a matter beyond our control..."[27]

In her diary that same day, she added a note of describing how she already missed her beloved only son:

"It is even worse than I had anticipated. I go into Howard's room and everything tells me he is gone..."[28]

A few days later, Sarah was pleased to receive word that, so far, Howard was safe:

"Received a short note from Howard, written in great haste at Camp King, three miles below Cincinnati on the Ohio river, on the Kentucky side. He is well. For this I am thankful. I knew they had no tents, and I feared the exposure would be too much for him, unaccustomed as he is to that kind of life..."[29]

Eugene Parrott was among the many Daytonians, including Howard Forrer, who headed to Cincinnati on September 5, to join a force of about several thousand so-called Squirrel Hunters.[30]

Eugene's diary entries for those days help bring the events to life, describing the sights and sounds that Howard Forrer likely experienced as well:

September 5, 1862:

"Left home after a hasty tea armed & equipped, a soldier of the Union. As soon as I got away & felt I was certainly going I felt I was in the right course, pursuing my highest duty. Our train got off amid the cheers of the people, at 8 P.M.; reported at Chamber of Commerce at <u>midnight</u>; were marched to 5th St. market space for supper, & returning turned in on the floor at 3 o'clock."[31]

September 6, 1862:

"At 5 A.M. having got about an hour & a half's sleep there was a noise commenced enough to awake the seven sleepers, so rose feeling pretty well on short rest. Breakfasted at Burnet with Charlie Clegg. Everybody said the call was a 'hum,' so got a discharge, but heard about dinner the attack was about to commence, so reported again at Mer Exch. My company had been ordered off so I fell in with a Dayton squad and we were detailed for Harrison's Body Guard, & ordered to North Bend, where the enemy was expected to cross the river. Didn't get a train till six P.M. Got to North Bend & found no enemy, apparently a false alarm. [Illegible] tonight by the river side."[32]

September 7, 1862:

"Rose at 5 A.M. quite refreshed by my first night's sleep on the ground. [Illegible] out with part of the squad foraging for breakfast. Fared pretty well at the Thirteen Mile House. We went into camp today on our regimental parade ground, which is on Gen Harrison's homestead, just in front of where his house stood. There was board yard here on the river which the men used for putting up very comfortable quarters."[33]

September 8, 1862:

"Rose at 6 A.M. after a broken night's rest—waked up at midnight by mosquitoes & kept up by the fun of the [squad?] until 2, then on guard until 4. The Guard made a forced march on Cleves, about a mile distant where we had ordered breakfast, & a good one we got from mine host

Kennedy. The impression seems to be that the danger is about over now, & as my business is too imperative to admit of my staying to play soldier I got a pass from Col. Harrison & left North Bend at 2:50 P.M. Reached home at 8, went to the office & looked over the business. Home at Ten. Our Guard was ordered down to the river on a scouting expedition this morning—going down on one of the river gun boats, & taking a [train?] into Kentucky, the enemy's country. When we got orders, Young & I who were going home, determined to go on the scout, even if we missed our train, but having to go back to camp after my ammunition, from Hd Qrs, I found on my return our Guard was about a quarter of a mile down the river, I went after them 'double quick,' but when I got within about a hundred yards of the boat she shoved off, leaving me very much discomfited.

"Last night about 5 o'clock, it was telegraphed to Hd. Qrs. from Camp Tippecanoe, 5 miles below here, that the enemy was in sight, & for a short time, we confidently expected a fight. We were ordered under arms ready to march, & supplied with ammunition. The Col. went down to see about the matters & returning in a few hours informed us that it was a party of our own men who had been foraging in Ky & were returning, which caused the alarm. Our boys seemed quite cool at the prospect of a fight, for myself I felt no apprehension, for I knew I had come out to fight & led by high & conscientious motives & if I fell it would be in a sacred cause. My greatest anxiety was for father, who I knew would sorely miss me in the business if I should fall."[34]

Howard Forrer wrote his version of the events of September 7 and 8 to his mother, which she summarized briefly in a letter to her daughters a few days later:

"I received both of your letters today, and one from Howard this morning. I had a short note yesterday, and a letter of 8 pages today. The first was dated Sept. 7th, Camp King, Ky., 3 miles below Ci—i [Cincinnati]. The one today at Camp 13 miles beyond Covington dated 8 Sept. In his first he said they had two calls to arms soon after entering the encampment, but they both proved false. They were ordered to march, and had a long hot march to their present camp. Some of the men dropped with fatigue and heat. Howard said he was well, and pretty near rested when he wrote..."[35]

On September 9, Eugene Parrott was back in Dayton, according to his diary: "Busy in the office part of the day, the other part fighting my battles (?) o'er on the street & telling about that 'gay & festiverous' corps, the 'Body Guard.' Slept at Aunt Margaret's tonight, the family wanting a protector during Charlie's absence."[36]

However, on September 10, all the Squirrel Hunters were called back to Cincinnati. (This was probably in response to a skirmish that took place at Fort Mitchel that day; the skirmish was the closest the Squirrel Hunters actually got to any real action.[37]) Eugene wrote of the call back:

"Another alarm from Cinti today. The Governor calls all the minute men back. As soon as we got the news I came home & got ready to go back, feeling if there should be a fight, I ought by all means to be with my company. We had a dispatch the eve from Joe, say'g that the enemy was in sight & they expected to hear their guns every minute, but having had some experience in Cinti scares, & not being in a condition to leave home except in a great emergency, I concluded to wait until tomorrow."[38]

Also on September 10, Sarah shared some additional Squirrel Hunter news with her daughter:

"Did I tell you Fin Harrison has command of a Regiment or in some way, I do not know how he has got to be a Brigadier, and is in command of our Dayton volunteers, and I suppose some others, at 'North Bend', his grandfather's old home. Joe Peirce and Brit Darst went to join his command today..."[39]

Apparently, Joe Peirce and Brit Darst were also friends of Eugene Parrott, because the three went to Cincinnati together, but on September 11, not the 10th:

"I woke this morning uncertain whether I ought to go back to North Bend or not, but Munger & Joe Peirce came into the office about eleven o'clock, & said they would go if I would, & not feeling willing to keep three men from the field when possibly we were much needed I consented to go. Left at 4 P.M. with Peirce & Brit Darst. Munger couldn't get ready. Reached Ludlow about six, & got off intending to go across the country to the river, & thereby avoid red tape in Cin, as we feared if a fight was in progress we should have difficulty in getting out on the O&M Rd. Couldn't get a horse for love or money, & couldn't learn that there was any road except through Cin, so we laid around until the next down train, nearly midnight. Darst and I took possession of a bench at the depot with our knapsacks for pillows, got two or three hours of very comfortable sleep. Went to bed at the Burnet House at 1:30 A.M."[40]

A "great battle" was apparently expected to take place on September 12, Eugene wrote:

"Rose at 4 & took the 5 o'clock train for Camp Harrison. The morning papers say that Kirby Smith was last night reinforced by 10,000 of Bragg's troops & there will certainly be a great battle today. Got to camp in time to go with the 'Guard' for one of Kennedy's good breakfasts. Fell easily into the routine of camp life, slept, smoked, eat, & speculated on the approach of the enemy. Our scouts inform us there were 300 rebel cavalry last night at Francisville Ky. 2 miles only from our Hd. Qrs., but they don't show themselves on the river. The news comes to us from Cin that Smith is retreating this afternoon, & Col. Harrison talks of taking his Brig tomorrow across the river, to hang on the enemy's rear & pick up stragglers."[41]

No great battle between Kirby Smith's army and the Squirrel Hunters ever took place:

"...whether Kirby Smith's soldiers would have been as easily brought down at the crack of their [the Squirrel Hunters'] rifles and shot-guns as squirrels had frequently been on previous occasions, was never demonstrated, as they [the Confederates] retreated southward without testing the valor of the Squirrel Hunters."[42]

On September 13, Eugene Parrott and many of the other Squirrel Hunters returned to their homes. The men returning to Dayton were apparently met with much fanfare, despite the fact that they had not participated in any actual combat:

"Today we end our bloodless campaign. The Cin papers & the Gov's proclamation say the danger is over & the minute men will be discharged. Tho' we have done nothing in the way of fighting, we came with willing hearts to do it, & probably after all it is the militia have saved Cin. The hosts of them that lined the banks of the Ohio would have made the crossing of the river a very severe undertaking. It has been a glorious sight to see; almost worth a man's life time, the great outpouring of the citizen soldiery, politicians & legislators in the ranks, & stout yeomanry from all quarters of the state with their squirrel rifles & blankets over their shoulders have been pouring into Cin by thousands & tens of thousands. It has not been so seen since Bunker Hill. Got home at eight o'clock—found a crowd at the depot & as much fuss made over us as if we were really blood stained heroes."[43]

Another photo of Howard Forrer.

Howard Forrer was not among those returning to Dayton on September 13, however. He stayed in northern Kentucky with his new-found regiment, the 112th. On the 15th, Samuel Forrer traveled down to

Kentucky to visit his son at camp. In one of the few surviving letters written by Howard Forrer himself, he tells his sister Elizabeth how pleased he was by the visit:

"Father came to see me yesterday and besides the delightful surprise of his own presence he brought his carpet sack full of good things from home, good in themselves and doubly good as reminders that I am not forgotten by the loved ones at home..."[44]

Howard was stationed at Camp Shaler, one of the fortifications built up on the Kentucky side for the defense of Cincinnati. (This camp is now part of Evergreen Cemetery in Southgate, Kentucky.) Sarah conveyed news of Howard's activities at Camp Shaler, as well as his regiment's recruitment situation, to her daughters on September 21:

"I had a very kind and pleasant letter from Howard from Camp Shaler or Taylor as they sometimes call it. He was well and seemed to enjoy his situation, since they are settled in this Camp, which is a pleasant place, in the Cemetery, only a few miles over the river. I did not mean to say he endured all the privations and hardships of a private. He has a horse, and was not so fatigued with the <u>long</u>, hot, unnecessary march as the poor men were, but he felt indignant on their account, and he <u>too</u> was much fatigued. We are trying to get them home to finish recruiting the regiment, but Gen. [Horatio G.] Wright says he has been sending so many away, that at present he cannot spare them. Mr. Odlin is making [exertions?] for them, in the way of recruiting, having obtained authority from the Gov. He intends to have Hunter for Lieutenant Col. Who they will have for Col. I do not know. They wish to get some one who will give [character?] to the Regiment and in this way aid in enlisting. Father says he does not think they will succeed[,] the time is so short. If they <u>do</u>, he thinks Howard will be the Adjutant. For my part, if the want of success is the means of disgusting Howard with the service, I hope they will not succeed... I hope he will be disgusted and leave..."[45]

Unfortunately, Sarah did not get her wish.

"...I think Howard will be at home soon though he has not said so. The 112th it is said, has been consolidated with the 63rd which is at Corinth, and pretty fully officered. If this is the case there will be no chance for Howard and I do hope he will return and settle down to some business, in civil life..."[46]

-Sarah Forrer to her daughter Mary, 4 Nov. 1862

"It is Howard's birthday, the eleventh November, 1862. He is twenty-one years of age. It seems but yesterday he was in my arms. And now, where is he?..."[47]

-Sarah Forrer's diary, 11 Nov. 1862

After Howard Forrer went with the Squirrel Hunters to Cincinnati in early September 1862, there was no stopping his momentum to join the army. He remained in northern Kentucky with the 112th Ohio Volunteer Infantry (or, the group of men who were hoping to be the 112th O.V.I. – their regiment had not yet been filled) until the end of September 1862.[48]

On October 1, 1862, Howard and a detachment from the 112th returned to Dayton to continue recruiting, hoping to fill their regiment. Sarah Forrer was thrilled to have her son close to home again (and safe).[49] She wrote on October 5:

"...we have him home every night, and though it is but little, we are very thankful for this nightly visit. He is very well, growing fleshy, and seems cheerful, though so uncertain as to his future prospects. I cannot but hope something will 'turn up' to prevent his going away..."[50]

About three weeks later, the 112th was sent to Camp Mansfield to continue recruiting. Sarah wrote:

"The 112th received orders to go to Camp Mansfield, and they went yesterday morning. Howard said he would go, and if things are not arranged to suit him he will leave and return to us, I hope he will..."[51]

It is clear from his family's correspondence—very little written by Howard himself survives—that Howard had his heart quite set on being an officer, particularly the adjutant. [Editor's note: An adjutant is a staff officer who assists the commanding officer of a regiment with administrative duties, also known as an aide-de-camp.] By early November, the 112th regiment was still not full, and so it was consolidated with an existing regiment, the 63rd Ohio Volunteer Infantry, which needed fresh recruits. At that time, Howard was commissioned as a full first lieutenant. On November 9, 1862, Howard's father Samuel Forrer wrote to daughter Mary of Howard's situation, which was still a bit undecided:

"Howard…is on his way to take the detachment of 112th regiment (of which he was adjutant) to Corinth [, Mississippi]. The 112th is consolidated with the 63rd Ohio V. I. [with] Col. [John W.] Sprague commanding… It will be a pleasant trip over a region of country new to your brother. And we hope he may return, probably as soon as you or soon after. And yet we must not be disappointed if he should spend the winter in that region. This he will not do unless he is made the adjutant of the 63rd Regt. Older Lieuts. may claim that place, and if so will and ought to have it. Do not[,] my dear child[,] let this piece of intelligence give you a moment's uneasiness. All will, I have no doubt, go well with us… I believe our armies will before long set matters right, whatever may be done by the administration or by the miserable democracy coming into power…"[52]

Howard's mother Sarah wrote her thoughts on the recent turn of events in her diary on November 11, 1862, Howard's twenty-first birthday:

"It is long since I wrote anything in this book. I have been too busy and my heart has been too full to write. Nor do I feel better now. Yet I will write. It is Howard's birthday, the eleventh November, 1862. He is twenty-one years of age. It seems but yesterday he was in my arms. And now, where is he?...

"The 112th regiment was never full and after staying at Camp Dayton a few weeks they were ordered to Mansfield with a hope they could there recruit in sufficient number to fill the regiment. They did not succeed. And they were consolidated with the 63rd, now at Corinth, Mississippi.

This regiment suffered greatly in the recent battle, and the 112th will supply the places of those who have fallen... Howard retains the adjutancy until they reach Corinth. And perhaps after that. As he wishes it I hope he will have it."[53]

Howard did receive the adjutancy of the 63rd O.V.I. and was evidently well-suited to the job. Several months later, Sarah wrote in her diary: "I hear from several sources that he is popular and makes a good officer."[54] But her November 11, 1862, entry continued:

"But it is all grief to me. I had hoped something would happen to keep him at home, and after every battle my first thought was, "Howard is safe at home." Now the thought that he is indeed gone comes between him and me like a stone wall, a great barrier, shutting out, I had almost said, hope itself..."[55]

The year 1863 held no major tragedies for the Forrer family. But at the time, of course, the family had no such knowledge, as things were just unfolding.

And back then communication was much slower and more difficult than today. They did have the telegraph, but that was not cheap, easy, or convenient. Unlike today, a soldier could not use Skype or a cell phone to call home and reassure his family from halfway around the world. People primarily relied on letters and the newspapers for news of loved ones in the war. Both of these communication methods might already contain outdated information by the time they were read, too. And newspaper reports were not usually specific enough to confirm the safety or whereabouts of a particular person anyway, so it was hard to ever really to know for sure if a loved one was safe or not.

Imagine the anxiety, waiting for the mail—hoping to receive good news, or, failing that, at least being relieved at not receiving bad news—or half fearing to open the newspaper every morning, afraid to possibly read the reason for a son's (or husband's) lack of correspondence, right there in the newspaper.

Having not heard from her son in over a month, Sarah Forrer was getting worried in mid-January 1863:

"We have not heard from Howard since the ninth December... We see by the papers that his regiment, the 63rd O.V.I., was in the fight with Forest at Cross Roads. But we have not heard from our dear one. I am anxious about him, wish to hear from himself that he is safe, and also how he felt during the fight..."[56] [The battle Sara referred to was that with Confederate General Nathan Bedford Forrest at the Battle of Parker's Cross Roads, on December 31, 1862, in Henderson County, Tennessee.] A few days later, Sarah's anxiety was temporarily relieved by news from her son:

"At last, after a silence of over a month, I have heard from Howard... He says of the fight with Forest, "I am pretty well satisfied with myself under fire." I had not a doubt of his bravery... Oh! That he was safe at home!..."[57]

Howard Forrer and the 63rd O.V.I. spent much of early 1863 in Corinth, Mississippi. In one of few surviving letters written by Howard himself, he described Corinth to his young niece Henrietta, in February:

"You have often noticed the name "Corinth" in the papers and have read of the battles that have been fought in and around it. Well that is the place near which we are at present encamped; and a most mean, insignificant little place it is, to be the center of so much glory—Earthworks thrown up by one party, or the other extend for miles in nearly every direction from the town—The forts are in and near the town—It has rained nearly every day since we came here; consequently the frog ponds which are almost innumerable about here at this season, are all full, and their occupants are in high glee if singing is any sign of mirth..."[58]

In March, Howard was still in Corinth. He wrote to his brother-in-law J. H. Peirce, thanking him for some money had had sent, for Howard had not received any pay since about the time he first joined the 63rd in November:

"If you only knew how much good it did me, to see my pocketbook wax fat with 'green backs.' I think you would feel amply repaid for your generous and timely aid. The Gov't is indebted to me for nearly four months, and a half pay; and there is no telling when I shall receive it..."[59]

Howard and the 63rd remained at Corinth until about April 1863. From May to August 1863, the 63rd was stationed at Memphis, Tennessee. Howard wrote another letter to his niece Henrietta from Memphis:

"We live here very quietly for soldiers—The only excitement we have, being the news, that we get by the papers, the reception of the mail every morning; and an occasional local affair of temporary interest…"[60]

Howard went on describing three such incidents, one of which involved the apprehension of a female spy. He signed the letter: "your affectionate Uncle Howard Forrer"

Howard returned to Ohio in August 1863 and seems to have remained in the state for most of the next several months, recruiting in Dayton, Cincinnati, and Marietta. (Meanwhile, the rest of the 63rd O.V.I. was in Tennessee and Mississippi.[61])

The main source for Howard's being in Ohio most of late 1863 is Sarah Forrer's diary, as follows:

August 9, 1863:

"Howard came home very unexpectedly, and much to our joy. He stayed with us a few days when he was taken with chills and fever and was sick near a week. He was with us two weeks. I see little or no change in him. Perhaps he is a little more staid than before he left home, more serious. I would be glad to keep him with us. I think one year for our only son quite enough. But he says, "No, not at this stage of the game." [This comment probably had something to do with the two major victories the Union had just won in July 1863, Gettysburg and Vicksburg.]

"He is now at Camp Dennison near Cincinnati, waiting for drafted men to fill the 63rd. We still hope for more of his company before he leaves the state.'"[62]

September 2, 1863:

"Howard returned last month, and he has been with us till this evening. He has apparently recovered his health. And this short visit has been a great blessing to us… Howard is to go to Marietta [to recruit] and left us this evening for that place. He thinks he will be with us before he leaves the state again…'"[63]

November 25, 1863:
"Thanksgiving. The excitement of the electioneering campaign was great and distressing. It seemed likely at one time that the Democrats would carry the state and elect Vallandigham. Howard was permitted to return home to recruit. Here is his home, and here he cast his vote against Vallandigham. I was overjoyed to have him with us, and glad he could give his vote in favor of the Administration…" [The Democratic candidate in the 1863 Ohio gubernatorial election was Clement Vallandigham, a Dayton lawyer, leader of the Peace Democrats or "Copperheads," and hated by pretty much everyone who supported the war effort. Vallandigham was defeated by the Republican candidate John Brough.]

Sarah continued her Thanksgiving, 1863, diary entry: "[Howard] has been expecting to go to his regiment soon for some weeks, and a few days since received orders to report, with his men, at Columbus… He left us at midnight… After a few days we received a dispatch which led us to believe he would leave for his regiment the next day. I thought I must see him once more, and Husband and I went to Columbus. He had just been detailed for office work by the provost-marshal. I was glad, but he did not seem pleased and thinks by absence he will lose his place as adjutant. I hope not if he returns to his regiment. I do hope peace will be declared and that he will not have to go again. The news is very good today."[64]

December 29, 1863:
"December 29th. We have had a pleasant Christmas. Howard came Christmas Eve and staid till next evening… Christmas a year ago he was far south… Where will he be a year hence?… He was much delighted with our bazaar. Says it is much finer than the Columbus one was.

"We hope to see Luther soon. I am glad for Augusta's sake. He has never seen Baby and she is now six months old. Sad. Strange times we have fallen upon..."[65]

Luther was Sarah's son-in-law Luther B. Bruen, who enlisted in the regular army – 12th U.S. Infantry – in May 1861. In a way, it is thanks to Luther that many of the primary sources used in telling Howard's story for the year 1862 even exist, for Sarah wrote many letters to her daughters Augusta (Luther's wife) and Mary, who were in New York City, along with Luther, who was stationed there at Fort Hamilton. Augusta and Mary apparently returned to Dayton in 1863, and in June of that year, Augusta gave birth to the couple's fourth child, daughter Mary Bruen, who (according to grandmother Sarah Forrer) was over six months old before her father ever laid eyes on her.

On Valentine's Day, 1864, Sarah wrote: "Yesterday dear Howard left us again to join his regiment. I do feel his loss... Luther...came, but his visit was so short he had hardly time to get acquainted with Baby. Still, though short, his visit was a great comfort to his family and to us all."[66]

All things considered, the year 1863 had been fairly calm for the Forrers, with son Howard Forrer spending most of the year either in camp or in Ohio recruiting, and son-in-law Luther Bruen spending most of the year as the commander of Fort Hamilton, New York, far behind Union lines.

However, when Howard and Luther left Dayton in February 1864, they were both ultimately headed for less safe assignments: Luther had been given command of a brigade in the Army of the Potomac. Howard was headed for Decatur, Alabama, returning to the adjutancy of the 63rd O.V.I. (probably much to his relief, as he had feared he might lose the position by being away so long). In May, the 63rd would join Sherman's Atlanta Campaign.

Sarah Forrer was not particularly diligent about keeping her diary on a regular basis. There were apparently large gaps in its coverage. After writing that February 14, 1864, entry, she did not write another for almost four years. But when she finally did write in her diary again, the entry began as follows:

"Dec. 27, 1867. I have not written, I could not write…until now. We never saw dear Howard again! And never saw Luther alive!…"[67]

"Do you hear from your Howard? And where is he? I am almost afraid to look over the lists of killed and wounded lest I should see his name among them… It is reported here that Atlanta is taken by our forces, though it is doubted by some…"[68]

-MARY AFFLECK TO HER SISTER SARAH FORRER,
24-25 JULY 1864

When Howard Forrer left his family to return to his position as adjutant of the 63rd O.V.I. on February 13, 1864, it was the last time his mother ever saw him alive.[69]

Howard headed to Camp Chase in Columbus to meet up with his regiment, and from there, they headed for Decatur, Alabama, on February 18, where the staff of the 63rd was stationed until the end of April.[70]

Howard kept a diary during his last campaign. It contains mostly notes on troop movements, weather conditions, and anecdotes about interactions with the locals. Unfortunately, it contains virtually nothing of his personal thoughts or feelings about the war (or anything else). This sample from one of his first few entries is typical of the entire diary:

"Left Camp Chase, Columbus, Little Miami RR (weather very cold) at 12 N Feb 18th 1864, arrived at Cincinnati at 8 PM. Quartered men in 6th St Barracks. I stayed at the Gibson House. Left Cinti 12:45 PM 19th on C&M RR very poor accommodations on cars, weather cold. Arrived at Jeffersonville, Indiana, opposite Louisville 5:45 A.M. 20. Crossed on ferry boat to Louisville at 7:15 AM. River full of floating ice, weather much warmer. Saw Kate McCook and the General at breakfast table at Louisville at Galt House. Left Louisville on L&N RR at 2:50 PM. Saturday 20th arrived at Nashville 3:50 AM 21st— Quartered in [seminary?] barracks Capt. E. C. Ellis 93rd Ohio of Dayton commanding—visited Dr.

McDermot at the field hospital near Nashville—went to theatre Monday and Tuesday nights."[71]

His description of the trek to Decatur, Alabama, continued:

"Left Nashville on cars at 8 A.M. Wednesday 24th Feb. Traveled finely until we reached a point five miles north of Linville station, which is 1-1/2 miles from Linville [Lynnville, Tennessee]—where the cylinders of the engine had the head burst out. This occurred about 2 P.M.—The train was taken to Linville at three trips—arrived at Linville station at about 5 P.M. and [illegible] for the night—I slept at the house of one Lt. Col Gordon formerly of the C.S.A. wounded at Donaldson [Donelson] now peacable at home. The regiment started on the march about 5:30 A.M. 25th. I stopped at Linville to get breakfast. The woman at whose house I took breakfast informed me that Col. Dan McCook burned the best houses in the town because his regiment had been fired upon from it.

"The Col. Q.M. & I got into a spring wagon & rode to Pulaski [TN] ahead of the Regt arrived at N. Regt arrived at 1.30 P.M. Camped 2 miles south of town. Left this camp at 5:30 A.M. 26th and arrived at the old camp of the Regt at Prospect [Tennessee] (the Col. & I riding ahead of the Regt 3 or 4 miles) about 11 AM. Left Prospect 7 A.M. 27th arrived at Athens [Alabama] 1.30 P.M. Camped about a mile south of the town. Left camp at 6.30 A.M. 28th- Cloudy- The Col and I left the regiment about 2 hours after we started and rode ahead to the camp of the 43d Ohio at a place called Decatur Junction [Alabama], where the Decatur branch R.R. comes in. It had commenced to rain in the meantime. We selected a camping ground & conducted the regiment to it—camped in a corn field because it was the only place where water was convenient. Monday, the 29th and the 1st and 2[d] of March were spent making out returns, and bringing up the papers of the regt... Decatur [Alabama] is on rather high ground and seems to be quite a pretty place..."[72]

At the end of April, Howard's regiment received orders that they would be joining Generals William T. Sherman and James B. McPherson on what would later be known as the Atlanta Campaign. Howard wrote of the news in his diary on April 24 and 25:

"24d... We received an order this morning issued to the army of the Mississippi by Gen'l Sherman directing the troops to be prepared to move in light marching order. This order is very strict and is only preliminary... 25' Received McPherson's order preparatory to a move—it is a little less stringent than Sherman's."[73]

On May 1, 1864, Howard's regiment (and several others) left Decatur, Alabama, and began traveling towards Georgia.[74] [Editor's note: the 63rd marched eastward to Huntsville and then on a bit further to Brownsboro, Alabama, where it boarded rail cars and was then transported by train to Chattanooga, where it arrived May 5. It then immediately marched south into Georgia with the rest of Sherman's army.]

The final entries in Howard's diary, dating from late May, follow:

"17' Laid in camp all day until 6.30 P.M. (illegible) moved by moonlight (foggy: but light) over the mills & camped the 2 brigades at 12 o'clock P.M. in a pasture field—Country much better than any we have passed through since we left Chattanooga—travelled 9 miles.~~& are 2 miles from Kingston~~. 18. Left Camp at 9.15 this a.m. Moved about 10 miles & stopped an hour or two giving me time to get over a slight chill & fever—then moved forward about a mile to where we are now (at 5.20 PM). We have been waiting for the 15d Corps to take the road ahead of us—They have been moving since yesterday on a road to the West of us. ~~Hooker's~~ The other corps have been ~~in sight~~ moving parallel with us on the East ~~side of the valley~~—We are said to be advancing in five columns—Our corps is on the direct road to Adairsville—started again at 10 PM & move about 8 miles in camp at 4 o'clock a.m. 19' very hard & tiresome march—19d moved at 10 a.m. for Kingston 8 miles camped within one mile of it at 4 P.M. having moved 7 miles. [illegible] yesterday a little skirmishing this a.m.—(beautiful spring). J. C. Davis took Rome [Georgia] yesterday & two trains of cars & report says 2500 prisoners. 20d Laid in Camp—received orders to be ready to move on 23d with 20 days rations."[75]

It's not clear why Howard decided to stop writing in his diary in May 1864. Perhaps he suddenly found himself too busy. (According to Hewett's Record of Events, there was a lot of "marching" and "skirmishing" after the 63rd joined Sherman in May.) Or perhaps he simply tired of keeping a diary; if he ever kept a diary previously, it seems that neither such a diary (nor any reference to one) have survived.

Whatever kept him from continuing his diary may have also kept him from writing home to his mother, who wrote on June 20: "We have had nothing from Howard and I almost fear to hear, I wrote to him yesterday but did not close it, and wait till I see how it terminates, or... when time, to him, is no more, I have written as cheerfully to him, as possible, and hope I shall not depress and unnerve him worse when he needs all the energy possible, Dear dear child! If we can only have him with us again!"[76]

As should be evident by this point, Sarah Forrer worried about her son quite a bit while he was away—not that anyone could blame her. She also worried about her son-in-law, Luther Bruen, who was seriously wounded in May 1864 and by June 20 lay dying in a Washington, D.C., hospital; he actually died the next day (June 21). This certainly must have breathed new life into all of Sarah's fears for the safety of her son Howard, whom she had not heard from and was still out there, somewhere.

For one with the benefit of history and hindsight, already knowing the fate of Howard Forrer, it is a bit chilling and eerie to read the following words from Mary Affleck to her sister Sarah Forrer, written July 24-25, 1864: "Do you hear from your Howard? And where is he? I am almost afraid to look over the lists of killed and wounded lest I should see his name among them... It is reported here that Atlanta is taken by our forces, though it is doubted by some..."[77] A Union victory had indeed been won in Atlanta (more specifically, Decatur), Georgia, a few days earlier. The July 29 issue of the *Cincinnati Gazette* carried an account of the battle, as well as a partial list of casualties. The blow they had all been dreading came when the Forrer family read that article in the *Gazette*, which included the following:

"Lieut.-Col. Brown, 63d Ohio, was wounded. The Adjutant of the regiment and Capt. Thorn were killed."[78]

Even though the adjutant's name was not given, the Forrers knew that there was only one adjutant of the 63rd Ohio—and it was their own precious Howard. This was how the Forrers first learned the fate of their only son: they read it in the newspaper. Unfortunately, and rather horrifically, this was not an uncommon way for people to learn of the death of a loved one. And yet, the article didn't explicitly *say* "Howard Forrer." What if a mistake had been made? It certainly would not be the first time (or the last) that a newspaper published inaccurate information, even in the casualty lists. These two scraps of correspondence from Samuel to his wife on the day the family first saw the report in the *Gazette* illustrate the frantic urgency and desperate hope they felt on that day, that perhaps the report was mistaken:

"My dear wife, Bro. John [Howard] has already telegraphed to the Editor of the Cin. Gazette to learn the name of the Adjt. No answer yet. Will wait here for answer and telegraph to Col. Sprague and others. Robt. Steele called on me and voluntarily said most sympathetically that he did not believe the statement. Odlin doubts its truth. Every body says if true we must have heard it before this time. Hope for the best. Wm. Howard says ["Ero"?] is Chamberlain of the 81st and classmate of theirs—believes he is mistaken. I will be out at 2 o'clock. [signed] S.F. Bro. John has some hopes as I have that it may be untrue for the same reason as others."[79]

"Bro. John" was John Howard, Sarah's brother, a prominent Dayton lawyer and former mayor. Samuel himself was a prominent civil engineer. And even if the Forrer family did not already have enough clout to warrant the attention of the *Gazette* editors in regards to their inquiry, son-in-law Luther Bruen, who died a few weeks earlier, had previously been one of the proprietors of the *Gazette*. So it seems reasonable to think the newspaper would be willing to give a little extra respect and consideration to *his* family.

"Col. Sprague" refers to John W. Sprague, who had commanded the 63rd O.V.I. since 1862 (when Howard joined it). By July 1864, he was in command of the entire brigade—2nd brigade, 4th Division, 16th Army

Corps—in which the 63rd was included. (Sprague was actually promoted to brigadier general and awarded a Medal of Honor for his actions in the Battle of Decatur.) And, according to an earlier letter, Samuel apparently knew Sprague from somewhere before the war, so it is not surprising that he felt comfortable contacting him directly.[80]

"Odlin" was likely James Hunter Odlin (referenced in some earlier letters as "Hunter Odlin"), another officer (Major) who had served with Howard in the 63rd O.V.I. At first this might seem confusing: *Wouldn't Odlin have been in Atlanta as well? How did Samuel ask Odlin about this?* But according to the Official Roster, Odlin had resigned from the regiment in 1863, so it seems he was probably back in Dayton in 1864.[81]

Robert Steele was a prominent Dayton educator who, as far as I know, had no particular ties to the war. William Howard was Samuel's nephew who had served in 1862-1863. "Ero" probably refers to the pen name of the war correspondent. There was a William H. Chamberlin who was a captain in the 81st Ohio, which was also in the 16th Army Corps at Atlanta.[82]

A few hours later, Samuel wrote a follow-up message:

"No answer from Cincinnati yet. Genl. McCook told Charles Anderson [lieutenant governor of Ohio] that He did not believe the statement in the Gazette in regard to Howard's death. Charley says that he does not believe it. But I confess that I have but little hope although [not] entirely without hope. 2 o'clock. S.F. Will come out as soon as things are in train."[83]

The Forrers obviously had ties to many prominent individuals and others whom they thought might have the correct intelligence on their son. Then again, even if they did not have personal connections to some of these people, it still would not be unheard of for a father to go to great lengths—including calling upon perfect strangers, if he thought it would help—in order to learn the fate of his child. Not surprisingly, many people were in shock, disbelief, and perhaps denial about the fate of Howard Forrer. "It can't be true," they said; they wanted to believe. But within a few days, that devastating news report was confirmed, and

Sarah Forrer's worst fear since the war began had come true. Her only son Howard was dead.

"His grave is made 'neath southern sod; / His feet no more will roam, / His soul stands at the bar of God; / But oh he's missed at home."[84]

-Lizzie Morton, 1864

"I have not written, I could not write...until now. We never saw dear Howard again!... The dear, dear son was killed instantly at Decatur, Georgia. I am almost destroyed by this great loss..."[85]

-Sarah Forrer's diary, 27 Dec. 1867

"How many hearts shall this war prepare for heaven by transferring all they loved to the far-off but beautiful land where the good dwell!"[86]

-Quincy [war correspondent], 10 Aug. 1864

The Forrers first learned of the death of their beloved son Howard via the *Cincinnati Gazette's* July 29, 1864, issue, which reported that the Adjutant of the 63rd O.V.I. had been killed in the Battle of Atlanta in Decatur, Georgia, on July 22. At first they held out hope that the news report might be mistaken, but alas, it was not. Within a few days, Samuel Forrer received a letter from Benjamin St. James Fry, chaplain of the 63rd O.V.I., giving a detailed account of Howard Forrer's death. Although the original letter was not included with the manuscripts in the Forrer-Peirce-Wood Collection, it was reprinted in the *Dayton Journal* on August 2, 1864:

"We were attacked at Decatur, on Friday, the 22d, after dinner, by [Joseph] Wheeler's whole force, at the same time that an attack was made on the left of our whole army, and were compelled to withdraw temporarily from the town. The attack was furious, and we lost many in prisoners, as well as by wounding.

"Howard was engaged with Colonel [Charles E.] Brown and Major Pfoutz [sic, John W. Fouts] in making a charge on our right. They had driven back the rebels, checking them, and were returning to their position, which was a good one, when Howard was killed instantly by a wound in the neck, for the rebels were coming forward in great force again. We could not get off his body, but when we returned on Saturday morning the citizens had buried him on the spot where he fell..."[87]

The chaplain's explanation of events refers to the attack of Confederate Gen. Joseph Wheeler's cavalry upon the Union's 2nd brigade, 4th division, 16th Army Corps, commanded by then-Colonel John W. Sprague. (He was promoted to brigadier general a week later for his actions in the battle.) Wheeler's men were attempting to capture a wagon train of supplies. Although the Union troops were pushed back, the wagon train was preserved.[88]

Major John W. Fouts (of the 63rd O.V.I.) wrote the following in his official reports of the battle:

"July 22, took part with the brigade in the engagement at Decatur, Ga. Two companies of this regiment by a charge upon a superior force of the enemy saved from capture a section of the Board of Trade Battery and a large wagon train of the Fifteenth Army Corps. The enemy attacked on all sides with a very superior force and, after two hours' hard fighting, we were finally driven out of the town with the loss of 1 commissioned officer (Adjt. Howard Forrer) killed, 4 wounded, and 1 wounded and taken prisoner..."[89]

In a more detailed report on the July 22 battle at Decatur, Fouts wrote:

"...The enemy advanced in greatly superior force and it became necessary for the battery to retire. While retiring the battery became entangled in a heap of old iron and was in danger of being captured. In order to save the battery[,] Company G, which had formed on the left of

[the] battery, and Company H fixed bayonets and made a determined charge on the advancing line of the enemy, causing it to fall back to the railroad and giving the battery time to get off, and giving a large wagon train of the Fifteenth Army Corps time to leave the field, which, but for this charge, would have fallen into the hands of the enemy. These companies, under command of Lieut. Col. Charles E. Brown, then fell back in good order to court square. Adjt. Howard Forrer was killed during this movement. The other companies of this regiment coming in at this time were rallied and formed on south side of court square with part of the Twenty-fifth Wisconsin Infantry, and held the ground until completely flanked on right and left, when we were ordered to fall back to ridge north of the town. In rallying the regiment at this point Lieut. Col. Charles E. Brown was severely wounded and carried from the field. The enemy continuing the attack with a much superior force in front and on both flanks obliged us to fall back to the cover of the woods, and we took position with the balance of the brigade..."[90]

A war correspondent called "Quincy" submitted not only some gory details regarding Howard's death, but also a touching, "beautiful tribute" to the young man, in a way that could only have been written by a fellow soldier who had known him well. While his identity is unclear, whoever he was, Quincy's "Beautiful Tribute" read thus in the *Western Christian Advocate*, August 10, 1864:

"Our commanding officer lies near me as I write with an amputated limb [Editor's note: Colonel Charles E. Brown, who lost a leg], maimed for life, and yet we are happy that his life is spared to us, and hope and pray for his restoration to health again. The Adjutant of our regiment [Howard Forrer], stripped by rebel hands, lies buried on the spot where he fell in instant death, his brain shattered by an unhappy bullet. There are but few men in the army whose death could affect me as his has done.

"Young, intelligent, carefully trained in virtue by parents of Quaker profession, not a stain had come upon the fair promise of his youth, and the future was a brilliant prospect, inviting him to advance and obtain the reward of honorable, energetic action. He was so brave that no one questioned his courage, yet so far from the recklessness of youth that you perceived at once it was moral, not physical, bravery that animated him. His character bore so plainly the graceful and tender teachings of female influence that you would suspect he was an only son, the youngest of the family, the idol of a devoted mother, and the pride of sisters. I dare not look toward the quiet home in the most beautiful town in Ohio, where he lived. But a few weeks ago in one of those fierce contests of the Army of the Potomac that initiated the campaign, a son-in-law [Luther Bruen], whose character, I have been told, was singularly fair and graceful, was wounded, and died in the hospital at Washington City. Now a second stroke, and a nearer one, flashes out of the war clouds, and I stop my ears to shut out the cry and groans of stricken hearts. At such times there is no refuge for one but in God. The mysteries of His providence lose all their terror and perplexity in the tenderness of His grace and love. How many hearts shall this war prepare for heaven by transferring all they loved to the far-off but beautiful land where the good dwell!"[91]

To Sarah Forrer and her family, certainly all the touching tributes in the world could not hold a candle to the devastating reality that Howard Forrer would never come home to Dayton alive. But even though Howard had died, he still could not yet return home. Remember what the chaplain wrote:

"...We could not get off his body, but when we returned [the following] morning the citizens had buried him on the spot where he fell..."[92]

Howard was buried on the property of Benjamin F. Swanton, near the spot where he had been killed. (This property is southwest of the county's old courthouse and the town square.) At the time, the Swanton house was being used as headquarters for Union Gen. James B. McPherson's Army of the Tennessee (which, incidentally, is probably the only reason the house—which still exists and is the oldest building in Decatur—did not meet the same fiery fate that many other area buildings did).[93]

As if to add insult to injury, as if the Forrer family had not already suffered enough for one year—with the loss of son-in-law Luther Bruen in June and now the loss of son Howard in July—they could not even bring Howard's body home for a proper burial, because the war was still raging.

"Who will survive is known only to Him who ruleth all things well."[94]

Howard Forrer was killed instantly, July 22, 1864, on the battlefield at Decatur, Georgia. His regiment, which was retreating at the time, was unable to retrieve his body immediately, and by the next day, the towns-folk had already buried him. Because of the ongoing war, even his family was unable to go and retrieve his remains. His mother later wrote in her diary: "We were obliged to leave him a year in Georgia..."[95]

Howard Forrer's remains would not come home to Dayton until November 1865, nearly 16 months after his death. In the meantime, the Forrer family commemorated Howard by having his portrait painted from a photograph, at cost of about $125 (about $1,700 in today's money). Several letters from Sarah Forrer to her daughter Mary in September 1864 dwell upon which photograph should be used, the precise shade of blue of Howard's army coat, and the color of his hair and eyes.[96]

Based on Sarah's descriptions and her mention of retrieving the photo negative from Cridland's photography studio[97], this may be the photograph from which the portrait was painted:

Howard Forrer photographed in his army uniform.

In these letters about the portrait, Sarah frequently refers to her son as "dear Howie," rather than "Howard," which was what she nearly always called him in all of her writings prior to his death.[98] The change is a little jarring but not entirely confusing. A nearly 23-year-old army officer might have insisted that his mother treat him like a man and refrain from calling him by a childhood nickname. Sarah had often written of putting on a brave face for her son, playing the patriotic mother and pretending to be fine when truly she was not. She likely still saw him as a child, as many mothers see their children even after those children become adults. When he died, he could no longer defend his adulthood; so in Sarah's mind, he reverted ever more back to being her baby, her beloved little boy, "dear Howie," whom she would never see again.

The Forrers of course continued to seek information about how they could retrieve their son's body. Samuel Forrer apparently wrote to A. C. Fenner, the Acting Assistant Adjutant General of Howard Forrer's brigade, asking for his assistance with the matter. It seems that the state of the roads and railroads near Atlanta—not to mention Sherman's March to the Sea and general "total war" on the South—greatly contributed to the inability to retrieve poor Howard's remains.

A. C. Fenner wrote to Samuel Forrer on January 11, 1865:

"...The R. R. was also broken up so that trains could not pass to Atlanta... Nov 15 the Army started on the recent campaign so that no opportunity has been afforded me of visiting Decatur Ga. Or getting any information from there since I was in Dayton. The troops who occupied it last[,] the 23d Corps[,] are as you have observed in Tenn. The R. R. south of [Chatt.?] Is all destroyed South of Kingston.

"Of course all prospects of visiting the place is now out of the question until the Road is rebuilt which will not be probably till after the war.

"I am extremely sorry it never was in my power to render such services in this case as know would greatly gratify you. My personal relations alone with Howard prompted me if it had been possible to have done all you had desired but the stern circumstances of war interfered..."[99]

The Forrers were sent a sketch showing the location of Howard Forrer's grave by the Swanton house in downtown Decatur. It shows how the Confederates were attacking down the hill from the railroad across an open field toward where the Federals were camped. In addition to Forrer's grave (a), it shows that two other Federal soldiers (Corporal Weston Ray and an unidentified third soldier) were killed at the same spot at the same time. The accompanying notes read:

1. An arbor in the open lot where Adjt. [Adjutant] Forrer was encamped. This was a rough arbor put up by the Soldiers. Stakes sit in the ground & bushes over the top.
2. Residence of the Mortons
3. ditto ditto Swantons

   a Adjt Forrer

   b Corp Ray

   c a third soldier

   d Adjt Forrer's horse toward which he was running when killed.

The Civil War finally ended a few months later with Robert E. Lee's surrender at Appomattox Courthouse on April 9, 1865. Although certainly relieved that the war was over, many on both sides still mourned what the war had cost. Among them were the sisters Mary Affleck and

Sarah Forrer, both of whom had lost sons (both named Howard, after the sisters' maiden name) in the war. Mary's letter to her sister Sarah on June 18, 1865, and the accompanying poem, "The Hour of Northern Victory" by Fanny Kemble, illustrate the what a bittersweet victory it was:

> "...*it almost seems as though the 'Old bright days had all come back again.' Will they ever come again? Not to thee, or to me, yet we may do much to brighten the pathway of the dear ones that are still left to us, and thus in some measure, relieve the 'blackness of darkness' that overshadows our own...*
>
> *"Has thee ever read 'The Hour of Northern Victory' by Fanny Kemble? I think it one of the grandest things I ever read, and will bear reading again, so I have copied it for thee...*"[100]

The poem was as follows:

"The Hour of Northern Victory"[101]
By Fanny Kemble

Roll not a drum, sound not a clarion-note
Of haughty triumph to the silent sky;
Hush'd be the shout of joy in ev'ry throat,
And veil'd the flash of pride in ev'ry eye.

Not with the Te Deums loud and high Hosannas,
Greet we the awful victory we have won,
But with our arms revers'd and lower'd banners
We stand—our work is done!

Thy work is done, God, terrible and just,
Who lay'dst upon our hearts and hands this task,
And kneeling, with our foreheads in the dust,
We venture Peace to ask.

Bleeding and writhing underneath our sword,
Prostrate our brethren lie, Thy fallen foe,
Struck down by Thee through us, avenging Lord,—
By Thy dread hand laid low.

For our own guilt have we been doomed to smite
These our own kindred Thy great laws defying,
These, our own flesh and blood, who now unite
In one thing only with us—bravely dying.

Dying how bravely, yet how bitterly!
Not for the better side, but for the worse,
Blindly and madly striving against Thee
For the bad cause where thou hast set Thy curse.

At whose defeat we may not raise our voice,
Save in the deep thanksgiving of our prayers,
'Lord! We have fought the fight!' But to rejoice
Is ours no more than theirs.

Call back Thy dreadful ministers of wrath
Who have led on our hosts to this great day;
Let our feet halt now in the avenger's path,
And bid our weapons stay.

Upon our land, Freedom's inheritance,
Turn Thou once more the splendor of Thy face,
Where nations serving Thee to light advance,
Give us again our place.

Not our bewildering past prosperity,
Not all thy former ill-requited grace,
But this one boon—Oh! Grant us still to be
The home of Hope to the whole human race.

Mary's letter continued:

"I have been looking over on the island [Wheeling Island], which is almost covered with tents of returning soldiers who are waiting to be discharged. A long train of army wagons passed through town a week or two ago, and another this morning. I feel thankful that so many of the poor fellows are permitted to return to their homes in peace but my heart aches to think of the thousands that never will return and of the <u>one</u> who was more to me than the whole army."[102]

By the time Mary Affleck wrote that letter, her son Howard had been dead for three years from the wounds he suffered at the Battle of Shiloh. Her younger son Edward had spent many months in a POW camp but had finally returned to her.

In the summer of 1865, the anniversary of Howard Forrer's death came and went, and the Forrers still had not been able to retrieve his remains, despite the war finally being over. On September 25, 1865, over 14 months after Howard had been killed, Maj. Genl. Thomas granted the necessary permissions to Samuel Forrer:

"Permission is hereby granted to Mr. Saml. Forrer to disinter the body of Lieut. Howard Forrer now buried at Decatur Georgia & to remove the same by Express or otherwise to Dayton Ohio, provided the disinterring is made at once after Oct. 15, 1865, & the body is shipped in a metallic coffin."[103]

Samuel Forrer inquired immediately about the cost of train fares and metallic coffins, apparently writing to Genl. Gates Phillips Thruston, a Daytonian stationed at Nashville, on October 1. Thruston wrote back on October 13, stating that the fare from Dayton to Atlanta would be about $30 (about $425 today) and sending a price list for coffins.[104] While Samuel Forrer was making his arrangements to finally retrieve his son from Atlanta, the U.S. Treasury Department forwarded the balance of Howard's back pay to his father: $797.89. The pay was for the time period of December 31, 1863, through Howard's death on July 22, 1864.[105] Apparently, he had not received any pay for several months, which was not uncommon.

That $797 in back pay amounted to about $11,000 in today's dollars.[106] However, it most certainly did not amount to much of anything to the Forrers, compared with the loss of their only son Howard.

Samuel Forrer and his brother-in-law John Howard finally made the journey in November 1865 to bring Howard Forrer home to Dayton at long last. It was a bittersweet relief. The son they remembered was of course not the son they brought home. Sarah wrote of it a few years later:

> *"...And then dear Husband and our dear, kind Brother John went and brought him home... There was nothing left but dry bones and some parts of his clothing, one piece showing his name written in indelible ink by me. They took a case with them and put the dear remains in and packed it with sweet pine boughs that it might carry safely. And so he came who left in health, radiant, enthusiastic... Oh, so lovely!!"*[107]

The *Dayton Journal* published a notice on November 14, 1865, announcing that Howard Forrer's remains had finally come home, as well as the funeral arrangements:

> *"The remains of the lamented Howard Forrer arrived here yesterday, in charge of the venerable bereaved father, Samuel Forrer, and John Howard, Esq. Lieut. Forrer was killed during a charge upon our lines near Decatur, Ga., on the 22d of July, 1864. He was truly an estimable and talented young man, and a gallant soldier. We cannot too highly honor the memory of the noble young men who offered up their lives for their country. The funeral of Lieut. Forrer will take place at the family residence, near Tate's Mills, northwest of the city, at 2 o'clock to-day, and his remains will be interred at 'Woodland.'"*[108]

On November 14, 1865, Howard Forrer was finally laid to rest in Woodland Cemetery in his hometown of Dayton, Ohio. The tombstone inscription reads:

> *"Howard, son of Saml. & S. H. Forrer. Adjt. 63rd Regt. O.V.I. Fell in Battle at Decatur Ga. July 22, 1864, in his 23rd year.*
> *"Young, lovely, brave, and true. He died a pure offering to duty and patriotism."*

About the author

Lisa Rickey is Archivist/ Collections Manager at Special Collections and Archives, Wright State University Libraries, Dayton, Ohio. Previously, she was a reference librarian and archivist in the Local History Room of the Dayton Metro Library. While at Dayton Metro Library, Lisa arranged and described the Forrer-Peirce-Wood Collection, an archival manuscript collection documenting several generations of a Dayton family, including at least six Civil War soldiers, one of whom was Howard Forrer.

Lisa has a Master of Arts in Public History from Wright State University and an MLIS from Wayne State University. She has been interested in genealogy, family history, and local history research for 20 years. The story of Howard Forrer originally appeared on Lisa's history and archives blog "Glancing Backwards," http://lisarickey.wordpress.com.

IX

The Life and Death of
Solomon Spitler

The story of a young Ohio man named Solomon Spitler, whose life was cut short at the Battle of Decatur, captures the experiences of many soldiers in the Civil War.

Solomon Spitler lived with his parents in Potsdam, Ohio, a little village in Miami County just northwest of Dayton, Ohio. The 160-acre farm of his parents John and Esther (Warner) was a mile south of the village. They had married on April 11, 1839, and their fruitful union produced a large family. By 1864 it included Oliver, age 23 and married; Barbra, 21; Elizabeth, 20; their fourth child Solomon, 19; Susana, 18; William, 16; Hannah and Lydia, 15; B.H., 14; and E.W., 3. [1]

Solomon had been born in December 1844 and was 19 at the beginning of 1864. Early that year, Solomon and three other young men secretly went to Dayton to join the army. At the time, the 63rd Ohio was home from the battlefield on furlough, having re-enlisted on January 1, 1864, as a veteran regiment along with the 43rd, 39th and 27th Ohio regiments (the so-called Ohio Brigade). Sergeants from the 63rd were out in the Ohio countryside actively recruiting, and it's likely that Solomon and his friends encountered one of these recruiters and thus wound up enlisting. [2]

On February 1, Spitler enlisted in Dayton for three years' service, listing his occupation as a farmer. We do not know what he looked like. The author has been unable to locate a photograph. But he was described as 5 feet 4 ½ inches in height with a dark complexion, dark eyes and dark hair. He was sent to Camp Chase in Columbus, Ohio, for training.

On February 4, 1864, he would write his family a letter:

"Dear father and mother, brothers and sisters,

"I will let you know that I have enlisted last Monday at Dayton and Monday night I started for Columbus and I got there at 4 o'clock in the morning and I will know that I am all right yet and hoping that when these few lines comes to hand that they may find you in the same state of health and further I will let you know that I got one hundred 25 dollars city bounty and yester day I drawed 75 dollars from the government bounty. We tried to get a furlough but I tried in vain we wrote back to our lieutenant fenner for a furlough and if he don't give us a furlough we are obliged to stay here. I like it first rate here. There is about 5000 soldiers here. We are in good barracks. Now I have about one hundred and 75 dollars to send home. Last night of my boots and socks in my bed so the money was safe. I think I will keep the money here till the old regiment comes here. Well I will tell you what we eat in the morning and evening. We have bread potatoes beef salt and coffee. At noon we have beef soup potatoes bread water and homney [sic]. O it is first rate enough of that. I drawed an overcoat pantaloons 2 pairs of socks one blouse knapsack blanket haversack canteen. I bought a vest and hat and a gum blanket hankerchief I am well supplied in close [sic, clothes].

"Yours truly from Solomon Spitler write soon Direct to Barraks Columbus Ohio. Lib, I am all right. Tell all the girls you see I send my best respects to them." [3]

Spitler was assigned to Company H of the 63rd Ohio, a veteran regiment that had been serving in northern Mississippi and Alabama. The 63rd's bloodiest battle had been the Battle of Corinth, Mississippi, where almost half of its men had been wounded or killed.

With the 63rd's veterans' furlough coming to an end, the soldiers of the 63rd gathered to return to the front. The new recruits for the 63rd, almost certainly including Spitler, were gathered at railroad stations on

February 15th, 1864, and taken to Columbus. There were more than 30 recruits, who were taken to the Tod Barracks to be mustered in and paid their enlistment bounties. [4]

On February 18 the regiment went by train to Cincinnati, then to Jeffersonville, Indiana, and on to Louisville, Kentucky, then on to Nashville, Tennessee, on the 21st. On February 24 they moved south again by train, getting to near Lynnville, Tennessee, when one of the train's engines blew a cylinder head. The regiment got out on foot and marched during the next couple of days through Lynnville and Pulaski, Tennessee, to Prospect, Tennessee, on the Elk River. This would have been Spitler's first experience with marching, one of the most basic aspects of soldiering.

Spitler would see his first action on March 8, 1864, when the 63rd Ohio, 43rd Ohio and 111th Illinois regiments made a bold nighttime amphibious assault to capture the strategic railroad town of Decatur, Alabama. At 1 a.m. in the morning, the Federals, who were on the north bank of the Tennessee River across from the town, boarded pontoon boats in the rain-swollen river and quietly began rowing across to the town on the south side. Thanks to the darkness and the noise of the high water, the Federals surprised the few Confederate sentinels on duty. The rebel guards fired a few shots and then fled. The Federals rushed out of their boats onto the river banks, formed up in regiments, and moved into the town at daylight. "It was one of the handsomest things I ever saw," [5] noted Capt. Oscar L. Jackson of the 63rd Ohio.

The next few weeks would be quiet for Spitler and the 63rd. But on May 1 the regiment's date with destiny arrived. By early spring 1864, Federal forces under General William T. Sherman were massing at Chattanooga, Tennessee, in preparation for a campaign to capture Atlanta, 110 miles south of Chattanooga. For the 63rd the campaign began on May 1 when it broke camp in Decatur, Alabama, and began moving on foot and by train northeast to Chattanooga, the Federal base from which the Atlanta Campaign would be launched. The 63rd arrived there on May 5, and the next day began marching south into Georgia along with 100,000 other Federal troops. On May 14th, Spitler would get his first real taste of combat at the Battle of Resaca, Georgia, where the Federals tried to break the railroad behind the Confederate army. Then in late May he would see more action in the Battle of Dallas, Georgia, as the Federals pushed south toward Atlanta.

Sherman's army would continue to close in on Atlanta during June and early July 1864. By July 17, 1864, the Federals were on the northern outskirts of the city. That day, the 63rd and other units of the 15th, 16th, 17th and 23rd Army Corps began a movement to cut the strategic railroad leading into Atlanta from the east, from which Sherman feared Confederate reinforcements might be sent to the city's defenders. This maneuver brought Spitler and the 63rd Ohio on July 19 to the village of Decatur, about six miles east of Atlanta. The Federals then turned westward to begin closing in on the city. But on Thursday July 21, the 63rd Ohio, 25th Wisconsin and 35th New Jersey were sent back to Decatur to guard the town, where the Federals had parked some 1,500 wagons loaded with supplies that were critical to the sustenance of the Federal campaign. The following day, Friday July 22, dawned with the three Federal regiments posted in an arc south and southeast of the courthouse in Decatur, with pickets posted well south of the railroad. The morning was quiet, but about noon, the boom of a cannon was heard to the south. Soon there were more. Word filtered into town that Confederates were seen south of town. It was the Confederate General Joseph Wheeler, who was fast approaching Decatur with some 3,000 men. Wheeler launched his attack at 1 p.m.

During the early stages of the battle, Spitler was shot in his left elbow and taken to the rear with other wounded. Solomon would die on August 8, 1864, in the division's hospital at Marietta – just six months after his enlistment. He was buried in the large military cemetery in the town. The captain commanding the 63rd Ohio, Oscar L. Jackson, filed a report stating that Spitler had left behind no personal property. In October, one of Spitler's friends – Corporal Henry Arnold, who had received a slight head wound during the battle of Decatur -- wrote to

Spitler's father. Since he was in the same hospital as Spitler, Arnold was on hand during Spitler's final days.

"October the Third 1864
     Marietta Hospital Georgia
     Mr. Spitler,
     "I received your kind letter and was much pleased to hear from you again. I have no doubt at all but what you did not expect such sad news. In my letter I wrote to Elizabeth, but such was the case at that time. I still thought your son would get well or I should of told you at the time I wrote, but this is the way things will happen. Sometimes life is uncertain in the Army and out of it. The 22nd of July in the afternoon was somewhat of a serious time for some of us Boys I ashure you. The fight commenced about 1 oclock and lasted till aboute three when the rebels commenced falling back. When Solomon was wounded was just when the rebels was coming out of the wood on the other side of the railroad. Our regiment was on this side of the railroad and Company H was ordered on them which they did. At the command charge the boys went for the Johnny rebs like true Yankees always do. Double quick the boys drove them back at that point but at the same time they was outflanking us on the left and right. In this Brave Charg Poor Solomon fell wounded in his left arm, shot in the elbow and out above it, breaking all the bones in boath parts of his arm. He was sent to the rear while we kept fighting until they drove us out of town where they left us. We then throwed up breastworks and received reenforcements. Moved all our wounded of[f] the field and buried our dead. I was slightly hit at the same time so that I was sent to the hospital with your son Solomon. Here in a few days I got so I could be up and around and at last they made me help nurse. Well I worked it so that I got in the same ward where Solomon was. Here I had all chances of nursing and taking the best care of him as I know how. I would ask him if he did not think it best to have his arm Amputated. He would always answer no, that he thought it would get well. He said it must get [well] without a doubt. At this I would still be satisfied and

would not insist on him having anything done that was against his will. In this way things still went on, till I became Ward master myself. Then I did not much else then tend Solomon and drew rations and have them fixed for the wounded Soldiers. At last I thought Solomon was getting worse fast. I went and had Doctor Gay and McDill to come in and see him which they did. All they said was that he had the ague and gave him some quinine powders. He after that had two Shakes, I saw that they was no ague shakes, the poison from his wound had worked all through his System and that Death was then takeing strong hold of him. I then asked him if I shouldn't write to his Father and Mother and Sisters and Brothers, and he told me I need not write for awhile yet. He told me he would like to see you all at the same time he said that they were far distant at home. Then he felt satisfied. After this he got delirious and out of his head. And 3 days later after he had the chills he died. He died the Eighth day of August at 5 oclock in the afternoon and was buried on the ninth about 7 oclock in the morning. Poor Solomon he is gone never to return. The cannons roar and the muskets rattle, will never call him forth to Battle, He harkened to a higher call, And for this Country gave his all. Solomon was always redy to do his duty and when he was on duty was always at his post. He was as brave a boy I ever saw on a Battlefield. He was beloved by all who knew him. By his Bunkmates and by all that knew him in the regiment, officers and all. He made no use of Profane language and did nothing but what was right. He is missed in the regiment, missed at the mess table, also in his Bunk, in the ranks and on the field, and left a large number of Soldiers friends to mourn his loss, notwithstanding he was left a kind Father Mother Brothers Sisters who will ever miss him at the old home. Before he died he handed me his Pocket Book containing $150 in Scrip, and Notes to the amount of $62 on the Boys in his Company. Also a small Day Book having three due Bills of $5 each also on the Boys. As I got worse and could not attend to his things I gave it all to Ervin Thomas and told him as they took me to the Hospital at Marietta to take and give those things to his Capt. O.L. Jackson and at pay day would collect his money and send it to you. Solomon is buried in the graveyard lying on the Decatur and Atlanta road, his grave is well marked and easy to find. I will send you General Sherman Orders concerning bring the dead body home then you will know more than I can tell you. I must close for the Present hopeing to hear from you all soon. My love and well wishes to you all and remain your soldier friend till Death. Good By to all Trust in Providence."

Henry Arnold

It's interesting to contemplate what Spitler must have been thinking as he lay in his cot in the hospital in Marietta. At 19 he was still just a boy with his entire future ahead of him. When he enlisted in the army, he may have viewed it as a great adventure that would get him off the family farm in Ohio. Did he really face the fact that he could be killed or maimed for life? Maybe he thought that's what happened to other unlucky guys, that he'd be the lucky one. When the bugle blew excitedly that afternoon in Decatur telling the soldiers of the 63rd Ohio to quickly get into line because the Confederates were attacking, as men grabbed their rifles and checked their cartridge boxes to make sure they had plenty of ammunition, did Spitler say to himself, "Well, here we go again. But it'll be ok. I made it through Resaca, Dallas, and Kennesaw Mountain. I'll make it through this, too."

And now here he was with his arm mangled, aching and bleeding, and doctors wanting to cut it off. Perhaps he worried about how he would be able to do the hard physical work on the farm with just one arm? He would be useless to his family, a burden. And perhaps most importantly, what woman would want a mangled man for a husband? Who would be attracted to a cripple? Maybe he decided that it would be better to die than live disfigured. He would roll the dice and win and prove the doctors wrong. Unfortunately for Spitler, and tens of thousands of other young men who got shot during the Civil War, the doctors treating him had no knowledge of the pathogens that were then invading and multiplying in his body, they had no knowledge of antibiotics. Their best option for treating infection in wounded limbs was often the saw. But

Spitler couldn't see a life like that. And so he died. His death would not have drawn great notice or attention. He was just one private in a hospital full of wounded privates where death was a hourly occurrence. As soon as his body was removed from the hospital to be taken to the burial ground, his cot would have been filled by another unfortunate young man.

Solomon's mother would live until 1888. His father John, who outlived his wife (who was perhaps worn out by child bearing and rearing), would later file a claim with the Bureau of Pensions in November 1896 for a pension based on Solomon's service and death on the battlefield.

X

The Civil War of John C. Fleming

Chicago resident John C. Fleming enlisted in the Chicago Board of Trade Battery, a unit of horse-drawn guns similar to this one shown here.

By Blaise J. Arena

Letters home give us a deeply personal view of war, and thoughts of home. From private to general, letters also tell us about the soldier and his, or her, state of mind. The letters to home of one soldier, Private John C. Fleming, give us such a picture.[1] Through them we can experience his everyday life as a soldier.

Fleming was 18 years old when he joined the army, and was a big fellow at 180 pounds. He was educated at The Chicago High School. This was an important thing since Fleming's era was long before the concept of free public education for all came into being. Not everyone got to attend the only high school in Chicago. And his education shows - he uses proper grammar, sentence structure and has good penmanship. He takes his letter writing seriously and is quite formal, always signing off as *"Your loving son, John C. Fleming"*; even to his mother. Maybe this is what was taught at the Chicago High School.

Fleming lived with his family - mother and father, younger brother Isaac and older sister Sarah. They lived in Chicago's central area, in what would someday become "The Loop". He occasionally refers to friends or relatives who lived on nearby streets. On an 1863 map of Chicago, before the great fire of 1871, the Fleming family probably lived in the area just south and east of the Chicago River, on or near Water Street. Fleming's parents also owned a store in this area.

Religion was important to Fleming. He often mentions his appreciation that his company captain organizes Sabbath services for the camp whenever possible. He even recounts to his parents what Bible readings were done.

As a new soldier, Fleming loved life in the Union Army, he frequently mentions various camp activities and schedules, and how well he has adjusted. He enjoys outdoor life and seems to have prospered - maintaining, or gaining weight and always seems in good spirits. Throughout his letters, across the span of the war, there is rarely a complaint about army life. Nor does he admit to loneliness or fear.

The first year of the war had gone badly for the North. Gradually it became clear that the Confederacy would not collapse after a few months, as many Northerners had assumed. Military failures and set-backs forced President Lincoln on July 2, 1862, to call for an additional 300,000 troops to bolster the Union Army. At that time the U.S. military didn't have the infrastructure to support and equip such a large addition. So, many organizations in the North recruited and organized their own army units and sent them off to war. One example of this was the Chicago Board of Trade. The Chicago Board of Trade (CBOT) established in 1848, and still in existence today, provided an open, public forum where its members could buy and sell agricultural grains - a central marketplace for a variety of grains such as wheat and corn. In a patriotic response to Lincoln's call, the members of the CBOT held a meeting on July 22, 1862 at the Board's facility on South Water and Wells streets. The object was to raise and equip a horse artillery battery for the Union Army. The members made an initial pledge of $5,000 toward this; and within days a complement of 150 young men had signed up. Fleming was among them. The newly-formed battery marched off to Camp Douglas on Chicago's south side to begin outfitting and training. There they were given 110 horses and six ten-pounder artillery guns. In early September they were off by train to Louisville, Kentucky, to join General Dumont's division.

The Chicago Board of Trade Battery goes to war

The artillery battery was trained to function rapidly and effectively in battle. The captain of the battery would direct a gun to be "raced" into position, guided by riders on the horses pulling the gun with its ammunition and cleaning equipment box (the "limber"). Once in position the gun crew would disconnect, or "unlimber", the gun from the ammunition carriage. The gun would then be aimed and fired in the desired direction. This process might repeat over and over as battle lines shifted.

The first major battle the CBOT Battery participated in was that of Stones River at Murfreesboro, Tennessee. This battle took place near

Nashville, over three days December 31 to January 2, 1863. Some historians mark this as a stalemate battle with little accomplished by either side. The battle involved a total of 76,400 soldiers, with total casualties of 21,645. Union dead: 1,677; Confederate dead: 1,254. [2] The details and strategy of this battle have been covered thoroughly by many others. We will simply see some of Fleming's thoughts about the battle as given in excerpts from his letters home. Generally the transcriptions of his letters will be shown, but it is interesting to see some of them in his own hand. In a following letter Fleming enclosed his hand-drawn map of the battlefield. He used this to give an account of the battle to his father. [3]

Letter to parents, January 9, 1863 – excerpt 1
"Next morning after partaking of rather a scanty meal, we were ordered out, our front having been driven in, and immediately took an active part in the battle. Gen'l Rosecrans assigned the Capt his position and we immediately opened a heavy fire, running our guns forward, and gaining ground inch by inch. We unlimbered, and came into line 3 times when we secured a good position on a commanding nole. Here Gen'l Rosecranz rode up to our Capt, and told him if he could hold that position for one hour he would win the day.

"An Ohio battery had been taken by the rebels in our track that morning, and right where we brought our gun into line, lay 6 horses and a limber which had been destroyed but a few moments before. The rebels made several charges to take our battery but we just more than mowed them down."

Letter to parents, January 9, 1863 – excerpt 2
"During the next hour we lost the following members of the battery
    Andrew Finney a married man on No 3 Gun. And WH Wiley (Single)
So both killed instantly by the same solid shot.
    Johnny S. Stagg killed by a shell.
    Sergt A L Adams (my sergeant) wounded in the right ankle.
    Corp A.H. Ganner (of our squad) shot through the thigh.

3rd Sergt T.D. Griffin badly wounded in the back while nobly performing duty

John C. Camberg slightly wounded in leg

JW Bloom face badly burnt

Corp Jackson D. Howard slightly cut by a piece of shell in the forhead

WHS. Odell, merely stunned by a bursting shell."

Letter to parents, January 9, 1863 – excerpt 3

"When everything was quiet we buried Wiley and Finney and cut their names on a couple of pieces of boards, leaving them for to be removed by their friends from Chicago. Stagg was buried farther down near the hospital. Next morning commenced firing at daylight from our old position and continued firing all day.

"That afternoon our left was driven in, and our battery was ordered out again, and made a famous charge beyond everything, and captured a rebel battery. We then moved across the river and had our hands full, to drink our horses, without running over the dead and wounded rebels who lay around us as thick as corn hulls."

Fleming gives an account of his experiences in the battle, some of which are gruesome. Here, and throughout the war, Fleming sends home the names of those killed or wounded. Most or all of these soldiers would be from Chicago, and some may be known to his parents. In excerpt 3 Fleming tells his parents of the dead Wiley, Finney and Stagg who they buried with wooden markers -"...*leaving them for to be removed by their friends in Chicago.*" We will return to the battery's handling of its dead later.

Below are excerpts from two letters where Private Fleming gives an account of additional casualties. At the bottom of the January 9 excerpt Fleming refers to George W. Gavitt [Editor's note: Fleming misspells his name at Gavit] who *"played the coward"* by deserting early in the battle. Fleming makes several remarks in his letters about individuals who, in his view, have behaved in a cowardly way. It is clear that he has no sympathy for such men. Similarly, he tells his father in the letter of January 18 excerpt about two more deserters – James H. Hildreth and Charles W. Johnston.

Letter to parents, January 9, 1863 – excerpt 4
"Lieut Griffin, Sergt Adams, Corp Carver, Camberg and Bloom have been taken to the hospital in Nashville. Lieut Griffin will never be able to join the battery again. [Editor's note: According to the battery's roster, Griffin returned to duty on June 21, 1863, and he later played an important role in the Battle of Decatur.] Adams maybe but not for quite a while.

"Corp [illegible] to whom all of you were introduced up at Camp in Chicago was one of our best men, and he now will never be able to join us. Camberg and Bloom will soon recover. Dr. Sand the company doctor, was so badly hurt that I suppose he will soon turn up in Chicago.

"In all the battle, but one of our men played the coward and that was G.W. Gavit a married man from Chicago, who ran away the first morning and has not been heard from since. Johnny Hall and I were with our guns every moment of the time and thanks to God were not so much as scratched."

Letter to father, January 18, 1863 excerpt 1
"Since coming to Murfreesboro 2 of our men have been discharged for standing disability, and sent home. Jacob Grosch, (blacksmith) and F.J. Favor, (the old horse doctor) 2 others J.H. Hildreth, and Chas. W. Johnston went out looking for horses and returned in a day or two with written paroles, which the Capt not considering genuine ordered them not to notice, but go about their duties as usual. Next day they ran away from camp, and are now considered as deserters."

Further in his January 18 letter to his father below, Fleming is able to "brag" a little about moving up to the position of Postillion in the artillery battery crew. The Postillion is the soldier who rides one of the horses that pull the cannon. Fleming describes the great advantages of having this role. And he has learned the proper way to care for a horse.

Letter to father, January 18, 1863 -- excerpt 2
"Mother wanted to know my position on the gun. Since leaving Louisville I have turned Postillion for a number of reasons, one is I never have to walk, never have to stand guard and so have all night to sleep and I have 2 horse blankets at night which I find very comfortable along with my own government blanket. I need not go foraging unless I wish to, and besides all I have the best team in the battery, and I have learned how to take care of them. I find I did not half take care of our mare at home."

Reverend Moody visits the camps

As mentioned earlier, Private Fleming took his religion seriously. He often comments to his parents about the camp's Sabbath services and Bible readings he has done. His comments in two excerpts below are interesting. The "Moody" referred to by Fleming is the Reverend Dwight L. Moody of Chicago. Although this was quite early in Moody's career, this is the very same Moody who went on to found the well-known Moody Bible Institute and Moody Church in Chicago. Both are still vibrant organizations today that also include the Moody publishing house and the large Moody radio network.

Letter to father, May 26, 1863
"Moody from Chicago was in our camp last Sabbath, but he never brings us any encouraging news. He would have had entirely discouraged the battery after our well-fought fight, but we knew he was a blowhard and paid no attention to him. The Capt said he ought to be kicked out of camp, but we let him go in peace."

Reverend Moody is known to have visited Union Army camps after major battles in order to spread his evangelical messages. Moody was not a conventional preacher. He was not educated, had never attended divinity school, and apparently had some controversial religious ideas and messages. Thus, he was out of the mainstream of preachers of his day, and it is to this that Fleming is probably reacting. He didn't like Moody and apparently many other soldiers didn't either.

Letter to father, Murfreesboro, May 26, 1863
"In regard to the man 'Moody,' himself and wife are now and have been for a week and more in Murfreesboro but there is no fear of him coming to our Battery to inquire for me or anyone else, although if he should, I shall treat him with due respect. He is held very low in the estimation of every member of the battery, officers not excluded."

Foraging for food, and plundering

Both soldiers and horses must be fed. The Union Army supplied train loads of horse feed (hay and oats, etc.) as well as food for soldiers. The quantities of each were rarely adequate. As in most wars, soldiers were expected to find additional food for themselves and their horses. It was a regular feature of camp life for groups of soldiers to make forays around the countryside hunting for live game. Or, they would often commandeer livestock (pigs, cows, chickens) from local farmers. Farmers were offered a receipt, redeemable after the war for reimbursement. Separate from necessary foraging was the abhorrent practice, common to all wars, of plundering. Though forbidden by Union Army regulations, some soldiers stole or destroyed personal property in homes or farms in occupied areas. Fleming comments on foraging and gives his low opinion of plunderers in his letter to his mother on October 7 and October 17, 1862 (see the excerpts below):

Letter to mother, Oct. 7, 1862
"One thing is extremely evident, which is that our Captain is a man, that is bound to see his men well taken care of, chickens, hogs ducks and C will do. In reading the orders regarding plundering, he remarked that

he thought his company was made up of men, who could help themselves without being caught. The infantry regiments, at least some of them do act shamefully.

"The other morning I saw one regiment completely ransack a house, which they heard was occupied by a seceshionist who had skedaddled, leaving his negroes in the charge of the house. They took everything they could lay their hands upon, taking even the cover from a splendid piano, which they scratched and cut most shamefully. We have a steer, hog or two, and chickens and ducks in abundance every day..."

Letter to mother, Oct. 17, 1862
"Were we to live on our government rations, we could not brag but to let you know we don't, I will tell you a day's rations we gobbled.

This is only our Squad's Gun:

First 1 hive honey, about 65 or 70, 4 Turkeys, 8 Chickens, Corn, Oats and Hay for the horses IA Pease well known to you, gobbled the honey receiving about 7 or 8 stings from the secesh bees. The people where we are now, are all secesh and they fed the rebels. So we help ourselves unasked and they never dare say a word. To gobble Chickens, Turkeys, and Geese is common....."

Letter to mother, Oct. 17, 1862
"Horse, oxen, pigs etc is not all uncommon. When a company are sent out under an officer to obtain fodder for the cattle they give the owner of it a receipt for whatever they take, which they can present after the war to the government, and after the gov finds out whether they have aided the rebels or not, they settle with them. If they have aided them their receipt is worthless, if not they are paid."

Camp life

Private Fleming often comments to his family about the activities and routine in his camp. Fleming is proud of his cooking ability and occasionally brags to his family about his creations. See the letters to sister Sarah and uncle below:

Letter to uncle, March 23, 1863
"Aunt Sarah, would no doubt be interested in hearing a word about my cooking. I make things containing dried fruits and numerous delicacies which I generally mange to get into a fit condition for eating. I can manufacture as good a pie as the ladies at home can brag of although they have better facilities for cooking and if the war lasts long enough so as to give me time to practice I am afraid I will beat them.

If Aunt Sarah desires it I can send her a recipe for making plum pudding out of dried apples"

Letter to sister, Nov 23, 1862
"It would amuse you greatly Sarah if you could only see me with my little sugar bag of my own manufacture containing the days ration of sugar, and my loaf of soft bread which thank goodness we get every day as long we remain in Bowling Green."

Fleming's letter writing

The tone of Fleming's letters home is respectful, upbeat and formal. As mentioned before, he signs all of his letters "John C. Fleming", as in *"your loving son, John C. Fleming"*. There is one exception to his gracious tone: On many occasions he expresses his pique when he has not received letters frequently enough from friends and family. He even expresses this to his mother. Somehow this seems out of character for him. But he takes his own letter writing very seriously, and he expects that others will respond in kind, and frequently. See the three letter excerpts below as examples:

Sept 12, 1862
"These few lines were scribbled off in a hurry which fact you have likely discovered before this and I beg of you not to show it outside of our

own family. I shall do better in my next. Burn it immediately after reading it."

April 18th, 1863
My dear Mother, If I haven't cause to complain, no one ever had. The 18th of april and no letters from home later than the 1st (by King). And yet you demand one letter, at least, every week from me, and so far your demands have been complied with. Now Mother, don't you think it is exceedingly trifling on my friends not to write me oftener. I do!"

May 17, 1863
"Mother I don't know whether I have a right to complain or not, but here I write home once a week and sometimes oftener, and yet I have not heard from home since the 27th of April and now this the 17th of May. But I am going to stop coaxing and scolding and let you write when you feel it.

P.S. Remember me kindly to all. If I do not receive a letter to-morrow, I shall begin to think my friends have gone back on me."

Fleming's brotherly advice
In 1864 Fleming's younger brother Isaac is accepted into the Chicago High School. Fleming is thrilled to learn of this and uses the occasion to talk to Isaac by letter. He gives Isaac passionate advice, telling him how fortunate he is to go to The High School. Fleming explains to Isaac how to conduct himself, the importance of good study habits, and how this will all pay off in the future. The advice still stands today as highly appropriate for any new high school student. See Fleming's letter below:

Letter to brother Isaac, August 5, 1864
"My Dear Brother, You cannot imagine how pleased I was when about a week ago I saw your name among the list of those admitted to the

High School. You are so young that you cannot rightly appreciate the position you have attained, but if you will listen to, and profit by, the advice which Father and Mother so often gave me and which they will willingly repeat to you, your four years in that institution will slip rapidly and pleasantly by and in after years when you have reached manhood, in looking back you will never regret the time spent in the High School. But if you let their advice pass almost unheeded, before you are out of School 6 months, you will regret it and looking back on your school days instead of a pleasure will always be a source of sorrow to you.

"Have regular hours for study, a time for each duty, and a set time for amusements, and under no circumstances if avoidable allow your order to be interfered with. Before entering the High School next September, or before commencing your studies there have a written plan to go by and if you follow my advice, when I return to Civil life in about 11 months from now, you will thank me for it. Obey your teachers, and do not aim to make sport for the members of your class and in the end you will be thought more of.

"I remain your loving brother,

John C. Fleming"

The Battle of Decatur, Georgia

Later in the war, over the course of about a week in late July 1864, Fleming and the CBOT battery had some intense battle experiences after they came under attack in their camp in Decatur, Georgia. These actions marked the beginnings of the battle for Atlanta that would rage until September. Of all the battles he described to his parents, these seem especially striking. Clearly these must have been terrifying, and deadly in their nature. Though he describes the deaths of friends, Fleming never expresses the horror of battle and mutilated bodies to his parents. This is typical for him. His descriptions of battle are always matter of fact. Does he want to spare his parents the feelings of his own fear and horror? Maybe he considers such feelings to be unmanly. Or, is he really just unaffected? We do not know. See excerpts below of two letters from this period[4]:

The Board of Trade Battery
Laying off 2 miles from Atlanta Ga - July 25th /64

"My Dear Parents
"It is now some time since I have heard from you and it is about some time since you have heard from me. My last being from Roswell nearly two weeks ago, which I suppose you have received before now. Although I have been well ever since we have been trolling around continually and I have not taken time to write. One section of our battery left us on the 20th, now 3 and 4 guns going on a raid with our division in the rear of Atlanta, and returned last night all safe having destroyed railroad bridges burnt government stores.

"Captured mules, horses and negroes and about 250 prisoners, and damaged the rebels generally. When they started they left the other 4 guns safe as they supposed now 1 - 2 - 5 and 6 reporting to Col Sprague's brig of infantry lying in Decatur Ga 6 ms from Atlanta and guarding a larger wagon train. About noon on the 22nd we were suddenly surprised by Wheeler's Corp of rebel cavalry and after a brief fight of half an hour driven out of Decatur.

"Our 4 guns went into the fight without orders, and am happy to say came out of it honorably, although we lost 8 men wounded inside of half an hour. Ed Field from Dunton Stn. and old acquaintance of John Fleming's is probably mortally wounded, being shot through the bowels. Tom McClallan had his left arm broken badly by a minnie ball and it has since been amputated. A.J. Close gunner on our piece was wounded in the jaw by a musket ball. W. H. Tinsley, J.D. Tommey, Chas Hollyland and J.B.Appleton and Geo Gackenhammer, the later two, new recruits were also wounded but none of them seriously. They are all 8 together in the hospital not 500 yds from here and are doing well, except Ed Field, who will probably not recover. It was the hottest place I have ever been in for over 1/2 an hour, but as luck would have it they only killed one horse and we got out with our guns all right.

"Next morning the 23rd we reoccupied Decatur and about 11 A.M. our battery was ordered back to the train where we belonged. As the division got back last night we will probably be on the move to-morrow again."

Camp near Atlanta, Ga Aug 3rd, 1864

"My dear Parents
Your joint letter of July 12th was received on the 1st Inst. accompanied by one from sister Sarah, a Chicago Journal, Banner of the Covenant and a new hat which suits to perfection. And as the mail goes in 15 minutes I am going to send you this hasty answer. When I wrote last, over a week ago, a part of our battery had just returned from a raid. And the next day after writing we started off on another raid in the rear of the rebel army and returned on the 31st. We went almost due south of Atlanta 30 ms accomplished our object and returned.

"The first day out we marched about 28 miles and went into camp on South River, at 11 o'clock that night we were routed out. heavy picket firing having commenced and harnessed up and remained so till morning. When morning came we found ourselves completely surrounded and so commenced fighting on every side. The rebs first used artillery, opening with two

12 pd brass howitzers on our rear. Our section was ordered out, and got in position under a shower of bullets, and in 3 minutes obliged the rebel pieces to make themselves scarce.

"We remained in this position about an hour and fired over 50 rounds of shell. When the rebs retreated from our front and at the same time our 2 regt of our Cavalry made a charge mounted and drove the force in our rear which proved to be only a strong skirmish line. The fight lasted about 2 Hrs and we then moved back about 5 ms and went into camp. Nothing more of interest occured till once again joined the left of our army, which we did by making a forward march of 35 ms on 31st. In the fight I have just mentioned the cavalry lost a few men wounded but our battery came off safe.

"Before going on this raid I went to the 60th Ill and saw Capt Kennedy and Lieut Miller I did not see Capt Dugurd his company being on the skirmish line that day. Chicago papers I see have Atlanta in our possession, but this is decidedly premature. Our lines extend from due north of Atlanta west in a semicircle almost due south the left resting on the Atlanta road and the right on the Atlanta and Macon RR Up to yesterday afternoon firing was continual night and day for several days, but since then it has be remarkably quiet all along the line and I do not know the cause of this silence."

The Chicago Board of Trade Battery comes home

Private Fleming and his CBOT artillery battery served through the end of the war. The battery arrived home by train in Chicago at 3:30 a.m. on June 27, 1865. They were welcomed home at the Chicago depot by a large crowd that had waited hours for their arrival. They were given a welcoming banquet the following night at Metropolitan Hall. The Chicago Tribune ran a 5,000-word piece describing the homecoming scene at the train station, and included a glowing account of the war exploits of the Battery. See excerpt below.

Chicago Tribune June 27, 1865

"It was touching, yet joyful, to see these scarred and weather-beaten men now as they defled from the station into the crowded streets. There were vehicles of all sorts in attendance, and numberless footmen and horsemen, all anxious to get a sight of their defenders, and to receive them with honor.

"It seemed but yesterday that they left us full of life, and hope, and courage; and yet nearly three years had elapsed from that time to the present, during which some of the most important events in the whole history of mankind had transpired..."

Bringing home the dead

Until the Civil War it had been common practice for armies to leave their soldiers to lie where they fell. It was considered glorious to be buried (or left to rot) on the field of battle, usually without any identification. If it was "glorious", it was also convenient. The carnage in the Civil War, the monstrous numbers of dead in single battles, changed all that. Early in the war families began to demand that their boys be brought home. The Union Army sent bodies home by train, when possible, but they were overwhelmed, as was the Confederate Army which had even fewer resources. Sometimes friends or family would make the trip to find their boy and bring him home. Thus, Fleming's reference to this practice.

The Chicago Board of Trade resolved to bring home all of their dead, and collected money from its members for that purpose. It is not known (to this author) how many they were able to bring home. However, it is an indication of their resolve in this matter that after the war, they brought home 21 dead who had been buried on "Southern soil". A memorial was held at Crosby's Opera House and the soldiers were laid to rest on January 7, 1866, in Rosehill Cemetery in Chicago. [5]

Fleming's Later life

John C. Fleming went on to live a long and prosperous life. He married a woman named Isabella, and had children. He became a successful businessman in the iron and steel industry. Fleming was one of the organizers of the Carnegie Steel Company in 1892 and held a minority ownership position in that company. In later life he kept an office in the Marquette Building, an early "skyscraper". [6] This building still stands today at 140 S. Dearborn in Chicago's Loop, just a few blocks from the neighborhood where he grew up before the War. He lived at 4351 S. Drexel Blvd in Chicago, where he died at age 87 in 1932.

Fleming is buried in his family plot in historic Oak Woods Cemetery on Chicago's South Side. His grave site is a short walk to the graves of, and monument to the Confederate soldiers who died as prisoners of war in Chicago's Camp Douglas.

About the author

Blaise J. Arena is a retired research chemist and project manager. He is the author of numerous scientific publications and patents. He is also a guitar player and teacher. Blaise and his wife live in suburban Chicago and have visited Civil War battlefields (Shiloh, Vicksburg, Murfreesboro, Mobile Bay) and cemeteries.

Author's note:

A few years ago I began participating in an online crowdsourcing project organized by the Newberry Library in Chicago, transcribing letters from Civil War soldiers. The work involved examining high definition digital images of letters and typing up the letter-writer's words for further review by the library. I chose to devote my transcription efforts to the letters of Private John C. Fleming, Union Army soldier from Chicago.

Fleming was a prolific letter writer home to his family. I transcribed about half of his 85 letters (others did the rest) in the Newberry's collection and learned a lot about Fleming and his experiences in the Civil War. I felt this was interesting enough to share with others.

I have not attempted to give an exhaustive discussion of all of Fleming's letters, but rather have chosen certain passages and comments written by him that I find interesting, or illuminating in some way.

XI

Aftermath, Part 2: New beginnings, new lives

As the horrors of July 22, 1864, passed into history, the struggle for Atlanta would continue for another six weeks. In Decatur there would be another skirmish on July 30, when a small body of Confederate cavalry arrived in town, only to be driven away by Garrard's troopers. [1] As the Federals moved in closer to Atlanta and swung around to its southwest, they left Decatur unoccupied during the first two weeks of August. Then on August 15, the cavalry brigade that included the 72nd Indiana of Garrard's cavalry was sent to Decatur, finding it occupied by Confederates who they drove out. The regimental history of the 72nd Indiana records this interesting event that occurred south of town, probably noted nowhere else in Civil War literature. "After getting to the town the brigade was sent out in detachments on different roads, the Seventy-Second taking a road running south, which we followed a mile and a half, ran out to the rebel picket posts and drove them back a mile further, where we stirred up the whole nest, and they came on to us by the thousand. As there were none of our brigade near us we concluded discretion was the better part of valor, and fell back, the rebels closing up on our rear guard lively; some members of Company D showing great coolness and courage in keeping back the rebels. The rebels were not only following us but pushing ahead on another road trying to cut us off from Decatur. After getting back past the intersection of the roads we stopped and formed line of battle on a high ridge, half a mile south of town, and dared the rebels to come on. It began to rain just as we commenced to fall back, and by the time we got our line of battle formed it poured down in torrents, and continued so till night. We had a good position, with an open field for a mile in front of us, sloping from our line nearly two-thirds of the way across it. The rebels were saucy and formed their line of battle in the open field in front of us and in plain view, and sent forward their skirmishers, who began to fire upon us when about half way across the field, their shots falling short 50 to 100 yards. Then we began to laugh at them and tell them to come closer; that their guns were no account; to come and get a piece of corn bread; and a hundred like expressions. They raised their accustomed yell and started, but a volley from our Spencers flattened them out on the ground in a minute. Then we had the laugh on them again and kept hallooing at them to get up out of the mud. This exasperated them so they made a second attempt, but a few shots from our lines sent them to grass again." The Federals held their position until it began to get dark, when they fell back slowly to the town, mounted their horses and road to camp on the south fork of Peachtree Creek north of Decatur. [2]

For the residents still living in Decatur, who were almost entirely women and children and the elderly, daily existence became a struggle as the hungry Federal soldiers with their hungry horses and mules occupied the town one day, and then even hungrier Confederates occupied it the next. Mary Gay writes frequently in "Life in Dixie During The War" about the hunger that stalked Decatur during the latter half of 1864 and her efforts to obtain food. Early on the morning of August 19, 1864, the 72nd Indiana's brigade of Federal mounted infantry rode back into Decatur, killing two Confederates and capturing two others. The regiment's history records the following incident which, although possibly exaggerated, illustrates what was probably the genuinely sad state of the residents. "We remained in town all day foraging on all the roads in every direction for two miles and a half from it. Just at noon most of our brigade were in town feeding their horses on roasting-ears [Editor's note:

raw corn on the cob] brought in from the country. A part of our regiment fed their horses on the north side of the square next the side-walk; as the men began to scatter and move off we noticed three little children come out on the side-walk who were the very picture of distress. After looking at our horses in astonishment for a while, the little boy, about three years old, happened to see the cobs where our horses had eaten, and immediately ran and picked up one of the cobs and began to gnaw and suck it as if his life depended upon it. The little girl noticed him and begged him to let her have some, but he could not be persuaded to part with it. She then asked him where he got it. Without stopping he motioned his head to the edge of the side-walk. She ran to the gutter and immediately uttered an exclamation of surprise, jumped down among the cobs and began to gather up her hands full, but seeing one with about half the corn left on she grabbed it up and exclaimed: 'Oh bubby! Bubby! Lookey here what a great big nice one!' Bubby threw down his cob and made a desperate effort to take the corn away from her, and perhaps would have succeeded but she threw him off his guard by saying: 'Oh bubby, less give it to the baby, and we'll get more.' The little fellow's wrath was appeased in a moment. They gave the corn to the baby a year and a half old, and set about hunting among the cobs for any chance one that might have a few grains upon it. Just a month ago our advance entered this town, killing a few rebel soldiers, and among the number was the father of these children. He had fallen, fighting as he supposed for his country, and now for more than three weeks this place had been inside the rebel lines. Yet his comrades were so base that they could see this wretched woman and her children starve, without making a single effort to help them. We acquainted our Colonel, who was one of the kindest hearted men in the world, with the circumstances, and he immediately sent for an ambulance [Editor's note: a type of horse drawn carriage with a driver] and had the widow and her children sent north, where it is to be hoped the children have grown up to love their country." [3]

General William T. Sherman's forces besieged Atlanta during August 1864 and, when Sherman's forces cut the last railroad into the city from the south, Confederate General John B. Hood withdrew his tattered army southward from the city and it surrendered on September 2, 1864. The battle-weary soldiers of Sherman's army then marched into the city and settled into camps for a much-needed rest. The 23rd Army Corps marched to Decatur and went into camp. [4] But most of Sherman's army would only get a few weeks' respite from marching and fighting. On September 29, Confederate General John B. Hood tried to make one last effort to force Sherman out of Atlanta by cutting the Federals' vital railroad supply line from Chattanooga. Hood led his 40,000 haggard men, then in camp south of Atlanta at Palmetto, Georgia, westward across the Chattahoochee River and up into northwest Georgia, repeatedly striking the Western & Atlantic railroad, tearing up track and attacking Federal garrisons. Leaving the 20th Corps as an occupying force in Atlanta, Sherman took the remainder of his forces – including the 63rd Ohio, 25th Wisconsin and 35th New Jersey -- and chased after Hood. [5] The Federals were able to quickly repair the damage to the railroad done by Hood's army, keeping supplies flowing into Atlanta. Unable to force the Federals out of Atlanta, Hood retreated into Alabama. Sherman, meanwhile, seeing no value in chasing Hood further, obtained permission from General Ulysses Grant to turn his back on Hood to do what Sherman really wanted: march to the sea. The Federal army returned to Atlanta, destroyed everything of military value and burned the town, and then on November 15 began the historic March to the Sea. Along for the journey were the 63rd Ohio, 25th Wisconsin and 35th New Jersey. Marching south out of Atlanta and crossing the South River at dusk, Captain Oscar L. Jackson of the 63rd Ohio looked back and saw Atlanta in flames. "It will be utterly destroyed," he wrote in his diary. "The glare of the light against the sky is beautiful and grand. A terrible but just punishment is meted out to the Gate City." [6] After reaching and capturing Savannah, Sherman's army turned north into South Carolina, blazing a path of destructive retribution through the state that began the war, north into North Carolina, where a Confederate army, then back under the command of General Joseph E. Johnston, surrendered following

Robert E. Lee's capitulation in Virginia. The war was finally over for the veterans of the 63rd Ohio, 25th Wisconsin and 35th New Jersey. With Sherman's army they marched north into Virginia and into Washington, D.C., where they took part in the Grand Review of the Armies on May 23 and May 24, 1865.

On June 1, 1865, the Second Brigade was discontinued and each regiment prepared to go home. Reaching Washington, the men of the 35th New Jersey were issued new Zouave uniforms and then mustered out several weeks later. [7] When the 35th left Washington in July 1865, its veterans went by train to Trenton, arriving on July 22 (one year to the day since the Battle of Decatur), completing the journey they had started nearly two years before when they left New Jersey for Washington on October 19, 1863. [8] "They have made a very thorough tour of the South, on foot, and they show the effects of it in their bronzed faces and hardened muscles," the Trenton State Gazette noted on July 25, 1865, on their arrival in the city. "They are soldiers every inch." [9] The soldiers were entertained at the Soldiers' Rest "where abundant provisions had been made for them," then paid off and discharged. The regiment, which had left New Jersey about 800 strong, then numbered about 530, according to the paper.

The 63rd Ohio on June 5 was ordered to Louisville, Kentucky. The men were sent by railroad to Parkersburg, West Virginia, then placed on a river steamer downstream to Louisville. [10] The regiment was mustered out on July 8, 1865, and it went by steamer to Cincinnati, then by rail to the nearby Camp Denison. There the men were paid off and discharged, and boarded trains for home. While at Camp Denison, the 63rd's Colonel Oscar L. Jackson was visited by Colonel Charles E. Brown, who had lost his leg at Decatur and returned home to Ohio. [11]

The 25th Wisconsin was mustered out on June 7, 1865, and then began the long journey back to Wisconsin by railroad and steamboat, arriving on June 11, 1865.

For Wheeler's Cavalry, perhaps their greatest moment of glory in the Civil War occurred just days after the Battle of Decatur. On July 27, having cut the rail lines into Atlanta from the east and west, General William T. Sherman was eager to cut the last remaining rail lifeline into the city from the south. Unable to get there with infantry, he launches a great cavalry raid, a two-pronged pincher movement. General Edward McCook is sent with 4,000 cavalry to ride around the west side of Atlanta, and General George Stoneman and about 2,000 troopers are sent to ride around the east side of the city, with the aim that they rendezvous on the rail line south of Atlanta at Lovejoy Station. McCook makes it to Lovejoy and destroys two and a half miles of track, when he learns that Wheeler's troopers are fast approaching. McCook's men start riding back toward the Chattahoochee to escape, but they are cornered by the Confederate cavalry at Brown's Mill near Newnan. Some 600 Federals are killed, wounded or captured, with the remainder escaping back to Federal lines near Marietta. Meanwhile, Stoneman's troopers make it as far south as Macon. At a nearby place called Sunshine Church they are surrounded by a superior force of Wheeler's cavalry commanded by General Alfred Iverson. Many of Stoneman's men manage to ride away and escape through Confederate lines, but Stoneman and about 700 of his men were captured. Stoneman earns the infamy of being the highest-ranking Federal officer to be captured by the Confederates during the Civil War. [12] Historian Edward G. Longacre notes that, "Surveying in later days these highly satisfying results – many of which had come about through his own energy and persistence – Wheeler would observe that 'thus ended in most ignominious defeat and destruction the most stupendous cavalry operation of the war.' Designed to win for him and his men the highest possible honors, this statement was a gross exaggeration even by Wheeler's standards. Yet his reasons for making it were both understandable and forgivable, as the laurels he sought were richly deserved. For the War Child and his worn-out but exuberant troopers, the devastating pursuit just ended would rank as the finest hour of their long, colorful, and eventful career." [13]

Just a week later, on August 10, 1864, Wheeler's forces were once again given a pivotal role, when they rode north toward Chattanooga to try to cut the railroad supplying the Federals in Atlanta, and thus cause the invader to retreat. So important was Wheeler's mission that Confederate General John B. Hood believed "this week will decide the fate of Atlanta." [14] Unfortunately for the Confederates, the damage done by Wheeler's troops to the railroad was quickly repaired and failed to halt the Federals. Wheeler's next major role would be to oppose Sherman's march to Savannah, the now famous March to the Sea. (During the March to the Sea, Wheeler's troopers, who were receiving no supplies from the Confederate government, earned a notorious reputation for plundering the homes of civilians who lived along the route of the march.) Wheeler's men would take part in the siege of Savannah and then, as Sherman's army headed north into South Carolina and North Carolina, the battles of Averysboro and Bentonville. [15]

The war finally came to a close for Wheeler in North Carolina after General Robert E. Lee surrendered his army in Virginia and Sherman's army closed in on the Confederate army that had battled Sherman through the Carolinas, leading to its surrender by General Joseph E. Johnston (who had been put back in command of the army following his ouster just before Atlanta's capture). On April 29, 1865, Wheeler gave a farewell address to his soldiers. "Gallant comrades – You have fought your last fight, your task is done. During a four years' struggle for liberty you have exhibited courage, fortitude, devotion. You are the sole victors of more than two hundred sternly contested fields. You have participated in more than a thousand conflicts of arms. You are heroes, veterans, and patriots. The bones of your comrades mark battle fields upon the soil of Kentucky, Tennessee, Virginia, North and South Carolina, Georgia, Alabama, Mississippi. You have done all that human exertion could accomplish. In bidding you adieu I desire to tender thanks for your gallantry in battle, your fortitude under suffering, and your devotion at all times to the holy cause you have done so much to maintain. I desire also to express my gratitude for the kind feeling you have seen fit to extend toward myself, and to invoke upon you the blessing of our heavenly Father, to whom we must always look for support in the hour of distress. Brethren in the cause of freedom, comrades in arms, I bid you farewell." [16] It was here that Wheeler disbanded all but a small number of hand-picked troopers. This small group followed Wheeler into South Carolina and Georgia as they rode trying to catch up to the party of Confederate President Jefferson Davis, who was then fleeing south trying to avoid capture by Federal forces. (Davis was ultimately captured by Federal cavalry near Irwinville, Georgia.) Having reached Washington, Georgia (a town about midway between Athens and Augusta), and unable to catch up to Davis, Wheeler and a few of his men turned west toward Atlanta, riding all night to try to escape themselves. While having stopped to catch a few hours of much needed sleep, they were surrounded and captured by a pursuing party of Federal cavalry near Conyers. They were sent first to Athens and then to Augusta, where they were confined with the party of Jefferson Davis. The Federals imprisoned Wheeler in Fort Delaware, a fortress holding many other Confederate prisoners in miserable conditions. He was kept in solitary confinement until July 1865, when he was paroled and allowed to return home.

The families and survivors

The war was now over. But for the families, wives and children of those killed at the Battle of Decatur, life continued. Beyond the immense loss of a loved one, for those left behind the soldiers' deaths often had tragic consequences.

Consider the case of 9-year-old William Daugherty, who was orphaned when his father, Thomas C. Daugherty of the 25th Wisconsin, was killed at Decatur. Thomas had married Emeline Scofield on October 1, 1853, and William was born on September 14, 1854. Emeline passed away in August 1859, and Thomas never remarried. He enlisted for three years in the 25th Wisconsin in August 1862, and when he died, William became the ward of Charles Daugherty, age 64, who must have been Thomas's father. [17]

Then there was the family of Amos Partlow. On October 3, 1861, just months after the Civil War began, Partlow, then 31 years old, enlisted for three years' service into Company C of the 63rd Ohio. When he died on the battlefield at Decatur, by then nearly 34 years old, he left behind a wife of 15 years, Mary Ann (who he had married on December 28, 1848) and a brood of seven young children. There is some confusion in pension records about the dates of birth of the children during the late 1840s and 1850s, but the first was apparently Mandana, born on December 20, 1849, almost exactly a year after Amos and Mary Ann's marriage (Mandana would have been 14 years old when her father died); followed by William Sylvester on February 26, 1851 (he would have been 13 when his father died); James Marcellus on July 7, 1855 (age 9 when his father died); Adam Granville on April 17, 1857 (age 7 when his father died); Emma Ardella on March 4, 1859 (age 5 when her father died); George B. McClellan (who had apparently been named for the then-commander of the Department of Ohio who went on to be a great Civil War general and political rival of Abraham Lincoln) on December 2, 1861 (age 2 when his father died); and lastly Alma Savannah, who according to one document was born August 11, 1864, 20 days after her father died. If this is true, Alma Savannah was conceived when the 63rd Ohio returned home during its winter 1864 leave after most of its men re-enlisted and prior to the start of the Atlanta Campaign. [18]

Private Henry W. Cressy of Company D of the 25th Wisconsin left behind a widow, Almira A., and four children: Effie L., who had been born on October 18, 1850, and so was almost 14 years old at the time of her father's death; Jason A., who had been born on June 29, 1856, and so was 8 at the time of his father's death; Anson H., who had been born on March 18, 1859 and was 5 at the time of his father's death; and Stephen W., who had been born on April 22, 1861, and was just 3 at time of his father's death. Henry and Almira had been married in 1848, and so had been together 13 years when the Civil War started. Henry enlisted in the 25th Wisconsin on August 2, 1862, and so had been in the service almost two years when he was killed at Decatur. Almira remarried in December

1867 to a George Jennings, who lived until April 1888. She would collect a pension for Henry's death until her own death in December 1906. [19]

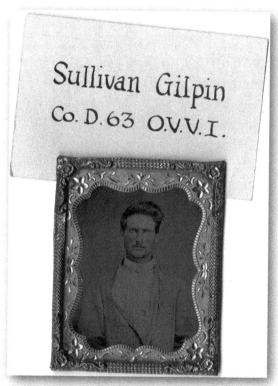

Sullivan Gilpin, one of four Gilpin family members who joined the 63rd Ohio Infantry. He survived the war and made it home. Matthew Gilpin was captured by Confederates at the Battle of Decatur and died a prisoner at Andersonville.

Private Matthew Gilpin of Company D of the 63rd Ohio was captured by the Confederates at Decatur, and his family never heard from him again. Gilpin had only enlisted in the 63rd Ohio in February 1864, just before the start of the Atlanta Campaign. A farmer, he was 27 years old. Three other Gilpin family members had previously joined the 63rd two and a half years earlier in October 1861: Jonas Gilpin Sr. (age 43 when he enlisted, he was discharged in May 1862 for disability); Jonas Gilpin Jr. (age 22 when he enlisted, he had died in May 1863 in the regimental hospital at Memphis, Tenn., from causes not shown in the 63rd's roster); and Sullivan Gilpin (age 18 when he enlisted, he survived the war and made it home.) When Matthew marched off to war, he left behind a pregnant 25-year-old wife, Nancy, who he had married the previous October. Nancy gave birth to the child, a son who was named Matthew Ellsworth, on July 5, 1864, as the Atlanta Campaign was raging and just three weeks before her husband's capture at the Battle of Decatur. Nancy later applied for a pension due to her husband's supposed death while in captivity. In the pension application, Samuel Coffee, another private in the 63rd Ohio who was also captured at Decatur, provided testimony in which he said that both he and Gilpin and others were taken prisoner and taken to Andersonville, and that Gilpin was "in a sick and emaciated condition" at the time Coffee was exchanged on September 22, 1864. Coffee wrote that he "never heard anything of him afterwards but believed he would die." There is no record of Gilpin's burial at Andersonville, so he is one of the many unknown soldiers buried there. Nancy herself lived on until 1909. [20]

Second Lieutenant William H. Gribble of the 25th Wisconsin, who was killed at Decatur, was a native of England who had emigrated to Platteville, Wisconsin, where he worked as a mechanic. He had enlisted in the 25th Wisconsin in August 1862 and risen through the ranks as sergeant, sergeant major and then second lieutenant. He left behind a wife, Mary M., who he had married on September 29, 1856. Mary remarried in 1884, and lived until January 1923. [21]

Corporal William J. Harris of Company C of the 63rd Ohio, the color bearer who was shot dead on the courthouse square in Decatur, left behind a wife, Olive, and 2 ½ year old daughter, Stella, who had been born on January 19, 1862. Harris and Olive J. Stafford had gotten married on March 26, 1861, in Erie County, Ohio (between Cleveland and Toledo). About a year and a half later in August 1862 he enlisted in the 63rd Ohio, survived its bloodbath at the Battle of Corinth, Mississippi, and other adventures, and he then re-enlisted with most of the regiment in December 1863, returning to its field post at Prospect, Tennessee, in January 1864. He was shot down just seven months later. Olive remarried in November 1865. Because of William's death, she applied for and was granted a pension of $8 a month from November 1865 through January 1878 as a war widow with a minor child. [22]

Jabez L. Huntley of the 25th Wisconsin left behind his wife, Amy, and four children. Jabez and Amy had married on September 14, 1848, and had been together 14 years when he enlisted in the 25th Wisconsin in August 1862. While there are some discrepancies in pension records, it appears that Amy was 36 at the time of his death and living in Rockford, Illinois. Their children were James Franklin, born July 23, 1849 (he turned 15 the day after his father died); Earnest, born May 26, 1857 (he would have been 7 when his father died); Jay M., born October 4, 1860 (almost 4 when his father died); and Jabez S., born January 15, 1862 (2 1/2 when his father died.) Amy became sick in July 1908 with pelvic peritonitis and passed away on September 10, 1909. [23]

Ohio residents George Milligan and his wife Sarah M. were married on November 21, 1861. Almost exactly a year later, on November 20, 1862, Sarah gave birth to a son who they named Charles. Fifteen months later, in February 1864, George, by then 25, enlisted for three years in Company H of the 63rd Ohio, just before the start of the Atlanta Campaign. He was only in the army five months before he was killed in action in Decatur. Just two weeks after George's death, Sarah, who was by then 20 years old, applied for an Army pension. The application noted about George that "He was shot through the head by a Rebel on the field." The infant Charles would have been just a year-and-a-half old. Pension records show that Sarah was still supporting Charles as of October 1866. But by April 1868, she had given Charles up to the care of a guardian, 38-year-old Andrew W. McCormick, a resident of Marietta, Ohio. The reason why is shown by a claim for a minor's pension which notes that "Probate judge certifies that satisfactory evidence of the immorality of widow has been produced before him. Widow gives her

Following the war, Sarah M. Milligan, the widow of Private George Milligan of the 63rd Ohio who was killed at the Battle of Decatur, lost custody of their son Charles for alleged "immorality." Charles' guardian later filed to obtain the pension due to Charles as the minor child of a soldier killed in action. A related affidavit by two women in the town where Sarah Milligan lived notes that "they are well acquainted with Sarah M. Milligan the widow of George W. Milligan late Pvt Co H 63rd Ohio and mother of Charles Milligan, minor child of said Geo W. Milligan, and know that said Sarah M. Milligan has had a Bastard child by a married man since the death of her said husband. They further make oath that said Sarah M. Milligan abandoned the support of said minor child on or about March 1st 1865, and that it has been supported by its Grandmother Milligan ever since and that her reputation in the community for immorality is very bad."

written consent to the transfer of Cert[ification] to Guardian." An affidavit signed by two women, Elizabeth Davis and Sarah Hylton, explains in more detail what the "immorality" was: "Sarah M. Milligan has had a <u>Bastard child by a married man</u> since the death of her said husband. They further make oath that said Sarah M. Milligan abandoned the support of said minor child on or about March 1, 1865, and that it has been supported by its Grandmother Milligan ever since and that her reputation in the community for immorality is very bad." [Editor's note: emphasis in original.] In January 1873, Charles, who by then would have been 11 years old, became the ward of a new guardian, a William H. Smith. [24]

Charles Richie of Co. E of the 25th Wisconsin left behind his wife of 15 years, Eliza (they had been married in Pennsylvania on January 25, 1849) and three daughters: Eva L., born on May 19, 1856; Ada May, born on January 8, 1859; and Luella J., born September 25, 1861. Richie had enlisted in the 25th on August 6, 1862, and had been wounded at the Battle of Resaca before being killed in action at Decatur. Because of Charles' death, Eliza began receiving a pension of $8 a month commencing on July 23, 1864. On November 11, 1866, Eliza, then living in Platteville, Wisconsin, and supporting herself by her own labor, placed Ada into the Soldiers' Orphan Home of Wisconsin. Little Ada was one of 133 children placed into the home that year. Eliza faced tragedy again three years after Charles' death: Ada May died February 22, 1867, and Luella J. died March 7, 1867. At the beginning of 1868 Eva L. was the only child still living. Eliza would receive a pension for Charles' death up until the time of her own passing four decades later on April 27, 1914. Eliza's passing left Eva, then married and known as Eva Greene and living in Long Beach, California, as the only surviving member of the family. [25]

Corporal Theodore Swartzel of the 63rd Ohio was killed at Decatur barely seven months after he joined the army. A resident of Germantown, Ohio, a town southwest of Dayton, Theodore had married Mary Frank on June 10, 1858. The reason why may have been pregnancy – on November

16, 1858, Mary gave birth to a daughter, who the new parents named Anna Laura. The couple had been together five and a half years when, in late 1863, Theodore enlisted for three years of service into Company G of the 63rd Ohio. He joined the regiment in winter quarters at Prospect, Tennessee, just north of the Alabama state line north of Huntsville, on January 1, 1864. The veterans of the regiment, most of whom had just re-enlisted, were then back in Ohio on furlough. Theodore's first few months in the service would have been uneventful, the biggest action being the regiment's March 1864 amphibious crossing of the Tennessee River and capture of Decatur, Alabama. But he would get his baptism of fire when the Atlanta Campaign began in May, with the battles at Resaca, Dallas, Kennesaw Mountain and then the crossing of the Chattahoochee River, leading to his death at Decatur. Mary applied for and was granted a widow's pension of $8 a month commencing in April 1866 (Anna Laura was by then seven years old) and ending in November 1874. The pension was later increased an additional $2 a month. Mary remarried in April 1866. [26]

The 63rd Ohio's Captain Daniel Thorne, who was wounded and captured at Decatur and then died in a Confederate prison in Savannah, Georgia, on October 5, 1864, left behind his wife Hannah and two children, Alonzo and Adelbert. Daniel and Hannah had married in January 1852. Alonzo was later born on Christmas Eve in 1852, and Adelbert was born on November 8, 1854. In December 1867 Hannah was remarried to a man named William S. Archer. In 1868, the Federal government granted the children a $20 a month pension because of their father's death. By that time Alonzo was 15 and Adelbert was 13.[27]

Now let's look at how some of the survivors from the Battle of Decatur spent the rest of their lives:

Charles H. Anderson, 25th Wisconsin

Sergeant Charles H. Anderson of the 25th Wisconsin, who was shot in his left hip at Decatur, would survive his wound and return home to Wisconsin. As of 1895 he was living in Omro, Wisconsin, west of Oshkosh. [28]

John F. Brobst, 25ᵗʰ Wisconsin

During the Atlanta Campaign, John Brobst of the 25ᵗʰ Wisconsin
exchanged letters with Mary, his girlfriend back home. He
survived the war, went home and married her. Here are John and
Mary with their children shown in an 1873 photograph.

One of the most remarkable stories in the aftermath of the Battle
of Decatur involves the 25ᵗʰ Wisconsin's John F. Brobst. When Wheeler's
Cavalry drove the Federals out of town, Brobst had lost his knapsack
which held his precious photographs of his sisters and his girlfriend
back home, Mary Englesby. Several weeks after the Battle of Decatur,
Brobst was hospitalized with another attack of malaria. "Her picture
had become a source of comfort; he especially missed it now that he was
separated from his friends," writes Margaret Brobst Roth in her edited

collection of Brobst's letters. "Adding to his loneliness was the fact that mail from home stopped coming through soon after he left the regiment [Editor's note: to go into the hospital]. It would be many more months before John received a letter from Mary." [29] Writing to Mary on September 15, 1864, from camp near East Point southwest of Atlanta, where the Federal army had moved in an effort to cut the last remaining rail line into Atlanta, Brobst looked forward to getting back home but lamented the loss of her photo. "Only eleven months from today and my time is out [Editor's note: his three-year term of enlistment would end], but that is plenty of time to get killed twenty times. .... But the rebs have got your picture, and another one would do me a great deal of good now. You say I have so many others to look at, but you accuse me wrongfully again, for I have not got any, for the rebs got them all. I had 4, 3 sisters and yours, and that is all I had." Brobst must have been feeling the loss of the photo acutely, because he mentions it again in a letter to Mary on September 27. Telling Mary about how some soldiers from the 25th Wisconsin who had been captured had been exchanged and returned to the regiment, Brobst wrote, "But they did not exchange your picture. I am afraid you are too spunky, and they will be very apt to keep you until the war closes, perhaps place you under the fire of guns, as they have the officers at Charleston [Editor's note: apparently a reference to a prison in that city that held Federal officers.] Lord, but I should like to kill the one that has that picture if they have it yet. I could kill him with a good heart and clear conscience." [30] The story of the photos would take a remarkable turn three months later. After the capture of Atlanta, General William T. Sherman would abandon the city and make the March To The Sea to Savannah. Sherman wanted only the strongest, combat-ready soldiers along for the risky and dangerous campaign, and sick or invalid soldiers were sent to the rear. Brobst was among these. He was sent to Dalton, Georgia, where, rather than killing Confederates, he killed time standing guard in camp. Writing to Mary on December 22, "another long, cold, and lonesome day," Brobst described how the day before he had struck up a conversation with a Confederate deserter named James Brown. "He is a very clever fellow. He is tired of war and has escaped and got safely inside of our lines. He is going home in a day or two. He lives in Tenn[essee]. He will stop a day or two with me yet. We have some friendly talk about the battles we have been in. We have been hotly engaged against one another several times. The 22nd of July was one day. We have talked the scenes of that day all over several times since he has been here." [31] The historian's heart weeps that Brobst did not put down on paper in this letter to Mary details about "the scenes of that day." Brown must have been in Wheeler's Cavalry during the Battle of Decatur, and we can only marvel at the odds that he would encounter and befriend Brobst in Dalton. It is also a remarkable fact, borne out in many Civil War diaries and letters, that private soldiers in the Federal and Confederate armies during the Atlanta Campaign like Brobst and Brown who tried to kill each other in battle could be very friendly at other times. While Brobst and Brown were chitchatting on December 22, naturally enough for two young men they got to talking about girls, and "something strange" occurred, Brobst wrote to Mary in a letter the next day. "I told him," Brobst said, "I thought the northern girls were the handsomest and while we were talking he told me he had pictures of four northern girls. At least, he supposed they were, for he got them the 22nd of July. I wanted to see them, so he let me see them, and it was your picture, with my three sisters. I told him so, and it was some time before I could make him believe it, but I told him all that there was in the knapsack that had them in, so he gave them back to me. I tell you I was glad to get them. They have been kept very nice, just as nice as I could have kept them myself and done my best, and the result is I have been taking a long look at you this morning. I told Brown what you had written to me, that you wished you had ahold of him and you would show him what a northern girl could do. He laughed and wants me to tell you that he sends his best respects and that he has carried you in his coat pocket five months

[Editor's note: from July 22 until that day in December 1864] and that you were docile and gentle as a lamb, never found a word of fault. He is going home this evening." [32]

Despite getting back his precious photographs, Brobst ended 1864 on a melancholy note, writing in a December 31 letter to Mary, "The old year will soon be gone forever. How many have gone to their long homes since one year ago today. Gay and happy one year ago today, but as sixty-four passes off in the sea of time it finds them mouldering in their cold graves. Many of my comrades that were all promising one year ago, today sleep under the soil of Georgia, but they have filled a hero's grave. They sleep in honor of their country, and all friends to our government should feel proud of their mouldering bodies." [33]

Following the 25th Wisconsin's participation in the March to the Sea, the regiment marched with Sherman's army northward into South Carolina and then North Carolina. Brobst would return to his regiment on February 8, 1865, in New Bern, North Carolina, as the war neared its end. With the Confederate surrender, the 25th Wisconsin marched to Washington, D.C., where on May 24, 1865, it took part in the Grand Review of the Armies. Brobst returned with his regiment to Gilmanton, Wisconsin, in June 1865. Six months after his return he married the girl with whom he had corresponded with for so long during the war, Mary Englesby, who had just turned 16 years old. Thankfully for history, Mary preserved John's war-time letters her entire life, and they were published in 1960. "John and Mary had a long and happy married life," writes Margaret Brobst Roth. "They raised three children and lived to celebrate their golden wedding anniversary in 1915. John was a farmer and [live]stock buyer, and is remembered by Ira Britton, a lifelong resident of Gilmanton, as being instrumental in bringing the first telephone line into that village." John died in 1917 at the age of 78. Mary would live on another 26 years, passing away in 1943 at the age of 93, outliving two of her three children. [34]

A photograph of Charles E. Brown, who lost a leg at the Battle of Decatur, taken after the war when he was a member of Congress from Ohio.

Charles E. Brown, 63rd Ohio

Colonel Charles E. Brown's life changed forever at the Battle of Decatur. The 30-year-old had been shot severely in his left thigh, requiring surgeons to amputate his left leg close to the hip, which during the Civil War was a dangerous and often fatal operation. (He was likely operated on at the Powell house just north of Decatur.) But Brown survived. Brown's wound may have made it unsafe to try to immediately transport him back north, because Colonel Oscar L. Jackson mentions in his diary that on August 12, 1864 – three weeks after the battle and while Federal forces were besieging Atlanta – he went to the hospital to visit Brown, "who is getting along splendidly." [35] Much later, back in Ohio and recovering from the loss of his leg, Brown would remain in the Army through the end of the war, serving as provost marshal of Cleveland, Ohio. He also received two military promotions, first to full colonel and then to brigadier general, in recognition of his service in the Atlanta Campaign. He resumed his law practice in Chillicothe, Ohio. He was later appointed U.S. pension agent in Cincinnati. Like many other former U.S. Army officers, Brown would next enter politics, being elected to the 49th Congress (March 1885 through March 1887) as a Republican. He was re-elected to the 50th Congress (March 1887 through March 1889). He did not stand as a candidate for re-election, but returned home to resume his law practice in Chillicothe. His political career was not over, though, and he served in the Ohio Senate in 1900 and 1901. Brown would live until May 22, 1904 [Editor's note: Two months shy of the 40th anniversary of the Battle of Decatur], when he died in College Hill, Ohio, leaving his wife and five children. In a short biographical article about Brown written for a history of Fuller's brigade in 1909, Colonel Oscar L. Jackson would say of Brown, "From his army wound and loss of his leg he was a great sufferer as long as he lived, and his death eventually resulted from it. Gen. Brown was a man of fine personal appearance, an honorable gentleman of strict integrity who was deservedly held in high esteem, alike by comrades in the Army and fellow citizens at home." [36]

John J. Cladek, 35th New Jersey

In September 1864, with the campaign over in Atlanta, Colonel John J. Cladek traveled home to New Jersey to recruit new volunteers for the 35th New Jersey. An advertisement in the Newark Daily Advertiser on September 9, 1864, called for 500 men to fill up the ranks of the 35th, and noted that applications could be made to Cladek, who was then staying for a few days at Kay's Hotel in Trenton. [37] Cladek was in Rahway, New Jersey, just outside Newark, by the first week of October. It was just a few weeks before the November presidential election in which the nation would decide whether to continue the war against the Confederacy, or seek peace after four bloody years. President Abraham Lincoln, a Republican who had vowed to prosecute the war until victory, was running in a very tight race against Democrat challenger General George B. McClellan, who was from New Jersey and who was the "peace candidate" who vowed to bring the war to an end. The North's belief in ultimate victory, and thus Lincoln's campaign, had been bolstered by General William T. Sherman's recent capture of Atlanta. In this agitated political environment, Cladek, who was himself a Democrat, attended a Friday night Democrat Party political meeting in Rahway. During the meeting, according to a newspaper account, one of the speakers, a Mr. Shann, "denounced the soldiers [of the Federal army] as Lincoln hirelings, at the same time looking at Col. C. The latter immediately resented the insult, and denounced the speaker for his language. The entire crowd then endeavored to force from Col. C. an apology, but failed to receive it, whereupon they denounced him as a coward, and threats were made of violence." Cladek later said of the event, "Censure from such a source is no small praise. My shattered Regiment and the commendations of Gen. Sherman will, I think, establish a reputation not to be shaken by a traitor... I have, as you know, always been a Democrat. I cannot, however, longer support a party which sneers at and insults Union Soldiers – which favors an armistice at the expense of national honor – which pronounces the war a failure on our part, and of course by insinuation a success on the part of the Rebels – and I shall, if we can be spared from the field, come home with my brave comrades and vote for Lincoln and [his vice presidential running mate Andrew] Johnson." [38]

In March 1865, Cladek was promoted to Brevet Brigadier General in the U.S. Army in recognition of his long, faithful and gallant service during the war. But this honor would soon be stripped from him. In August 1865, Cladek was arrested and court martialed for fraud, his rank revoked, and dismissed from the service. Cladek was guilty of "conduct to the prejudice of good order and military discipline" for allowing a civilian named George H. Moore "to come within the limits of the camp... and take the pay rolls thereon, and did knowingly allow the said George H. Moore to deduct and retain ten per cent from the amount of local or state pay or bounty due, ... at the same time knowing that the regiment was to be paid by the regular paymaster within a few days, thereby permitting some of the men to be defrauded of a part of the money justly due them... and did receive in consideration thereof the sum of $335." [39] It's unknown what Cladek did following his ouster from the army, but he only lived 20 years after the war, passing away in Rahway in April 1884 at the young age of 59. [40]

Chauncey H. Cooke, 25th Wisconsin

Chauncey H. Cooke of the 25th Wisconsin would return home at the end of the war, now age 19. Of the seven other boys he had enlisted with in 1862, all would make it home safely except for his friend John W. Christian who was killed in action at the Battle of Decatur. [41] Cooke would become a teacher and teach for several years in Freedmen's schools in Texas. He then returned to Wisconsin and became a farmer. He would live to be 73, passing away in 1919, having outlived his good friend killed at Decatur by 55 years. He was buried in the family cemetery where "a reddish granite tombstone proudly summarizes the life of Chauncey H. Cooke," noted William H. Mulligan Jr. in an introduction to Cooke's collection of letters: "Cooke, Chauncey H., 1846-1919, A Soldier of the Civil War for the Union of the States, Freedom of the Slaves, A Friend of the Colored Races, The Indian and The Negro." [42]

Charles Croft, 25th Wisconsin

Private Charles Croft of Company C of the 25th Wisconsin, who was wounded in arm and side in the Battle of Decatur, survived the war to become a farmer with 240 acres of land, and a minister in the United Brethren Church. Croft's heritage was different from most of the other soldiers of the 25th Wisconsin. He had been born in 1840 in Yorkshire, England. His parents moved to America when he was two, settling in Wisconsin. Croft was married in 1860 to a woman named Sarah Hutchison. In 1864 he enlisted in the 25th Wisconsin and served 17 months in the army. He was in four battles, the last of which was Decatur where he was wounded. Back at home, he and his wife would have eight children: Mary R., William J., Ferguson A., Flora E., Charles E., John W., Bertha J., and Ethel A. [43]

Captain Augustus Dusenberry, 35th New Jersey

Captain Augustus Dusenberry, who was captured for a second time by Confederates at the Battle of Decatur, survived his harrowing escape from the Confederate prison and winter journey through the mountains of North Carolina and Tennessee to reach Federal lines at Chattanooga. He then returned home to Newark, New Jersey. Following the end of the war he got involved in politics, becoming an alderman in Newark and member of the New Jersey State House of Assembly from Essex County. [44] He was also active in veterans' affairs, serving as treasurer of the 35th New Jersey veterans group in 1892 [45] and making annual pilgrimages to Gettysburg in the 1890s. [46] In 1900 he became president of the Police Board of Newark. [47] He lived to age 76, passing away in March 1914, and is buried at Mount Pleasant Cemetery in Newark.

Samuel Wragg Ferguson, Wheeler's Cavalry

After the Federal capture of Atlanta, Confederate General Sam Ferguson's cavalry opposed General William Sherman during the now-famous March to the Sea. Today the March to the Sea may be perceived as having been a cakewalk for the Federal invaders, who faced no significant Confederate opposition and ate their way across Georgia, enjoying the harvest season bounty of the state's farms. But Ferguson noted how he and his soldiers dealt very harshly with Federal soldiers caught robbing the homes of Georgia civilians, committing – with his approval –what we today would condemn as war crimes. "I followed Sherman and picked up hundreds of prisoners, many of them stragglers out plundering," Ferguson wrote in his memoirs. "I had no idea how many of the latter class were killed on the spot, for they were robbers and not entitled to the benefits of the rules of war." [48] Ferguson recounts how one Federal soldier had been captured in the possession of a lady's handsome opera cloak, opera glasses and other plunder. "I made use of some expression of disgust at such a fellow being taken prisoner," Ferguson said, turning the prisoner over to one of his men. "The next day was Sunday and a most lovely day. The population came to the river bank to see the command crossing the stream. I noticed that groups would walk up the bank a short distance, look at something and then come back. At last I asked what was the attraction and learned that it was a dead Yankee. I then remembered to have heard a shot in that direction the night before, soon after the prisoner had been started to the guard, and I did not doubt that he was the dead Yankee."

After the March to the Sea, Ferguson's troops would continue to oppose Sherman's army as it turned north from Savannah and blazed a path of fiery retribution into his home state of South Carolina. As the war reached its end in April 1865, Ferguson was called to Greensboro, North Carolina, where the Confederate army there received news of Robert E. Lee's surrender in Virginia. "Old soldiers could be seen by hundreds, weeping as though their hearts would break, my feelings I cannot attempt to describe," Ferguson wrote. Ferguson and his men would then escort Confederate President Jefferson Davis, who was trying to escape westward across the Mississippi River, from Charlotte, North Carolina, to Washington, Georgia, a town between Athens and Augusta. It was there that Ferguson's command broke up, many of his men going to surrender to the Federals. "So on the 6th of May 1865, near Washington Georgia ended my career as a soldier, which had been continuous, from the first day of June 1852, without a day's intermission, for I entered the service of the Confederacy on the day that my resignation from the United States Army was accepted." Ferguson and his wife would move to her home in Greenville, Mississippi, and he took up the practice of law.

A number of years after the war, Ferguson traveled to Washington, D.C., where he went to the War Department to see his friend and former West Point classmate, General Orlando M. Poe, who had been chief engineer on the staff of General William T. Sherman during the Atlanta Campaign and March to the Sea. (Poe oversaw the Federal army's burning of Atlanta.) At the time of Ferguson's visit, Poe was serving as an aide to General Sherman, who was then commanding general of the U.S. Army. Poe "insisted on taking me to Gen. Sherman's office to see his Chief and I had a chat with the man I had fought so often." [49]

In 1894, while serving as treasurer of the Delta Levee Board, Ferguson was caught embezzling money. He fled to Ecuador. There, in April 1900, at the age of 66, he would begin to write his memoirs, starting off on a somber note. "I am very often sad and lonely, for in my old age I have no home and am in a foreign country, separated from my family and from all that is dear to me, but most sad at the thought that my good wife and loving daughters are not provided for and are dependent entirely upon what my son DuGue and I can furnish from our salaries. I am thankful that I have the blessing of good health and that I am still active and capable of undergoing much fatigue." [50] Ferguson ultimately returned to Mississippi, where he died in 1917 at the age of 83.

Mary Gay, Decatur resident

With the end of the Civil War, Mary Gay devoted the remainder of her long life to memorializing the Confederacy and its noble dead. One of her most notable deeds was raising money for the Confederate cemetery at Franklin, Tennessee, outside Nashville, where her half-brother Thomie had been killed in battle and was buried. Her mother was devastated by grief at Thomie's death and would die herself in the spring of 1866 at the young age of 59. Gay's family had lost their slaves and much of their financial assets during the war. They were also left to raise Thomie's son. "The postwar task of rebuilding was as daunting for Mary as it was for most southerners. Not only must she and her sister reconstruct their lives without their brother and their mother, but they must shore up their home," [51] notes Michele Gillespie in a 2009 essay about Gay. Gay went to work to earn money, traveling long distances around the South by railroad peddling Bibles from which she made small commissions. "Indeed, Gay was among the first generation of Victorian women in the South to defy cultural sanctions against train travel for elite women," Gillespie notes. "Despite public images of the train as a masculine space, where danger for women predominated, Mary Gay remained undaunted by the alleged risks." She "was able to defy the confines of the new domesticity of postwar southern white women. Her life on the road allowed her to escape the pettiness and frustrations of running a household on a shoestring without the help of servants, as expected of so many white women of her class in the postwar South."

Gay also became "a celebrated guardian of Confederate heritage," "peddling the memory of the Confederate dead and the attendant suffering." In 1892, at the age of 61, Gay published what would become her best known book, "Life in Dixie During The War", in which she portrays herself as a saucy, fiercely independent heroine. "I have long felt that it was the duty of the South to bequeath to posterity the traditions of that period; for if we do it not ourselves they will be swallowed up in oblivion," [52] she wrote in the preface to the book. Gillespie asserts that Gay was "a moderate racist. She remained sympathetic to the tenets of white supremacy, like so many white southerners of her time, even as those tenets crescendoed into Jim Crow segregation late in her life." Gay's persona portrayed in "Life in Dixie" is famous worldwide today as the character Scarlett O'Hara in "Gone With The Wind." Atlanta author Margaret Mitchell, in a letter to a movie reviewer in July 1936, discussed the diaries and memoirs she used to create O'Hara's character. "Of course, I used everybody from Myrta Lockett Avary to Eliza Andrews and Mary Gay and Mrs. Clement Clay and Miss Fearn and Eliza Ripley and the Lord knows how many unpublished letters and diaries." [53] Gillespie writes that "Margaret Mitchell, creator of Scarlett O'Hara, perhaps the most enduring female figure in southern fiction, was influenced by at least one of Mary Gay's books, Life in Dixie during the Civil War [sic]. Certain scenes in Gone with the Wind (1936) are drawn directly from Gay's memoir." [54] Gay would publish her third book in 1907, a novel about the antebellum period entitled "The Transplanted". She died on November 6, 1918, shortly before her 90th birthday, and was buried in the Decatur cemetery beside her mother and sister Missouria.

George Knox Miller, 8th Confederate Cavalry

Knox Miller of the 8th Confederate Cavalry of Wheeler's Cavalry, whose eloquent letters to his wife Cellie provide the historian with such great insight into the Atlanta Campaign, is believed to have taken part in the battle of Decatur, although a letter he wrote near Decatur in late July 1864 which might have described it has been lost. [55] Miller would serve with Wheeler's Cavalry through the siege and capture of Atlanta and as it opposed General William T. Sherman's March To The Sea. In a vicious fight with Kilpatrick's Federal cavalry at Waynesboro, Georgia, during which Miller freely used his revolver and saber and shot one Federal soldier in the face at point blank range, Miller was himself shot in the left elbow. Surgeons wanted to amputate his arm, but another physician believed, correctly it turned out, that his arm could be saved (a reminder to always get a second opinion). He spent months recovering from his wound. With the end of the war, Miller and Cellie moved back to Talladega, Alabama, where he became an attorney, county judge, mayor and local newspaper editor. Cellie bore five children, the first – a daughter – born in June 1866. "Over the ensuing decades Knox Miller filled the role of a respectable, late nineteenth-century, upper-middle-class, white Southern urban professional. His life came to revolve around his family, his profession, and his community," notes Richard M. McMurry, who edited a collection of Miller's letters. Miller would outlive Cellie – she passed away in 1889. "She was to me all that a wife should be, and left, at her death, a wide circle of friends who sincerely admired and loved her," Miller noted in a 1895 letter. Miller remarried in 1892. He would pass away in November 1916 – a month shy of 80 years old -- at his home in Talladega. [56]

Milton Montgomery, 25th Wisconsin

Despite having been captured by Wheeler's Confederates and crippled by the loss of his right arm at the Battle of Decatur, the 25th Wisconsin's Colonel Milton Montgomery survived captivity and was exchanged by the Confederates. He returned to his regiment to finish out the war during February and March 1865, then was discharged from the army in July 1865. He returned to Wisconsin and then went on to build a highly successful postwar life. There, in June 1873, his son Carroll, also known as "C.S.", would follow in his father's footsteps, receiving a law degree from the University of Wisconsin. For reasons now unknown, in November 1873, Montgomery, by then 48 years old, and C.S., age 21, moved to Lincoln, Nebraska. The state was then just six years old and the first rail line connecting the east to the west had been laid across the Missouri River the year before. [57] There the Montgomerys opened a law practice known as Montgomery & Son. In 1879, C.S. moved to Omaha to practice law. The town was growing as a center of agriculture, transportation and finance. Today the firm the Montgomerys founded, now known as Baird Holm LLP, may be the oldest continuously existing law firm in the state. During his years in Nebraska, the elder Montgomery was known as "General Montgomery." Fifteen years after the war ended, the sword that Montgomery had been wearing when he was captured at Decatur was returned to him. Montgomery had been in declining health and just turned 72 when he passed away in May 1897 in his son's home in Omaha. [58]

John A. Nourse, Chicago Board of Trade Battery

John Nourse, shown in a post-war photograph, became very
prominent in the lumber business in Chicago.

John Nourse served through the remainder of the war and returned
home to Chicago. There he had a "long and honored career" in the lumber business, starting in 1867 as a lumberman, then with the firm of
Wheelock, Dean & Hermann. By 1871 he was manager of another lumber
company, Bates & Co., then as manager for Sawyer, Goodman Company.
When that business closed, Nourse in 1900 entered the yellow pine trade
as a wholesaler and then formed Nourse-Taylor Lumber Company in
1903. [59] He sold his interest in that business in 1910. "John A. Nourse is
one of the older lumbermen of the Chicago trade and, while youthful in
appearance and vigorous in physique, few of his friends realize that he
served with credit during the War of the Rebellion and has been actively
identified with the Chicago lumber trade ever since the close of hostilities," noted an April 1910 article about Nourse in the trade publication

"The Lumber World." The article went on to say that, "There are few men in the Chicago trade who possess the standing and character generally accorded to John A. Nourse." [60] He would pass away in 1913, aged 68. [61]

William L. Nugent, Ferguson's Brigade of Confederate cavalry

William Nugent, the Confederate cavalry officer who poured out his heart into his letters to his wife Nellie, survived the war to return home to become a prominent leader in post-Civil War Mississippi. Unfortunately, his "grief-filled personal experiences" followed him from the battlefields. With the surrender of the Confederate army in 1865, Nugent returned to Greenville, Mississippi, and found it had been almost completely destroyed during the war. Riding out to his home, he found his Nellie working in a field chopping weeds. "Reportedly this sight moved him to sit on the ground and weep," note the editors of Nugent's letters. "The hardships and heartaches endured by Nellie were evident in the autumn of 1865 when her health began to fail, and she died January 1, 1866." Nugent began rebuilding his career as an attorney and remarried in May 1867, but his second wife died within a year. He would remarry a third time in 1870. Nugent enjoyed growing fame as a lawyer and went on to become active in the prohibition movement. The daughter he bore with his first wife, also known as Nellie, went on to become a national women's suffrage leader and the first woman elected to the Mississippi legislature. Nugent would pass away in 1897 after a brief respiratory illness at the age of 64, his death perhaps hastened by his hard war time experiences. [62]

David S. Oliphant, 35th New Jersey

After his escape from a Confederate prison in South Carolina and a perilous journey over the Appalachian Mountains to Federal lines at Knoxville, Tennessee, in January 1865, David S. Oliphant returned home to Freehold, New Jersey, and devoted himself to business pursuits and veteran's affairs. In July 1867 he was married to Elizabeth Hale and they had a daughter. He would live to almost 77 years old, passing away in Freehold in 1918. [63]

Balthasar Regli, 25th Wisconsin

A member of the 25th Wisconsin who fought at Decatur, Balthasar Regli was the last surviving Union veteran of Eau Claire, Wisconsin. He lived to be almost 100 and was still living in June 1943. A native of Switzerland, Regli volunteered for the Union Army at the age of 19 on a "dare" of fellow wheat threshers as he was working on a brother's farm near Alma, Wisconsin. He took part in the Vicksburg campaign, Sherman's campaign through Tennessee and Alabama, and then fought at Resaca, Kennesaw Mountain, Decatur and Atlanta and then took part in the March to the Sea. A 1943 article in the Milwaukee Journal-Sentinel noted that, "He drove his automobile until he was 85, and after that, until five years ago, walked the two miles from his home to the downtown area to transact his business and visit friends." [64]

Isaiah R. Rose, 63rd Ohio

Isaiah R. Rose of the 63rd Ohio, seated center, survived the Battle of Decatur and imprisonment at Andersonville. After the war he returned home to Ohio and became active in state and local politics. Here he is shown in a photograph with his family taken around 1895.

After being captured by Confederates at Decatur, the 63rd Ohio's Isaiah R. Rose was imprisoned at Andersonville for seven months. He later escaped, but, when trying to get back into Union lines was shot in the leg by a Federal sentry. Rose survived his wound. When he was able to travel, Rose left the army hospital and was sent home to Coal Run, Ohio, where he arrived on crutches but rapidly regained his health. He returned to the 63rd Ohio just as the war was ending, but in time to take part in the Grand Review of the Army in Washington, D.C. With the war over, Rose returned to Ohio where he became active in veterans' organizations. He went to school to get an education, then engaged in the produce and insurance businesses. He later bought a farm where he and his family lived. In the 1880s Rose became active in Republican politics and served two terms as sheriff of Washington County, Oho. Beginning in 1890 he served four years on the board of managers of the Ohio state penitentiary. A photo taken around 1895 of Rose, his wife and their eight children, shows him with a stern, mustachioed face. In 1906, he was elected a state senator, in which role he became active in the temperance movement. He would pass away on Thanksgiving Day in 1916, aged 74. [65] Rose's Civil War service might have remained obscure if not for his great-great-great granddaughter, singer Kelly Clarkson of American Idol fame. In 2013, Clarkson filmed a TV show called "Who Do You Think You Are" for the TLC cable channel which explored Clarkson's Ohio ancestry and Rose's war time service. [66]

A photograph of Jeremiah "Uncle Jerry" Rusk when he was serving as governor of Wisconsin.

Jeremiah M. Rusk, 25th Wisconsin

With the end of the Civil War, Jeremiah Rusk, now 34 years old, immediately restarted his career in government that he had placed on hold in September 1862 when the 25th Wisconsin was organized. Over the next three decades, propelled by his military fame, he would rise to the highest levels of state and national politics. Having ended the war a colonel, Rusk soon received an honorary promotion to general. Just months after returning home to Wisconsin, Rusk was elected the state's bank comptroller, a position he would hold until the beginning of 1870. In August of that year he was encouraged by the state's Republican party (the party of Abraham Lincoln, and the favored party of many Midwestern Civil War veterans) to become a candidate for Congress. [67] He won the election and entered Congress in 1871, winning two more elections and serving until March 1877. He then returned to his Wisconsin farm and re-entered the banking business. In 1880 he would play a prominent role in getting one of his boyhood friends, James A. Garfield, now a prominent veteran Federal army general, nominated for president. When Garfield won the election, he offered Rusk positions in his administration, but Rusk opted to return home to Wisconsin and run for governor. He won the election and entered office in January 1882. He would serve until the beginning of 1889.

While serving as governor in 1886, Rusk played a key role in what is now one of Wisconsin's landmark historical incidents. Labor unrest was then roiling the rapidly industrializing Midwest, with workers – many of them foreign-born immigrants stoked by German anarchists and socialists -- demanding shorter work days. The work day at the time was typically 10 or 12 hours, six days a week. Strikes became increasingly common. "As the spring of '86 wore on the signs of coming trouble were incessant," [68] noted Rusk's biographer Henry Casson. "A concerted effort was to be made by the labor leaders all over the West [as the Midwest was then called] to compel employers to reduce the number of working hours to eight, even while maintaining the day's wages on the ten hour basis. Aided by the anarchists and socialists of Chicago and Milwaukee, and fired by the speeches of demagogues and fanatics, hundreds of honest and hitherto law abiding men had been drawn into the turmoil. The governor, coolly watching the symptoms from his office at the capital [Editor's note: in Madison, Wisconsin, 79 miles west of Milwaukee], gave no sign. He had one horror, -- that of being considered an intimidator; but through his adjutant general and through a staff officer stationed in Milwaukee, he was kept constantly informed of what was happening in the metropolis." Ten days before the trouble had begun, Rusk had stores of ammunition moved into the Milwaukee national guard armories.

At the beginning of May 1886, mobs of workers gathered in Chicago, Milwaukee and other cities, calling for factory strikes to demand eight-hour work days. In Chicago on May 4, the unrest would explode when a bomb was thrown at police, leading to the deaths of at least eight people in what became known as the Haymarket Square riot. The trouble began in Milwaukee on May 1. May 2, May 3 and May 4 were filled with processions, meetings, "fiery and furious speeches," and demonstrations that forced workshops to close. When the owners of factories and workshops asked for guards, detachments of militia were sent. On the night of May 4, leaders of the strike announced plans to march the next day on the Bay View Rolling Mills, then the Milwaukee area's biggest manufacturer. [69] Being told of their plans, Rusk ordered two companies of state militia to the factory to bolster a battalion already there. The next morning, May 5, at about 9 a.m. an estimated 1,500 workers marched on the Bay View Rolling Mills. "The Governor was early at his post at the armory and close to the telephone," Rusk's biographer Casson would write. "He had already given his instructions to Major Traeumer [Editor's note: Major George P. Traeumer, who commanded the militia guarding the rolling mill] to receive them with a volley if they refused to halt at his demand. He had long since made up his mind that the true way, the most merciful and effective way to put a stop to mob violence was to hit it sharply at the start and end it then and there. Suddenly came the call from Bay View, 'The mob's coming, sir, in full force.' And back went the answer in the chief's stentorian tones, 'Very well, sir. Fire on them.' And two minutes later crashed the single volley that scattered the south side mob like so many sheep and practically blew the back bone out of anarchy in our midst." Seven people were killed in what became known as the Bay View Tragedy. Rather than facing condemnation for the deaths, commendations and endorsements of his actions poured into Rusk's office, according to Casson. [Editor's note: One can only imagine what the reaction would be today to a similar incident.] The site is today marked with a historical marker, and the anniversary of the incident is still commemorated.

In 1888 Rusk declined a nomination for a fourth term as governor. He was considered as a potential Republican presidential candidate in that year's election. Instead, Benjamin Harrison, who had been a colonel in the Federal Army, was nominated and won election, taking office in 1889. Rusk, who had been on farms since he was a child in Ohio, was among the first considered for a cabinet position. Rusk wanted to be Secretary of War. [70] Instead, Harrison chose Rusk for the brand new cabinet position of Secretary of the Department of Agriculture, which was created in February 1889. Rusk worked to make U.S. agriculture more scientific, to expand markets for American farm products such as corn, to develop new products such as cane sugar, and to get European governments to drop barriers to imports of live cattle and meat products from the United States.

Rusk left the Department of Agriculture in March 1893, retiring to his 400-acre farm in Viroqua, Wisconsin. Later that year he was stricken by malaria and other illnesses, and he died on November 21, age 63. A front-page story about his death in that day's The Milwaukee Journal recounted Rusk's key Civil War experiences, noting his dramatic experiences at the Battle of Decatur. "When McPherson fell in front of Atlanta, on July 22, 1864, Rusk was leading the advance, and in that hard-fought contest lost one-third of his men. At one time in this battle he was cut off from his command, surrounded by the enemy and ordered to surrender; but by a chivalrous dash he broke through the confederate line and escaped to his regiment with only a slight wound and the loss of his horse, which fell riddled with bullets." [71] Rusk's death made national news and his funeral on November 24 was "attended by thousands," including Wisconsin's governor, lieutenant governor and other top elected officials. He was carried to his final resting place by 10 former members of the 25th Wisconsin. A salute was fired over the grave by a detail of Grand Army veterans. The lead story in The Milwaukee Journal on November 24 called Rusk "a man of the people on whose life was a constant exemplification of that grit and energy, that sterling honesty, that undaunted patriotism that are part and parcel of the characteristics of the typical American..." [72]

David Schreiner, 25th Wisconsin Infantry

Private David Schreiner of the 25th Wisconsin, who was very slightly wounded at Decatur (so slightly, apparently, that he does not appear on the list of wounded), would not be so lucky a month later when, in front of Atlanta in August 1864 he was severely wounded and lost his left arm. Schreiner was 22, a native of Hesse-Darmstadt, Germany, who had moved with his family to America and settled in Wisconsin in 1855. He would survive his wound and return home to become a court clerk and town treasurer, marry and have two children. [73]

John M. Shaw, 25th Wisconsin Infantry

John M. Shaw, 25th Wisconsin Infantry

With the capture of Atlanta in September 1864, Captain John M. Shaw of Company E of the 25th Wisconsin received a month's furlough, and returned home to marry a childhood friend, Ellen Eliot. Shaw then returned to the war in Georgia. Following the Atlanta Campaign, March To The Sea and the campaign through the Carolinas, Shaw was in the spring of 1865 named judge-advocate and acting provost marshal of the First Division of the 17th Army Corps, duties he held until his company was mustered out at the end of the war in June 1865. "His military experiences having undermined his health, upon return from the war, he sought its restoration in the invigorating atmosphere of Minnesota, and in February, 1866, located as an attorney in Minneapolis." [74] Shaw would become one of the leading lawyers in the city. He was appointed a judge by the governor of Minnesota, and he spent the rest of his life as a judge and corporate attorney. [75] He and Ellen would go on to become parents of two daughters and a son. Shaw died of heart failure on December 6, 1897, just shy of turning 64 years old.

John W. Sprague, 16th Army Corps

Following the Civil War, John W. Sprague, who led the Federal forces at the Battle of Decatur, helped found the city of Tacoma, Washington. In 1893 he was awarded the Medal of Honor for his victory at the Battle of Decatur.

John W. Sprague distinguished himself in the years after the Civil War as one of the pioneers of America's great northwest. At the close of the war, now-General Sprague left the Army and, undoubtedly because of his army service and connections, was appointed the first agent of the Bureau of Refugees, Freedmen and Abandoned Lands for Arkansas. The posting must have seemed very remote for the native New Yorker and former businessman. The Freedmen's Bureau was then led by General Oliver O. Howard, who had served along with Sprague in General William T. Sherman's army during the Atlanta Campaign. Because of the Arkansas's distance from Washington, its bad roads and frontier-like conditions, and the limited number of Federal soldiers in the state, the Freedmen's Bureau faced a daunting task of reconstructing Arkansas and empowering the state's 110,000 former slaves, notes historian Randy Finley in a 1999 history of the Bureau. "Sprague faced the obstacles of creating the Freedmen's Bureau bureaucracy in Arkansas," Finley writes. "His ideology and activism crucially shaped the attitude and policy of the Bureau toward freedpeople, white loyalists, and Confederate sympathizers. Like so many white Americans, he displayed an ambivalence toward blacks that often hampered the Bureau's mission. At his worst, he wrote a Chicago editor that he had nearly concluded that it might be better to let freedmen 'perish from the earth.' At other, less despairing moments, however, he reminded local agents that blacks had to be treated as 'white free men and in no other way.' He repeatedly cautioned his subordinates against controlling the freedpeople too much and warned Bureau agents that 'they are in no sense the masters or overseers of the freed people. All are free.' 'Make sure your civilians know,' he admonished local officials, 'that they are not the Negroes' master.' " [76]

Finley goes on to write that "Sprague viewed the Freedmen's Bureau as a temporary expedient to boost black freedom in the South. Economic power rather than government agency, Sprague believed, was the surest route to freedom. As a result, Sprague urged Arkansas freedmen to work hard and become self-reliant. Fearful that southern whites would attempt to resurrect slavery 'under some new name,' he sought to counter this by demonstrating to both blacks and whites exactly what 'a free laborer is.' Ironically, the implementation of his free-labor ideology often provided much needed field hands for planters ... From the beginning, Bureau Chief Sprague tried to harness Arkansas blacks to the plantation system that had produced so much cotton during the years before the war. Although Sprague hoped to restore a reconstructed Arkansas where the majority of blacks still planted and picked cotton most of the time, he did not countenance a return to chattel slavery. Even if his faulty economic analysis allowed planters to regain substantial control, he defended black rights in other areas." In addition, Finley writes, "Sprague promoted schools as a means of encouraging black self-reliance."

"Although, in many cases, Sprague favored black independence, his underlying paternalism often thwarted black freedom," Finley writes. "Abstractly, he said he believed blacks could and should take care of themselves, but his actions belied his theory because he often tried to shape black attitudes and behavior. He, along with many other Bureau agents, often saw blacks as problems and not as people." [77]

In November 1865, Sprague returned home and – like many other Federal generals -- entered the railroad business, which shaped his postwar life. He spent four years running the Winona & St. Peter railroad, and then in 1870 became general manager of the western division of the Northern Pacific Railway. [78] Construction of the Northern Pacific was begun in 1870, with funds for the project raised by Philadelphia financier Jay Cooke, who had been extraordinarily successful raising money for the U.S. government to fight the Civil War. [79] The transcontinental railway would stretch through thousands of miles of wilderness, from the shores of Lake Superior in Minnesota to the Pacific Ocean, the aim being to spur trade between Asian countries and the east coast. When the decision was made to build the railroad, one of the big questions was where its western terminus should be. The terminus would be somewhere on Puget Sound in what would later become the state of Washington, and the then-pioneer towns of Seattle, Steilacoom, Olympia and Tacoma competed to win it because of the enormous economic development and wealth it would bring. In 1870, Sprague was one of three men appointed to choose the western terminus. Tacoma, then just a rough frontier village hewed from the wilderness, was selected. Sprague became one of the pioneers of Tacoma "and one of the best known men in the Pacific Northwest." [80] "He came to Tacoma as a representative of the [Northern Pacific's] Land company but soon became an important factor in the railroad building and after its completion into Tacoma he was the general superintendent," notes a history of Tacoma. "He was an able executive and likeable man and soon he had not only this but all communities along the new railroad at his shrine. His simple dignity and the importance of his position with the railroad made him the foremost figure in the community and he was treated with great respect." [81] When the "Ohio Brigade" held a reunion in 1878, Sprague was invited but begged off on making the long railway journey back east, writing, "My lot seems to have been cast in a remote corner of our country, yet I can say 'my lines have fallen in pleasant places,' but they are so remote from the place of your meeting, and my duties are so pressing at this season of the year, that I am compelled to deny myself the pleasure and honor of attending the reunion." [82] Suffering from ill health in 1883, Sprague resigned from the Northern Pacific, but after a short rest he was busy again, founding the Tacoma National Bank, where he served as the first president. He was also president of the Union Savings Bank & Trust Company. In December 1883 at the age of 61 he was elected mayor of Tacoma. [83] In 1884, Sprague became the first president of the Tacoma Chamber of Commerce. [84] Sprague's influence and stature was shown again in 1889 when Washington was admitted into the union as a state, and he was presented as a candidate for the U.S. Senate. [85]

Sprague would recall the Battle of Decatur in a letter he wrote in September 1892 to the veterans of the 63rd Ohio for their reunion in Dayton, Ohio. Sprague recounted that he still had the brigade's flag which had been rescued from the Confederates as it flew over the courthouse in Decatur. Another flag had been purchased by the brigade and the old one presented to him. "I have it yet and cherish it as a precious momento," Sprague told his honored comrades. [86]

In 1893, 29 years after the Battle of Decatur, Sprague would be awarded the Medal of Honor at the request of General Grenville M. Dodge. Dodge had been commander of the 16th Army Corps, of which Sprague's brigade was a part. On November 29, 1893, Dodge sent a letter to General John M. Schofield, then-commanding general of the U.S. Army, asking that the medal be awarded to Sprague. Case No. 1899 (378064) noted that "Decatur, Ga., July 22, 1864. With a small command defeated an overwhelming force of the enemy and saved the trains of the corps." The award was granted on December 14, 1893, and the medal issued on January 18, 1894. [87] But the medal would arrive too late across the country in Washington state. After several years of poor health, Sprague had died at his home in Tacoma on December 24, 1893, age 77. The significance of the Battle of Decatur in the life of Sprague is apparent in an obitu-ary about him published by the Oregonian newspaper on December 26, 1893. It notes that he "won his star as a brigade commander" at Decatur. Most significantly, the obituary carries a letter that Sprague wrote to his regiment in September 1892 in which he "retold the story of this fight." [88]

Charles Weittenhiller, 25th Wisconsin

Charles Weittenhiller of Company E of the 25th Wisconsin was one of the unfortunate Federal soldiers captured at Decatur and sent to Andersonville prison. But luckily for Weittenhiller and for reasons unknown, he was discharged from the prison after just two months and returned home. Like many other recent European immigrants who filled the ranks of the Northern army, Weittenhiller had been born in Bavaria, Germany, in 1844. His parents moved to America in 1853, settling in Platteville, Wisconsin. Weittenhiller followed in his father's footsteps, becoming a barrel and cask maker. At the age of 20 in February 1864, he enlisted in the 25th Wisconsin. Thus his entry into the service coincided with the beginning of the bloody Atlanta Campaign. After his capture by the Confederates at Decatur on July 22 and two months in Andersonville, Weittenhiller apparently returned to the 25th Wisconsin and finished out the war. With the end of the war, Weittenhiller by 1867 had gone into business and married a woman named Jennie Marshall, and they had four children: Cora, Addie, Marenus and Charles. [89]

After the end of the Civil War, Confederate General Joseph Wheeler became a member of Congress and helped guide the South away from its past and towards a prosperous future. With the outbreak of the Spanish American War, he returned to active service with the U.S. Army. Here Wheeler is shown (in front, third from the left) in Tampa, Florida, in 1898 with Theodore Roosevelt, far right, and the staff of the 1st U.S. Volunteer Regiment at the beginning of the Spanish-American War.

Joseph Wheeler, Wheeler's Cavalry

Following the Civil War, General Joseph Wheeler led a life of public service, helping guide the devastated South away from its past and toward
a more prosperous and industrialized future. Wheeler settled in northern Alabama, married and raised a family, and became a farmer. He
then became a lawyer. In 1880, amidst a very turbulent political period
during Reconstruction, he was elected to Congress during a bitter campaign in which Wheeler and his campaign were charged with voter
fraud. He would be re-elected in 1882 and 1884 and then seven subsequent terms, serving until 1899. As a congressman, rather than hold
on to the Old South, Wheeler turned toward a bright future. He would
work to promote better feelings between the North and defeated South,
and for measures to help the South prosper and industrialize as the
United States grew its supremacy in world affairs. [90] Then, in 1898, 33
years after the Civil War had ended and now age 61, Wheeler returned
to his original profession as soldier.

With the outbreak of the Spanish American War, he offered his services to President William McKinley, and they were happily accepted. A
U.S. invasion fleet was sent to Cuba, and Wheeler was among the first
American soldiers to set foot on Cuban soil. There, during the Battle of
Santiago as the Spanish forces retreated, Wheeler famously reverted to
the ways of his younger days. Rising up in his stirrups, Wheeler reportedly yelled, "Boys, give the damn Yankees hell." Asked later if he actually said it, Wheeler reportedly answered, "Well, I did not say damn."
When the questioner pressed him about whether he had indeed called
the Spaniards "Yankees," Wheeler replied, "Yes, I said it several times.
I could not help it. Things did not look so different from what they did
during the War Between the States, and I forgot where I was." [91] With
the surrender of the Spanish army in Cuba, Wheeler and other U.S.
soldiers returned home. He returned to Congress, and then embarked
on a speaking tour of the East. "The general sentiment was that Wheeler
was a living illustration of the fact that the South was loyal again after
her great mistake in 1861," [92] historian John Dyer notes. Then, it was

back to the Spanish-American War. Wheeler and his daughter traveled to the war's other theater in the Philippines, where he took part in some of the fighting. He then returned home to the United States, retired from Congress and traveled widely. He died in New York City in January 1906 while visiting his sister, at the age of 70. He is buried in Arlington National Cemetery in Virginia.

Reunions of the units

With the end of the war, the soldiers of the Federal and Confederate regiments that fought at Decatur made their way home. Some would never see their comrades again. After the passage of a decade or two, others would begin to hold reunions.

The 25th Wisconsin

The 25th Wisconsin held its first reunion on June 8-9, 1887, in Sparta, Wisconsin, 22 years after it was mustered out of the Union army in Washington, D.C., and sent home to Madison, Wisconsin. The event was attended by about 150 of its veterans. Colonel Jeremiah Rusk, who had by then become governor of Wisconsin, and who had narrowly escaped death or capture at the Battle of Decatur, called the meeting to order. Not in attendance was Colonel Milton Montgomery, who had been shot and captured at Decatur, losing his right arm. "Meetings and cordial greeting of comrades separated for nearly 22 years, was the order of the day," noted a pamphlet later published to mark the occasion, "and every new arrival was a source of joyous hand shaking indulged by every comrade, while more demonstrative scenes, when the hearty embrace, quivering lip and moistened eye, spoke more than lips could express of the heart-felt happiness of the meetings, were not unfrequent.... Every train brought veterans from near and far, who, registering at the Secretary's tent, procured a badge and then engaged in looking up old chums with whom to renew a recital of war associations." With the opening of the

reunion, Governor Rusk gave a "recital of the life of the regiment," where he spoke at length about the Battle of Decatur, showing how significant it had been for the men gathered before him. Rusk described how the great Battle of Atlanta began on the morning of July 22, 1864. "My comrades, you will all recollect the 22nd of July...In this terrible conflict the 25th played its part. We occupied the extreme left of the line, covering the trains five miles from Atlanta. The enemy attacked us a little after noon, and continued the fight upon us till nearly five o'clock. Here the regiment's loss amounted to one-fourth of the whole number engaged. The list of casualties shows fifteen killed, fifty-seven wounded, twenty-five missing, and three prisoners. After the war, and during my service in congress, I met Col. Price, a member of congress from Alabama, who commanded one of the rebel brigades in this fight, and when I told him we had less than a brigade of infantry and a company of artillery he could hardly believe it. He stated that when he attempted to cross around to the rear of Decatur, he met reinforcements in large numbers coming up from Roswell Mills. I informed him that it was only one regiment of our brigade, the 43rd Ohio, under Col. Swain. He stated that two brigades of cavalry, one brigade of infantry and two companies of artillery formed the rebel forces at Decatur, and that had they known their superior numbers, would have captured the Union troops."
[93] Dr. M.R. Gage, who had served as the 25th Wisconsin's regimental surgeon, spoke later, describing how the 25th's commander at the Battle of Decatur, Colonel Milton Montgomery, "upon the bloody battle-field of Decatur, left his torn and mangled good right arm as sacrifice to the government he so ably and patriotically served; and who to-day bears, in his maimed person, a terrible testimony of the interest he had in the maintenance of the complete integrity of the Union of all the States, and in the spread and perpetuity of free institutions throughout the world." [94] W.C.S. Barron, who had been a private, second lieutenant, first lieutenant and then captain of Company B, recalled for his fellow veterans, "Who that was there will ever forget the 22nd day of July 1864... [When the Confederates attacked] all our camp equipage was left, the

officers left most of their private property and worse than all, we left some of our best men and officers, dead and prisoners...and Lieut. Col. Rusk performed his herculean feat with the Johnnies, lost his sword, shot the Johnny and skipped, and Capts. Ferg and Whittleton composed and sang that never-to-be-forgotten song, hymn or psalm, one verse of which runs something like this [Editor's note: It was apparently sung to the tune of Yankee Doodle]

> Oh! Col. Rusk he lost his sword,
> Fort Bowls, Fort Bowls
> Oh! Col. Rusk he lost his sword,
> Fort Bowles, says I,
> But he shot the Johnny right in the goard,
> And we will all drink stone blind,
> When the 25th comes marching home. [95]

William G. Willoughby, also with Company B, recalled, "It is almost painful to reflect that a few more circling years will wipe out all, save the memory of those gallant names and the deeds associated with them. But let us teach our children to trace the history of our regiment from Minnesota to Vicksburg, thence to Chattanooga, and on to 'The wild hills of Resaca,' to frowning Kenesaw, and on to the ever memorable 22nd of July, when the regiment bled at every pore, and when the gallant McPherson fell." [96]

The 63rd Ohio and 43rd Ohio

Members of the 63rd Ohio and 43rd Ohio held their first reunion on October 3-4, 1878, in Columbus, Ohio, as part of a reunion of "The Ohio Brigade." The two regiments had been part of The Ohio Brigade (which also included the 27th and 39th Ohio regiments) prior to their reorganization in the spring of 1864 into the Second Brigade of the Fourth Division of the 16th Army Corps along with the 35th New Jersey and 25th Wisconsin. The 63rd Ohio's Colonel Charles E. Brown, who had lost his leg at Decatur, played a prominent role in the 1878 reunion. [97] The veterans of the 63rd would continue to hold annual reunions. For the reunion in 1892, General Sprague wrote them a letter from Tacoma recounting the dramatic events that hot day in July 1864. "The bravery and excellent conduct of the infantry and artillery under my command on the 22d of July, 1864, won a star for me," Sprague noted. [98] The 63rd held their 12th reunion on October 5-6, 1897, in Corning, Ohio.[99]

The 35th New Jersey

After the war, the veterans of the 35th New Jersey met at intervals and renewed old friendships and memories. But survivors of the 35th New Jersey would not hold their first formal reunion for 26 years. They finally came together on October 22, 1890, at the Lincoln Post of the Grand Army of the Republic in Newark, N.J. Seventy "responded to the call and greeted one another with that heartiness peculiar to men who have braved all sorts of perils together," [100] reported the Trenton Evening Times. The old soldiers agreed to form a permanent organization and chose officers, and then held a banquet. [101] "After the dinner the veterans returned to the hall and indulged in speeches, songs and stories to their heart's content," the Trenton Evening Times reported. (Unfortunately for the historian, any discussion of their experiences at the Battle of Decatur was apparently not recorded.) But demonstrating the signifi-cance the Battle of Decatur had had on their lives, they agreed to meet next in Elizabeth, N.J., on July 22, 1891, the anniversary of the battle of Decatur, "where the regiment did gallant work," the Trenton Evening Times noted. They would meet again in Newark, N.J., on July 22, 1897, the 33rd anniversary of the Battle of Decatur, with a banquet, business meeting and sightseeing.
[102]

With the passage of more years, the ranks of the veterans of the Battle of Decatur would grow thinner and thinner, until by the 1940s all had passed into history.

Epilogue: Traces of the Past

I grew up a few miles north of Decatur in the 1960s and 1970s. In my early teens I was seriously bitten by the Civil War bug. My hobby, which became an obsession, was supported by my parents who bought me books about the war. My father drove me up to Kennesaw Mountain. One year we took a family road trip to Washington, D.C., to the Smithsonian Institution where I got to see its incredible Civil War collection. On the way home we stopped at the Wilderness battlefield park in Virginia. I remember seeing a long row of trenches running into the woods.

Back home, I joined a teen history group sponsored by the DeKalb Historical Society, then led by Executive Director Dr. Gordon Midgette. This would have been about 1975 or 1976. One Saturday afternoon, Midgette led a small group of us kids – most of them bored to death -- on a walking tour of downtown Decatur, showing us the historic buildings and reciting the lives of famous citizens and events that had occurred there. The tour took us to the old Decatur Cemetery. We walked down a sunken dirt road on the southwest side of the cemetery, behind where the Kroger grocery store is now. I recall Gordon Midgette saying the sunken dirt road had protected soldiers during the Battle of Decatur. How he knew this I don't know. But walking down that sunken road with the other kids, I looked down and saw a small grayish white object lying in the dirt. From my obsessive study of the Civil War, I recognized immediately what it was. I stopped and picked it up. It was a heavy, three-ring .58 caliber Minie ball, a bullet fired by rifled muskets used in the war. (I am quite sure I was the only kid in the group who would have recognized what it was!) I yelled out with delight my discovery and the other kids came to see the dirty bullet I held in my hand. Gordon Midgette came over, with a big smile on his face. I looked down at the mud to see if there were more, and a short distance away quickly found another bullet. This one was different though – a smooth-bore slug with a conical base, dented on its nose. I later learned it was for a Confederate Enfield rifle. I proudly gave the two bullets to Midgette. No others were found.

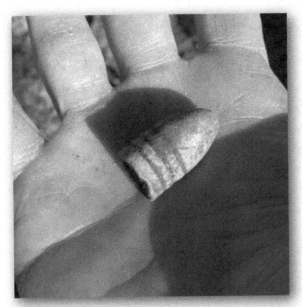

A .58 caliber bullet, commonly known as a "Minie ball," found by the author in downtown Decatur where Commerce Drive meets West Howard Avenue.

Those two bullets transformed the Battle of Decatur from an abstract subject – spoken or printed words that weren't quite real – into tangible proof that could be held and touched. Finding these traces of the past ignited a lifelong desire in me to know more about the battle, which is scarcely mentioned in most books about the Battle of Atlanta. I have since found other evidence of the battle. A few years ago, just north of the intersection of Clairmont and North Decatur roads, I found a .58 caliber Williams Cleaner bullet. These distinctive bullets were issued to Federal soldiers along with the more common .58 caliber "Minie balls," but are different because they have a zinc plug in their base which, when fired from a rifled musket, would scrape the bore of black powder fouling, hence their name. This was probably dropped by a Federal soldier as they advanced into Decatur on July 19, 1864, battling Wheeler's Cavalry. In downtown Decatur by the railroad, on top of the hill where Commerce Drive meets West Howard Avenue – the high ground from which the Confederates drove the Federals on July 22, 1864 -- I found a .58 caliber Minie ball, possibly dropped by a young and very scared Federal soldier as he ran for his life. Why and how did these bullets come to be lying there in the dirt? This book is an attempt to answer that question, and I hope I have succeeded.

David Allison

Notes and sources

Notes to Introduction

1. "become so hardened": William T. Sherman To Ellen Ewing Sherman, June 30, 1864, in "Sherman's Civil War: Selected Correspondence of William T. Sherman, 1860-1865", edited by Brooks D. Simpson and Jean V. Berlin, The University of North Carolina Press, 1999, Page 660.

2. "the continuous roar": "The Crime At Pickett's Mill", in "Phantoms of a Blood-Stained Period", edited by Russell Duncan & David J. Klooster, University of Massachusetts Press, 2002, Page 219.

3. "zero in on the silences" : "Ron Chernow's New Chapter: Ulysses S. Grant," by Alexandra Wolfe, The Wall Street Journal, September 15, 2017.

Notes to Chapter 1: The Civil War Comes to Decatur

1. a history of Morgan's great raid : John Hunt Morgan and His Raiders, by Edison H. Thomas, The University Press of Kentucky, 1975, Page 92.)

2. "other soldiers were frequently represented" : Life in Dixie During The War, by Mary A.H. Gay, Mercer University Press, 2000, Page 72.

3. "all four sides": The Central Courthouse Square In The American County Seat, by Edward T. Price, *Geographical Review*, Vol. 58, No. 1 (Jan., 1968), pp. 29-60.

4. 22 years old in 1864: The Story of Decatur, 1823-1899, by Caroline McKinney Clarke, Higgins-McArthur/Longino & Porter Inc., Atlanta, 1973, Page 9.

5. "with teams thus hitched." : The Collections of the DeKalb Historical Society, Volume 2, Page 17.

6. hotels and private homes : 1866 map of Decatur Court Square, DeKalb New Era, August 6, 1970.

7. "DeKalb Light Infantry": Life in Dixie During The War, by Mary A.H. Gay, Mercer University Press, 2000, Page 26.

8. built of granite blocks : The Collections of the DeKalb Historical Society, Volume 2, Page 17.

9. "one of the nicest houses in Decatur" : The History of DeKalb County, Ga., 1822-1900, by Vivian Price, DeKalb Historical Society, Chapter 26, Page 354. Price recounts this interesting tale. "During the Battle of Decatur, the Swanton cellar was considered one of the few safe places in town. Walter Alonzo Sexton, whose family was friends with the Swantons, later recalled: 'When cannon balls began to strike our house and go through it my father said to my mother: 'Our only hope is to try to make it over to Swanton's house and get in his cellar. You carry the baby (which was me), and I will carry your mother (who was very feeble and blind). A cannon ball passed through our house and struck my cradle and knocked it into fragments. A few days after that we left Decatur and I did not return until 20 years later when I went back on a visit.' The Swanton house, described as one of the nicest houses in Decatur, was in the thick of the fighting. The first time it was re-roofed after the war, a dishpan full of minie balls [Editor's note: bullets] was removed from the roof and walls of the house." During the battle, the 63rd Ohio's adjutant, Howard Forrer, was killed and later buried just a short distance south of the Swanton house.

10. "has 1,000 inhabitants": History of the 72nd Indiana Volunteer Infantry of the Mounted Lightning Brigade, written and compiled by B. F. McGee, edited by Wm. R. Jewell, S. Vater & Co., 1882, page 344.

Notes to Chapter 2: The Federals

1. a total of 2,548 soldiers : Report of Brig. Gen. John W. Sprague, Official Records, Series 1, Volume 38, Part 3, Report No. 557, Page 505.

2. formed (September 1863) : The Union Army: A History of Military Affairs in the Loyal States 1861-1865, Federal Publishing Company, Madison, Wis., 1908. Volume 3, Page 64; Volume 4, Page 60; Volume 2, Page 398

3. Sprague named its colonel : The Union Army: A History of Military Affairs in the Loyal States 1861-65, Volume 2, Federal Publishing Company, Madison, Wis., 1908, Page 398.

4. "took it very cooly" : The Colonel's Diary, by Colonel Oscar L. Jackson, Sharon, Pennsylvania, 1922, Page 45.

5. the New Madrid area : The Colonel's Diary, by Colonel Oscar L. Jackson, Sharon, Pennsylvania, 1922, Page 42-84

6. including the Battle of Decatur : The Colonel's Diary, by Colonel Oscar L. Jackson, Sharon, Pennsylvania, 1922, Pages 51, 165.

7. Grant wrote in his memoirs : Autobiography of Ulysses S. Grant, New York, Charles L. Webster & Company, Chapter 24.

8. "or in calm meditation" : The Colonel's Diary, by Colonel Oscar L. Jackson, Sharon, Pennsylvania, 1922, Page 64.

9. "a remarkable thing in a battle" : The Colonel's Diary, by Colonel Oscar L. Jackson, Sharon, Pennsylvania, 1922, Pages 69-76

10. "superhuman exertions to hold our position" : Report of Colonel John W. Sprague, Sixty-third Ohio Infantry, First Brigade, Second Division, Army of the Mississippi, cited in The History of Fuller's Ohio Brigade, 1861-1865, by Charles H. Smith, Cleveland, Ohio, 1909, Press of A.J. Watt, Page 107.

11. a total of 90 at Corinth : The History of Fuller's Ohio Brigade, 1861-1865, by Charles H. Smith, Cleveland, Ohio, 1909, Press of A.J. Watt, Page 99.

12. two thirds were killed or wounded : The Colonel's Diary, by Colonel Oscar L. Jackson, Sharon, Pennsylvania, 1922, Page 76.

13. no doubt saving his life : The Colonel's Diary, by Colonel Oscar L. Jackson, Sharon, Pennsylvania, 1922, Page 77.

14. and 35th New Jersey Volunteer Infantry : History of Fuller's Brigade, 1861-1865, by Charles H. Smith, Cleveland, Ohio, 1909, Page 140.

15. mustered in on September 14, 1862 : The Union Army : A History of Military Affairs in the Loyal States 1861-65, Volume 4, Federal Publishing Company, Madison, Wis., 1908, Page 60.

16. elected to the Wisconsin legislature : "Uncle Jerry": Life of General Jeremiah M. Rusk, by Henry Casson, Madison, Wisconsin, Junius W. Hill, 1895, Page 114.

17. arrived in June 1863 : The Union Army : A History of Military Affairs in the Loyal States 1861-65, Volume 4, Federal Publishing Company, Madison, Wis., 1908, Page 60.

18. and 35th New Jersey Volunteer Infantry : The History of Fuller's Ohio Brigade, 1861-1865, by Charles H. Smith, Cleveland, Ohio, 1909, Page 140.

19. mustered in in September 1863 : The Union Army, A History of Military Affairs in the Loyal States 1861-65, Volume 3, Federal Publishing Co., Madison, Wis., 1908, Page 64.

20. then just three in 1863 : Jersey Blue: Civil War Politics in New Jersey, 1854-1865, by William Gillette, Rutgers University Press, 1995, Page 158, 159.

21. "in comparison with many other states" : Jersey Blue: Civil War Politics in New Jersey, 1854-1865, by William Gillette, Rutgers University Press, 1995, Page 243.

22. the 13th New Jersey and 33rd New Jersey : Jersey Blue: Civil War Politics in New Jersey, 1854-1865, by William Gillette, Rutgers University Press, 1995, Page 173.

23. in the north of New Jersey : "Scoundrels from New York and Philadelphia: A Look at New Jersey's Zouave Regiments," by Joseph G. Bilby, in Military Images magazine, September/October 1988, Volume X, Number 2, Page 16. For more on the environment in which the 35th was raised, see "The Mutinous Regiment: The Thirty-Third New Jersey in The Civil War," by John G. Zinn, McFarland & Company Inc., Publishers, 2005; and "The Thirty Fifth" in Trenton State Gazette, Trenton, New Jersey, Volume LXXXIII, Issue 169, Page 3, accessed on GeneaologyBank.com.

24. just days after they were mustered in : Complete roster of the 35th New Jersey is in "Record of Officers and Men of New Jersey in the Civil War, page 1054; Record of Officers and Men of New Jersey in

the Civil War, 1861-1865, Volume 2, Trenton, New Jersey, 1876. See Page 1063 for a good example.

25. a shocking 450 deserted : Record of Officers and Men of New Jersey in the Civil War, 1861-1865, Volume 2, Trenton, New Jersey, 1876, Page 1094.

26. was shot by an officer for insubordination : Record of Officers and Men of New Jersey in the Civil War, 1861-1865, page 1073.

27. through many brutal campaigns" : Jersey Blue: Civil War Politics in New Jersey, 1854-1865, by William Gillette, Rutgers University Press, 1995, Page 173-174.

28. "Arab" inspired uniforms : The Ninth Regiment New York Volunteers (Hawkins' Zouaves), by Matthew J. Graham, New York, 1900, Page 22.

29. "a good regiment for service" : For the regiment's total strength see Record of Officers and Men of New Jersey in the Civil War, 1861-1865, page 1054. The newspaper account comes from the Newark Daily Advertiser, October 21, 1863, Column 5, "The 35th Regiment at Washington", accessed on Geneaologybank.com

30. but no heavy combat : Official Records, Series 1, Volume 32, Part 1, page 205.

31. arriving March 1 : Official Records, Series 1, Volume 32, Part 1, page 195.

32. and 25th Wisconsin Volunteer Infantry : History of Fuller's Brigade, 1861-1865, by Charles H. Smith, Cleveland, Ohio, 1909, Page 140.

33. volunteer organizations to respond : Historical Sketch of the Chicago Board of Trade Battery, Horse Artillery, Illinois Volunteers, Chicago, 1902, The Henneberry Company Printers, Page 6.

34. grew to 63 names : Historical Sketch of the Chicago Board of Trade Battery, Horse Artillery, Illinois Volunteers, Chicago, 1902, The Henneberry Company Printers, Page 18.

35. badges for their uniforms : Detailed history of the Chicago Board of Trade Battery, 1862-1865, John A. Nourse papers, Chicago History Museum Research Center, Page 66.

36. the battery's wartime experiences : Detailed history of the Chicago Board of Trade Battery, 1862-1865, John A. Nourse papers, Chicago History Museum Research Center.

37. "on which the right and centre rested" : Historical Sketch of the Chicago Board of Trade Battery, Horse Artillery, Illinois Volunteers, Chicago, 1902, Page 21-24.

38. "I cannot write them" : John A. Nourse papers, Detailed history of the Chicago Board of Trade Battery, 1862-1865, written in diary form, Chicago History Museum, Research Center, Page 47.

39. "southern states to secede" : Well Mary: Civil War Letters of a Wisconsin Volunteer, edited by Margaret Brobst Roth, The University of Wisconsin Press, Madison, 1960, Page 9.

40. attorney for Ross County : Biographical Directory of the United States Congress, 1774-2005, U.S. Government Printing Office, Page 718.

41. not killed or wounded : Report of Colonel John W. Sprague, Sixty-third Ohio Infantry, First Brigade, Second Division, Army of the Mississippi, October 9, 1862, cited in "The History of Fuller's Ohio Brigade, 1861-1865," by Charles H. Smith, Cleveland, Ohio, 1909, Page 106. The 48 percent casualty figure cited is on Page 108.

42. the beginning of the Atlanta Campaign : The History of Fuller's Ohio Brigade, 1861-1865, by Charles H. Smith, press of A.J. Watt, Cleveland, Ohio, 1909, Pages 349-351.

43. an artillery officer in the Austrian army : Colonels In Blue: Union Army Colonels of the Civil War, by Roger D. Hunt, Stackpole Books, Mechanicsburg, Penn., 2007, Page 195.

44. "enlisted to end slavery" : A Badger Boy In Blue, The Civil War Letters of Chauncey H. Cooke, Wayne State University Press, 2007, introduction, Page ix.

45. "the sweetest voices I ever heard" : A Badger Boy In Blue, The Civil War Letters of Chauncey H. Cooke, Wayne State University Press, 2007, Page 51.

46. "just to fight them" : A Badger Boy In Blue, The Civil War Letters of Chauncey H. Cooke, Wayne State University Press, 2007, Page 64.

47. re-enlisted in other units : The Ninth Regiment New York Volunteers (Hawkins' Zouaves), by Matthew J. Graham, New York, 1900, Page 460, Page 532.

48. with a distinctive uniform : Record of Officers and Men of New Jersey in the Civil War, 1861-1865, Volume 2, Page 1084, Trenton, 1876. Findagrave.com, http://www.findagrave.com/cgi-bin/fg.cgi?page=gr&GRid=15200930_accessed on October 17, 2017

49. with the rank of colonel : Baird Holm's First Century, by Michael G. Lessmann, November 2007, Page 6. Manuscript provided to the author by Baird Holm LLP.

50. and 27th Wisconsin : Official Records, Series 1, Volume 24, Part 2, Page 155.

51. erected in 1913 : Vicksburg National Military Park, https://www.nps.gov/vick/learn/historyculture/col-milton-montgomery.htm]

52. a bouquet of flowers : Chicago History Museum, John A. Nourse Papers, diary, typewritten manuscript, Page 3, July 23rd 1862.

53. "they returned to the woods" : Chicago History Museum, John A. Nourse Papers, diary, typewritten manuscript, Page 17.

54. was no stranger to combat : The New Jersey Coast In Three Centuries, William Nelson, Editor, Vol. III, The Lewis Publishing Company, 1902, Page 107, 108

55. also enlisted in Company F : "Isaiah R. Rose," by Betty K. Rose, in Reflections Along The Muskingum, Lower Muskingum Historical Society, Waterford, Ohio, Volume 36, No. 3, July-August-September 2010, Page 7.

56. would become the 25th Wisconsin : "Uncle Jerry": Life of General Jeremiah M. Rusk," by Henry Casson, Madison, Wisconsin, Junius W. Hill, 1895, Pages 25, 63, 97, 108, 111, 118.

57. a biography of Shaw : Encyclopedia of Biography of Minnesota, Volume 1, by Judge Charles E. Flandrau, Chicago, The Century Publishing And Engraving Company, 1900, Page 150.

58. "the 25ᵗʰ Wisconsin Regiment" : History of the City of Minneapolis, Minnesota, Part 1, by Isaac Atwater, Munsell & Company, Publishers, 1893, Page 436, 437.

59. the Atlanta Campaign : Roster of Wisconsin Volunteers, War of the Rebellion, 1861-1865. Volume II, Madison, Wis., Democrat Printing Company, State Printers, 1886, Page 294.

60. producing four sons : For biographical sketches of John W. Sprague see "Still Another Gone: Death of General J.W. Sprague," Oregonian, December 26, 1893; Ohio in the War: Her Statesmen, Her Generals, and Soldiers, Volume 1, Page 864, by Whitelaw Reid, Moore, Wilstach & Baldwin, 1868; and The History of Fuller's Ohio Brigade, 1861-1865, by Charles H. Smith, Cleveland, Ohio, 1909, Press of A.J. Watt, Page 344, Biographical Sketch by Colonel Oscar L. Jackson.

61. keeping the latter's name : The Union Army: A History of Military Affairs in the Loyal States 1861-65, Volume 2, Federal Publishing Company, Madison, Wis., 1908, Page 398.

62. "he had influence with Governor Todd" : The Colonel's Diary, by Oscar L. Jackson, Sharon, Pennsylvania, 1922, Page 42.

63. "brought them again into line" : Report of Colonel John W. Fuller, October 13ᵗʰ, 1862, cited in "The History of Fuller's Ohio Brigade, 1861-1865, Page 98.

64. "portray an officer in battle" : History of Washington County, Ohio, With Illustrations and Biographical Sketches, H.Z. Williams & Bro. Publishers, 1881, Page 213.

65. "with a hearty good will did they respond" : The Colonel's Diary, by Oscar L. Jackson, Sharon, Pennsylvania, 1922, Page 73.

66. the Atlanta Campaign : The History of Fuller's Ohio Brigade, 1861-1865, by Charles H. Smith, Cleveland, Ohio, 1909, Page 346.

67. "one of the best officers in the regiment" : The History of Fuller's Ohio Brigade, 1861-1865: Its Great March, with Roster, Portraits, Battle Maps and Biographies, by Charles H. Smith, Press of A.J. Watt, Cleveland, Ohio, 1909, Page 363.

Notes to Chapter 3: The Confederates

1. delay the approach of the enemy : Fightin' Joe Wheeler, by John P. Dyer, Louisiana State University Press, 1941, Page 43.

2. a month later : Fightin' Joe Wheeler, by John P. Dyer, Louisiana State University Press, 1941, Page 76.

3. moving south out of Chattanooga : Decision In The West: The Atlanta Campaign of 1864, Albert Castel, University Press of Kansas, 1992, Page 119.

4. and then Decatur : Campaigns of Wheeler & His Cavalry, 1862-1865, edited by W.C. Dodson, Hudgins Publishing Company, Atlanta, Georgia, 1899, Page 363.

5. as of July 10, 1864, included: Official Records, Series 1, Volume 38, Part 3, Page 657-658.

6. attack at Decatur : Official Records, Series 1, Volume 38, Part 3, Page 660.

7. "little regard for the source" : Fightin' Joe Wheeler, by John P. Dyer, Louisiana State University Press, 1941, Page 76.

8. "a brutal master" : Mary Gay: Sin, Self, and Survival in the Post-Civil War South, by Michelle Gillespie, in "Georgia Women: Their Lives and Times", Volume 1, edited by Ann Short Chirhart and Betty Wood, The University of Georgia Press, 2009, Page 201.

9. from a neighbor : Lincoln, by David Herbert Donald, Simon & Schuster, 1995, Page 48.

10. and line drawing : Samuel Wragg Ferguson Papers, Mss. 1416, 1576, Louisiana and Lower Mississippi Valley Collections, LSU Libraries, Baton Rouge, La., Part 1, Page 9-10.

11. "happiest part of my life" : Samuel Wragg Ferguson Papers, Mss. 1416, 1576, Louisiana and Lower Mississippi Valley Collections, LSU Libraries, Baton Rouge, La., Part 2, Page 6.

12. on May 1, 1861 : Samuel Wragg Ferguson Papers, Mss. 1416, 1576, Louisiana and Lower Mississippi Valley Collections, LSU Libraries, Baton Rouge, La., Part 3, Page 14.

13. friends at the fort : Samuel Wragg Ferguson Papers, Mss. 1416, 1576, Louisiana and Lower Mississippi Valley Collections, LSU Libraries, Baton Rouge, La., Part 4, Page 1.

14. a relative of Confederate General Robert E. Lee : Samuel Wragg Ferguson Papers, Mss. 1416, 1576, Louisiana and Lower Mississippi Valley Collections, LSU Libraries, Baton Rouge, La., Part 4, Page 18.

15. a brigadier general of cavalry : Samuel Wragg Ferguson Papers, Mss. 1416, 1576, Louisiana and Lower Mississippi Valley Collections, LSU Libraries, Baton Rouge, La., Part 4, Page 37.

16. a collection of Miller's letters : An Uncompromising Secessionist: The Civil War of George Knox Miller, Eighth (Wade's) Confederate Cavalry, edited by Richard M. McMurry, The University of Alabama Press, 2007, Page xii, xxiii-xxiv.

17. "to submit to Yankee rule" : My Dear Nellie: The Civil War Letters of William L. Nugent to Eleanor Smith Nugent, University Press of Mississippi, 1977, Page 132.

18. as "War Child" : An Uncompromising Secessionist: The Civil War of George Knox Miller, Eighth (Wade's) Confederate Cavalry, edited by Richard M. McMurry, The University of Alabama Press, 2007, Page 206.

19. "iron nerves and endurance" : Decision In The West: The Atlanta Campaign of 1864, Albert Castel, University Press of Kansas, 1992, Page 111.

20. "with skill and dogged determination" : A Soldier to the Last: Maj. Gen. Joseph Wheeler in Blue and Gray, by Edward G. Longacre, Potomac Books Inc., 2007, preface pages xi and xii.

21. for the coming conflict : Fightin' Joe Wheeler, by John P. Dyer, Louisiana State University Press, 1941, Page 20.

22. Shiloh in Tennessee in April 1862 : General Joseph Wheeler and The Army of Tennessee, by John Witherspoon DuBose, The Neale Publishing Company, New York, 1912, Page 54; Confederate Veteran magazine, Volume 14, No. 4, April 1906, Page 154.

23. "did not like the man" : General Joseph Wheeler And The Army of Tennessee, by John Witherspoon DuBose, The Neale Publishing Company, New York, 1912, Page 91.

24. "with separate commands" : Fightin' Joe Wheeler, by John P. Dyer, Louisiana State University Press, 1941, Page 51.

25. supplies and provisions : A Soldier to the Last: Maj. Gen. Joseph Wheeler in Blue and Gray, by Edward G. Longacre, Potomac Books Inc., 2007, Page 77.

26. to major general : Fightin' Joe Wheeler, by John P. Dyer, Louisiana State University Press, 1941, Page 90.

27. horses shot out from under him : Campaigns of Wheeler and His Cavalry, 1862-1865, edited by W.C. Dodson, Hudgins Publishing Company, Atlanta, Georgia, 1899, introduction, Page 363.

28. wounded or killed during the war : Campaigns of Wheeler and His Cavalry, 1862-1865, edited by W.C. Dodson, Hudgins Publishing Company, Atlanta, Georgia, 1899, Page 371.

29. "leading from the front" : A Soldier to the Last: Maj. Gen. Joseph Wheeler in Blue and Gray, by Edward G. Longacre, Potomac Books Inc., 2007, Page 71.

30. "the swollen river below" : Fightin' Joe Wheeler, by John P. Dyer, Louisiana State University Press, 1941, Page 106.

31. "the opposite bank in safety" : General Joseph Wheeler And The Army of Tennessee, by John Witherspoon DuBose, The Neale Publishing Company, New York, 1912, Page 177.

32. "false, misleading intelligence" : Decision In The West: The Atlanta Campaign of 1864, by Albert Castel, University Press of Kansas, 1992, Page 111, Page 490.

33. "even by Wheeler's standards" : A Soldier to the Last: Maj. Gen. Joseph Wheeler in Blue and Gray, by Edward G. Longacre, Potomac Books Inc., 2007, Page 168.

34. "grooming their horses" : An Uncompromising Secessionist: The Civil War of George Knox Miller, Eighth (Wade's) Confederate Cavalry, edited by Richard M. McMurray, The University of Alabama Press, 2007, Page 195.

Notes to Chapter 4: Chattanooga to the Chattahoochee

1. then up the Tennessee River : Official Records, Series 1, Volume 32, Part 1, page 575.

2. at that time totaled 2,548 men : Report of Brig. Gen. John W. Sprague, Official Records, Report No. 557, Series 1, Volume 38, Part 3, Page 504.

3. "from all directions" : A Badger Boy In Blue, The Civil War Letters of Chauncey H. Cooke, Wayne State University Press, 2007, Page 84.

4. of Confederate cavalry : Official Records, Series 1, Volume 38, Part 3, Report of Major General G.M. Dodge, Page 375.

5. "join in the retreat" : A Badger Boy In Blue, The Civil War Letters of Chauncey H. Cooke, Wayne State University Press, 2007, Page 87.

6. "in these hot days" : Well Mary: Civil War Letters of a Wisconsin Volunteer, edited by Margaret Brobst Roth, The University of Wisconsin Press, Madison, 1960, Page 54.

7. "opened a brisk fusillade fire on us" : Official Records, Report of Col. John J. Cladek, No. 558, Series 1, Volume 38, Part 3, Page 509.

8. "I am a good shot" : A Badger Boy In Blue, The Civil War Letters of Chauncey H. Cooke, Wayne State University Press, 2007, Page 92.

9. "with one man wounded" : Official Records, Report of Col. John J. Cladek, No. 558, Series 1, Volume 38, Part 3, Page 510.

10. until about 8:30 p.m. : Official Records, Report No. 452, Series 1, Volume 38, Part 2, Page 143; Official Records, Report No. 465, Series 1, Volume 38, Part 2, Page 191; Official Records, Report No. 473, Series 1, Volume 38, Part 2, Page 214.

11. 24 killed and wounded at Resaca : Official Records, Series 1, Volume 38, Part 3, Report No. 452, report of Brigadier General C.R. Woods, Page 143.

12. had come to his aid at Resaca : Official Records, Series 1, Volume 38, Part 3, Page 144.

13. 20 men wounded plus one missing : Official Records, Series 1, Volume 38, Part 3, Report No. 559 of Lieut. Col. William A. Henry, Page 511.

14. "Many were the sleepless nights" : Samuel Wragg Ferguson Papers, Mss. 1416, 1576, Louisiana and Lower Mississippi Valley Collections, LSU Libraries, Baton Rouge, La., Part 4, Page 45.

15. "satisfaction never experienced before" : An Uncompromising Secessionist: The Civil War of George Knox Miller, Eighth (Wade's) Confederate Cavalry, compiled, edited and annotated by Richard

M. McMurry, The University of Alabama Press, Tuscaloosa, 2007, Page 202.

16. "death and destruction all around" : An Uncompromising Secessionist: The Civil War of George Knox Miller, Eighth (Wade's) Confederate Cavalry, compiled, edited and annotated by Richard M. McMurry, The University of Alabama Press, Tuscaloosa, 2007, Page 200.

17. "as the rebs have to live" : Well Mary: Civil War Letters of a Wisconsin Volunteer, edited by Margaret Brobst Roth, The University of Wisconsin Press, Madison, 1960, Page 60.

18. "the hardest sights of the battlefield" : Well Mary: Civil War Letters of a Wisconsin Volunteer, edited by Margaret Brobst Roth, The University of Wisconsin Press, Madison, 1960, Page 61.

19. "start for the north as prisoners" : Chicago History Museum, John A. Nourse Papers, diary, typewritten manuscript, Page 78.

20. on the evening of May 26 : Official Records, Series 1, Volume 38, Part 3, Report No. 557 of Brigadier General John W. Sprague, Page 505. Sprague says the brigade arrived at Dallas on the evening of the 26th. See report of 35th New Jersey's William A. Henry, who says 35th arrived on the 27th.

21. Sprague would recall : Official Records, Series 1, Volume 38, Part 3, Report No. 557 of Brigadier General John W. Sprague, Page 505.

22. "what this afternoon will bring forth" : Well Mary: Civil War Letters of a Wisconsin Volunteer, edited by Margaret Brobst Roth, The University of Wisconsin Press, Madison, 1960, Page 66.

23. "the closest call I have yet had" : John A. Nourse Papers, Chicago History Museum Research Center, typed manuscript of written diary, May 27, 1864, Page 79.

24. eight wounded and one missing : Official Records, Series 1, Volume 38, Part 3, Report No. 559 of Lieut. Col. William A. Henry, Page 512. Henry says the 35th arrived in Dallas on May 27.

25. return to their main line to rest : A Badger Boy in Blue: The Civil War Letters of Chauncey H. Cooke, with an introduction and appendix by William H. Mulligan Jr., Wayne State University Press, Detroit, 2007, Page 95.

26. "since yesterday two weeks" : An Uncompromising Secessionist: The Civil War of George Knox Miller, Eighth (Wade's) Confederate Cavalry, edited by Richard M. McMurry, The University of Alabama Press, 2007, Page 202-204.

27. "horrified at the sacrifice necessary" : An Uncompromising Secessionist: The Civil War of George Knox Miller, Eighth (Wade's) Confederate Cavalry, edited by Richard M. McMurry, The University of Alabama Press, 2007, Page 211-212.

28. 53 captured and 81 missing : Official Records, Series 1, Volume 38, Part 3, Page 949.

29. "would answer back the challenge" : A Badger Boy In Blue, The Civil War Letters of Chauncey H. Cooke, Wayne State University Press, 2007, Page 95-96.

30. skirmishing with the Confederates followed : Official Records, Series 1, Volume 38, Part 3, Report No. 557 of Brigadier General John W. Sprague, Page 505.

31. seven killed and eight wounded : Official Records, Series 1, Volume 38, Part 3, Report No. 559 of Lieut. Col. William A. Henry, Page 512.

32. "continually uttered all around" : My Dear Nellie: The Civil War Letters of William L. Nugent to Eleanor Smith Nugent, University Press of Mississippi, 1977, Page 179.

33. "until it was relieved" : Official Records, Report of Gen. G.M. Dodge, Series 1, Volume 38, Part 2, Page 381.

34. on June 8th, 9th, 11th, 15th, 18th, 20th and 27th : Historical Sketch of the Chicago Board of Trade Battery, Horse Artillery, Illinois Volunteers, Chicago, 1902, Page 28.

35. "wounded around and on all sides of me" : An Uncompromising Secessionist: The Civil War of George Knox Miller, Eighth (Wade's) Confederate Cavalry, edited by Richard M. McMurry, The University of Alabama Press, 2007, Page 218.

36. "when the opportunity offers" : My Dear Nellie: The Civil War Letters of William L. Nugent to Eleanor Smith Nugent, University Press of Mississippi, 1977, Page 182.

37. "the sickening theme" : My Dear Nellie: The Civil War Letters of William L. Nugent to Eleanor Smith Nugent, University Press of Mississippi, 1977, Page 185.

38. "I shall be all right soon" : A Badger Boy in Blue: The Civil War Letters of Chauncey H. Cooke, with an introduction and Appendix by William H. Mulligan Jr., Wayne State University Press, Detroit, 2007, Page 106.

39. "near enough to the battery" : John A. Nourse Papers, Chicago History Museum Research Center, typed manuscript of written diary, June 27, 1864, Page 86.

40. around Kennesaw until July 3 : Official Records, Series 1, Volume 38, Part 3, Report No. 557 of Brigadier General John W. Sprague, Page 505.

41. Sprague would later write : Official Records, Series 1, Volume 38, Part 3, Report of Brigadier General John W. Fuller, Page 485; Official Records, Series 1, Volume 38, Part 3, Report No. 557 of Brigadier General John W. Sprague, Page 505.

42. firing 85 rounds : Diary of John A. Nourse, Chicago History Museum Research Center, typewritten manuscript of diary, July 4, 1864, Page 88.

43. "a victim of southern fever" : A Badger Boy In Blue, The Civil War Letters of Chauncey H. Cooke, Wayne State University Press, 2007, Page 107.

44. "for killing their comrades" : A Badger Boy In Blue, The Civil War Letters of Chauncey H. Cooke, Wayne State University Press, 2007, Page 109.

45. "but got no reply" : Diary of John A. Nourse, Chicago History Museum Research Center, typewritten manuscript of diary, July 4, 1864, Page 89.

46. completed on July 13th : Official Records, Series 1, Volume 38, Part 3, Report No. 557 of Brigadier General John W. Sprague, Page 505.

47. "Atlanta will soon be ours" : Well Mary: Civil War Letters of a Wisconsin Volunteer, edited by Margaret Brobst Roth, The University of Wisconsin Press, Madison, 1960, Page 75.

48. joined the 5th Georgia Cavalry : In the Saddle: Exploits of the 5th Georgia Cavalry During the Civil War, by Timothy Daiss, Schiffer Publishing Ltd., 1999, Page 100.

49. "very well satisfied" : In the Saddle: Exploits of the 5th Georgia Cavalry During the Civil War, by Timothy Daiss, Schiffer Publishing Ltd., 1999, Page 106.

50. "No casualties in my Regt" : An Uncompromising Secessionist: The Civil War of George Knox Miller, Eighth (Wade's) Confederate Cavalry, edited by Richard M. McMurry, The University of Alabama Press, 2007, Page 231.

51. "one of the most impressive scenes I ever witnessed" : An Uncompromising Secessionist: The Civil War of George Knox Miller, Eighth (Wade's) Confederate Cavalry, edited by Richard M. McMurry, The University of Alabama Press, 2007, Page 235.

52. "have not done so yet" : In the Saddle: Exploits of the 5th Georgia Cavalry During the Civil War, by Timothy Daiss, Schiffer Publishing Ltd., 1999, Page 107.

53. also crossed the river : Official Records, Series 1, Volume 38, Part 3, Report No. 439, Reports of Maj. Gen. Oliver O. Howard, Page 38.

Notes to Chapter 5: The Civil War Comes To Decatur

1. to Decatur on July 19 : Official Records, Series 1, Volume 38, Part 5, Page 166, Special Field Orders No. 36.

2. "swing toward Stone Mountain" : Official Records, Series 1, Volume 38, Part 5, Page 108, Major General William T. Sherman to Major General McPherson, July 10, 1864.

3. "to work out the solution" : Official Records, Series 1, Volume 38, Part 5, Page 123, Major General W.T. Sherman to Lieutenant-General Grant.

4. "or of Atlanta itself" : Official Records, Series 1, Volume 38, Part 5, Page 142-143, Special Field Orders No. 35, July 14, 1864.

5. "sending troops to Johnston first" : Official Records, Series 1, Volume 38, Part 5, Page 143, Lieutenant-General U.S. Grant to Major-General Halleck, July 15, 1864.

6. "by you and General Garrard" : Official Records, Series 1, Volume 38, Part 5, Page 147, Major-General W.T. Sherman to General McPherson, July 15, 1864.

7. "as far to the east and south of you as possible" : Official Records, Series 1, Volume 38, Part 5, Page 149, Lieutenant-General U.S. Grant to Major-General Sherman.

8. "against such increase of rebel force" : Official Records, Series 1, Volume 38, Part 5, Page 150, Major-General H.W. Halleck to Major-General Sherman.

9. "All well" : Official Records, Series 1, Volume 38, Part 5, Page 150, Major-General W.T. Sherman to Maj. Gen. H.W. Halleck.

10. "we have moved out from the Chattahoochee" : Official Records, Series 1, Volume 38, Part 5, Page 158, Major-General W.T. Sherman to Maj. Gen. H.W. Halleck.

11. Cincinnati Daily Commercial, Volume XXV, No. 19, July 30, 1864, "Left Wing, 16th Army Corps, In The Field, Four Miles From Atlanta", Page 1, Column 8, accessed through GeneologyBank.com.

12. "they abandoned the town" : Report of Major General John M. Schofield, Army of the Ohio, No. 296, Official Records, Series 1, Volume 38, Part 2, Page 516, September 10, 1864.

13. "a difficult, time-consuming process" : Decision In The West: The Atlanta Campaign of 1864, by Albert Castel, University Press of Kansas, 1992, Page 193.

14. "a large amount of tobacco, was burned" : Report of Brigadier General Milo S. Hascall, No. 309, Official Records, Series 1, Volume 38, Part 2, Page 566, September 10, 1864. The tobacco was probably newly harvested by Georgia farmers and at the depot awaiting shipment to the coast to be sent overseas, where it could be readily sold by the Confederate government to raise much needed hard currency.

15. fighting from the south fork of Peachtree Creek into Decatur : Report of Col. Peter T. Swaine, 99th Ohio Infantry, Report No. 302, Official Records, Series 1, Volume 38 Part 2, Page 550; Report of Lieutenant Colonel John E. Cummins, Official Records, Series 1, Volume 38, Part 2, Page 565, July 30, 1864.

16. "encamped in an open field" : Report of Colonel C.A. Zollinger, 129th Regiment Indiana Infantry, August 12, 1864, Official Records, Series 1, Volume 38, Part 2, Page 560.

17. "drove them from the place" : Report of Captain J.C. Shields, 19th Ohio Battery, Official Records, Series 1, Volume 38, Part 2, page 673, September 9, 1864; Official Records, Series 1, Volume 38, Part 2, Page 666, No. 346, Report of Capt. Joseph C. Shields, 19th Ohio Battery, September 9, 1864.

18. "worthy of a better position" : Report of Major John W. Tucker, 80th Indiana Infantry, Official Records, Series 1, Volume 38, Part 2, No. 329, Page 627.

19. "back on a road and camped" : Diary of Isum Gwin, July 19, 1864, typed manuscript, Indiana Historical Society. Gwin was 37 years old at the time of the Atlanta Campaign. According to a biographical sketch of Gwin prepared by the Indiana Historical Society (http://www.indianahistory.org/our-collections/collection-guides/isum-gwin-diary-1864.pdf), Gwin was born on October 17, 1826, in Harrison County, Indiana. He volunteered for the Federal army on August 9, 1862, joining the 80th Indiana Volunteers, Company D. "He had a distinguished service record, rising in rank from first sergeant in September 1862, second lieutenant in January 1863, first lieutenant in February 1864, and finally captain on 1 July 1864. Isum mustered out of the army 22 June 1865 in North Carolina," the Indiana Historical Society's biographical sketch says. Gwin survived the war and returned home, marrying on Christmas day in 1870. He died on April 4, 1907, aged 80 years old, in Shoals, Indiana, and is buried in the South Martin Cemetery in Rutherford Township of Martin County, Indiana.

20. "firing when we neared the town" : Report of Lieutenant Colonel J.M. Rusk, Official Records, Series 1, Volume 38, Part 3, Sept. 8, 1864, Page 524.

21. "and everything quiet" : E.B. Quiner Quiner Scrapbooks: Correspondence of the Wisconsin Volunteers, 1861-1865, Volume 10, 25th Infantry, Number 320, Wisconsin Historical Society.

22. "was becoming fearfully alarming" : Life in Dixie During the War, by Mary A.H. Gay, Mercer University Press, 2001, Page 125.

23. "sorry I should be so disappointed" : Life in Dixie During the War, by Mary A.H. Gay, Mercer University Press, 2001, Page 126.

24. "from any cavalry dash" : Official Records, Series 1, Volume 38, Part 5, Page 194, Special Field Orders No. 72.

25. "an immense army train of wagons commenced rolling in" : Life in Dixie During the War, by Mary A.H. Gay, Mercer University Press, 2001, Page 128.

26. "the Nero of the nineteenth century" : Life In Dixie During The War, by Mary A.H. Gay, Mercer University Press, 2001, Page 168.

27. going to be attacked soon : Decision in the West: The Atlanta Campaign of 1864, by Albert Castel, University Press of Kansas, Page 367.

28. "and think so today" : Samuel Wragg Ferguson Papers, Mss. 1416, 1576, Louisiana and Lower Mississippi Valley Collections, LSU Libraries, Baton Rouge, La. Part 4, Page 46. Ferguson goes on to say in his memoirs, "Some time afterward I spent a day with him (Editor's note: General Johnston) in Macon, Ga., he explained to me his plans and his reason for the moves he had made, with this explanation, and my personal knowledge of the country, and of the condition of our Army; I do not doubt that had Johnston not been removed from Command, Sherman would have met a crushing defeat at Atlanta."

29. "without the formality of a demand" : Official Records, Series 1, Volume 38, Part 5, Page 193.

30. medical director of the 23rd Army Corps : Harper's Weekly, August 27, 1864, Page 558; Official Records, Series 1, Volume 38, Part 2, Report No. 297, Page 522. [Editor's note: Dr. Shippen was the sixth generation in a line of famed Pennsylvania surgeons. He was born in Farley, Pennsylvania, on June 23, 1827, so he would have been 37 years old in 1864. He was a graduate of the University of Pennsylvania, class of 1846, and received his M.D. in 1857. He was a distinguished surgeon during the Civil War, serving in Washington,

D.C., when he at one point had 1,000 wounded men under his care. Later he served as a surgeon in the Fifth Army Corps, and then as medical director of the 23rd Army Corps. He died April 22, 1895, in Baltimore, Maryland. He is not to be confused with another Dr. Edward Shippen of the same family and generation who served in the U.S. Navy during the Civil War. See "Seven Generations of Physicians," by George Schuyler Bangert, in New York Medical Journal, August 28, 1920, Vol. CXII, No. 9, Page 279.]

31. pushed into Decatur : Harper's Weekly, August 27, 1864, Page 557, "General Sherman's Campaign – Sherman's Head-Quarters, Near Decatur, July 19, 1864. – Sketched by T.R. Davis." [Editor's note: Caroline McKinney Clarke's 1973 book "The Story of Decatur: 1823-1899" has a photograph on Page 53 of a two-story wood frame house she believed to be the Powell house. The photo is from the front of the house (chimney on the right) and shows a yard with large shade trees. The photo agrees well with Theodore R. Davis's sketch from the rear of the house (chimney on the left). The photo also shows a picket fence around the house, which also appears in Davis's sketch. In 2016 the author conducted a metal detector survey of the area of the Powell house just south of where the railroad now crosses Clairmont Road. On the point where the land rises above Clairmont Road, and very close to the road, I located numerous square-cut nails and pieces of 19th century ceramics. This would seem to indicate that the Powell house was close to Clairmont Road. Because of his knowledge of the Atlanta Campaign, Theodore Davis later helped with the creation of the Atlanta Cyclorama. [New Georgia Encyclopedia, http://www.georgiaencyclopedia.org/articles/history-archaeology/cyclorama, accessed October 15, 2017.] Davis was apparently in Decatur at the time of the Battle of Decatur, as he provided details about the battle in a June 13, 1886, story in the St. Paul Daily Globe about the painting of the Atlanta Cyclorama. [Atlanta's Big Fight,

St. Paul Daily Globe, June 13, 1886, Page 10, accessed through the Library of Congress, Chronicling America.]

32. was Surgeon J.T. Stewart : Report of Lt. Col. M.W. Manning, Official Records, Vol. 38, Part 3, Page 494.

33. parked in Decatur : Official Records, Series 1, Volume 38, Part 5, Page 209, W.T. Sherman to General Garrard, July 20, 1864.

34. "until the return of the cavalry" : Official Records, Major General James B. McPherson to Major General G.M. Dodge, July 21, 1864, Series 1, Volume 38, Part 5, page 220.

35. leading south and east of town : Official Records, Series 1, Volume 38, Part 3, Report 557 of Brig. Gen. John W. Sprague, September 3, 1864, Page 506.

36. to guard the town : Report of Lieutenant Colonel J.M. Rusk, September 8, 1864, Official Records, Series 1, Volume 38, Part 3, Page 524.

37. south toward the railroad : Official Records, Series 1, Volume 52, Part 1, Page 108, Report of Lieut. Trumbull D. Griffin, Chicago Board of Trade Battery, of operations July 22.

38. "having been captured by said cavalry" : E.B. Quiner Scrapbooks: Correspondence of the Wisconsin Volunteers, 1861-1865, Volume 10. 25th Infantry, Number 320, Wisconsin Historical Society.

39. and retook the breastworks : Report of Major General Joseph Wheeler, October 9, 1864, Official Records, Series 1, Volume 38, Part 3, Page 952.

40. has been lost : An Uncompromising Secessionist: The Civil War of George Knox Miller, Eighth (Wade's) Confederate Cavalry, edited by Richard M. Mcmurry, The University of Alabama Press, 2007, Page 241.

41. "a great deal better than I expected" : In the Saddle: Exploits of the 5ᵗʰ Georgia Cavalry During the Civil War, by Timothy Daiss, Schiffer Publishing Ltd., 1999, Page 110.

42. "as soon thereafter as possible" : Official Records, Series 1, Volume 38, Part 3, Page 631, report of General J.B. Hood.

43. "to strike the enemy in flank" : Official Records, Series 1, Volume 38, Part 3, Page 699, Report of Lt. Gen. W.J. Hardee, April 5, 1865.

44. Hood refused : Decision In The West: The Atlanta Campaign of 1864, by Albert Castel, University Press of Kansas, 1992, Page 394.

Notes to Chapter 6: The Battle of Decatur

1. by approximately 1,000 soldiers : The Official Records do not report the exact number of soldiers present in the regiments on July 22. A September 3, 1864, report by Colonel Sprague gives the regiments' strengths on May 3 at the beginning of the Atlanta Campaign as an aggregate of 1,744. By the time of Atlanta's surrender on September 3 the aggregate had fallen to 909. Official Records, Series 1, Volume 38, Part 3, Page 509.

2. from that direction : Official Records, Series 1, Vol. 38, Part 1. Report of General William T. Sherman, Pages 72.

3. "a matter of time" : Life in Dixie During the War, by Mary A.H. Gay, Mercer University Press, 2001, Page 137. In "Life in Dixie During

The War," Mary Gay contends the Federals at her home were completely surprised by the sudden arrival of the Confederates. "Garrard and his staff officers were in our parlor – their parlor pro tem. – holding a council; the teamsters and army followers were lounging about promiscuously, cursing and swearing and playing cards, and seeming not to notice the approaching artillery until their attention was called to it, and then they contended that it was their men firing off blank cartridges. I intuitively felt that a conflict was on hand... 'Impossible,'" one of the Federals said, "and yet, with a bound he was in the yard, followed in quick succession by each member of the conclave. A signal, long, loud, and shrill, awakened the drowsy, and scattered to the four winds of heaven cards, books and papers; and, in a few minutes, horses and mules were hitched to wagons, and the mules, wagons and men were fairly flying from the approach of the Confederates. Women and children came pouring in from every direction, and the house was soon filled. Before Garrard's wagon train was three hundred yards away, our yard was full of our men – our own dear 'Johnnie Rebs.'" Gay's account is clearly intended to make the Federals look stupid and incompetent, and is clearly fiction, as Garrard and his staff were not even in Decatur, but away on the raid to Covington. All accounts make it indisputable that the Confederates did not reach the northern edge of the town where Gay's home was until after two hours or more of intense fighting.

4. "We were not, however, alarmed" : Cincinnati Daily Commercial, Vol. XXV, No. 21, August 2, 1864, Column 4, "Left Wing 16th Army Corps, Colonel Sprague's Brigade, Near Atlanta, Ga, July 23, 1864"

5. would later recall : Newark Daily Advertiser, August 16, 1864, "Correspondence of the Newark Daily Advertiser from the 35th Regiment," accessed through GeneaologyBank.com.

6. get nearer and nearer : "Who Saved the Trains at Decatur?", The National Tribune, July 19, 1883, Page 7, Library of Congress.

7. "or suffer by neglect" : John A. Nourse Papers, Detailed history of the Chicago Board of Trade Battery, 1862-1865, written in diary form, Chicago History Museum, Research Center, Page 91.

8. south of town : Report of Lieut. Col. J.M. Rusk, Sept. 8, 1864, Official Records, Series 1, Volume 38, Part 3, Page 524.

9. "I ordered the section limbered" : Official Records, Series 1, Volume 38, Part 3, No. 569, Report of Lieut. Henry Shier, July 26, 1864, Page 536.

10. how the battle began : Report of Brig. Gen. John W. Sprague, No. 557, Sept. 3, 1864. Official Records, Series 1, Vol. 38, Part III, Page 504.

11. old Fayetteville Road : After the Federals has occupied Decatur on July 19, on the morning of July 20 they moved west toward Atlanta in "two columns", the 15th and 16th Corps on the "direct road," that is today's DeKalb Avenue along the railroad, and the 17th Corps on a road south of the railroad. Official Records, Series 1, Volume 38, Part 3, Page 38.

12. four companies of the 63rd : Official Records, Series 1, Volume 38, Part 3, Report No. 562, Lt. Col. J.M. Rusk, Page 521.

13. "quiet until noon" : Wisconsin Historical Society, E.B. Quiner Scrapbooks: Correspondence of the Wisconsin Volunteers, 1861-1865, Volume 10, 25th Infantry, Number 320, "From the 25th Wisconsin, In The Field Near Atlanta, Ga, July 25th, 1864".

14. "to the left of our camp" : Official Records, Series 1, Volume 52, Part 1, Page 108, Report of Lieut. Trumbull D. Griffin, Chicago Board of Trade Battery, of operations July 22.

15. "a division of Wheeler's cavalry" : "Who Saved the Trains at Decatur?", Library of Congress, The National Tribune, Vol. II, No. 49, July 19, 1883, Page 7, Column 2.

16. "all around us" : John A. Nourse Papers, Detailed history of the Chicago Board of Trade Battery, 1862-1865, written in diary form, Chicago History Museum, Research Center, Page 91.

17. "it reached the railroad" : Official Records, Series 1, Volume 38, Part 3, Page 516, Report No. 561, Reports of Maj. John W. Fouts, Sixty-third Ohio Infantry, July 26, 1864.

18. "known to be fearless" : George Stoneman: A Biography of the Union General, by Ben Fuller Fordney, McFarland & Company Inc., Publishers, 2008, Page 90.

19. "occupied the town" : Official Records, Series 1, Volume 38, Part 3, Page 952, Report of Major General Joseph Wheeler, October 9, 1864.

20. "patented multidirectional assaults" : A Soldier to the Last: Maj. Gen. Joseph Wheeler in Blue and Gray, by Edward G. Longacre, Potomac Books Inc., 2007, Page 163.

21. "the entire line of works was carried" : Editor's note: The erroneous statement by Wheeler that the Federals were entrenched when he attacked Decatur has unfortunately made its way into published accounts of the battle, such as Edward G. Longacre's "A Soldier

to the Last". [A Soldier to the Last: Maj. Gen. Joseph Wheeler in Blue and Gray, by Edward G. Longacre, Potomac Books Inc., 2007, Page 162.] The Federals did entrench at Decatur a month and a half after the battle, following the capture of Atlanta when the 23rd Army Corps camped in the town in September 1864. In his 2003 pamphlet about the Battle of Decatur, Albert Rauber addresses the question of entrenchments and makes a plausible case that Wheeler was probably describing the sunken cuts in the railroad bed as it passes near Agnes Scott College. "These cuts could have served as impromptu quasi-trenches for the Union troops and may have been what Gen. Wheeler refers to... These pre-existing railroad cuts may be the basis for the legend that the Yankees fought from 'hastily dug entrenchments.' Unexpected strength in the center of the out-numbered Union line was an important factor in Gen. Wheeler's decision to direct his main thrust at the Union right." [The Battle of Decatur, by Albert Rauber, pamphlet published by the DeKalb Historical Society, June 7, 2003, Page 21.] Rauber also addresses a Civil War-era sketch appearing to show Federal soldiers entrenched a short distance from the courthouse. The sketch was later pub-lished in Battles and Leaders of the Civil War [The Struggle for Atlanta, by Oliver O. Howard, Battles and Leaders of the Civil War, The Century Co., 1884, 1888, Volume 4, Page 314], as well as in the June 3, 1909, edition of The National Tribune newspaper. In a short note in his pamphlet, Rauber addresses the sketch and states that the view is from the southeast corner of the square. "It was prob-ably drawn during the September rest period," Rauber says. Maps of Decatur contained in the Official Atlas of the Civil War show the Federal trenches dug after the battle. None of the maps show any trenches near the courthouse.

22. "both on my right and left" : Official Records, Series 1, Volume 38, Part 3, Page 506, No. 557, Report of Brig. Gen. John W. Sprague, September 3, 1864.

23. "the enemy's plan of action" : Official Records, Series 1, Volume 38, Part 1, Page 73, Report of Major-General W. T. Sherman, September 15, 1864.

24. "surrounded and captured by the enemy" : Official Records, Series 1, Volume 38, Part 3, Page 506, Report No. 557 by Brig. Gen. John W. Sprague.

25. along the railroad : Official Records, Series 1, Volume 38 Part 3, Page 521, Report of Lieutenant-Colonel J.M. Rusk, July 26, 1864.

26. "shot from under him" : The Military History of Wisconsin, by E.B. Quiner, Clarke & Co., Chicago, 1866, Pages 740-741.

27. Rusk's escape uninjured was miraculous : Twenty two years after the Battle of Decatur, in an 1886 story in the St. Paul Globe newspaper ("Atlanta's Big Fight," St. Paul Daily Globe, June 13, 1886, Page 10, Column 4, accessed through the Library of Congress, Chronicling America), sketch artist Theodore R. Davis, who had accompanied Sherman's left wing and who was apparently in Decatur at the time of the battle on July 22, recalled Rusk's role in the fight. Davis was being interviewed because of his involvement in the painting of the Atlanta Cyclorama. The article says, "Gen. Wheeler, with his entire cavalry corps, accompanied Gen. Hardee, and before noon on the 22d, attacked Decatur, which was held by Sprague's brigade of three regiments, the Twenty-fifth Wisconsin, Thirty-fifth New Jersey and Sixty-third Ohio, where a battle ensued, which for unequal numbers and bitterness, was and is one of the notable conflicts of the war. Had this little brigade suffered defeat, Sherman's army would have lost almost its entire transportation. Mr. Davis, in speaking of this, says that to the gallantry of Gov. Rusk, then lieutenant-colonel of the Twenty-fifth Wisconsin, is largely due the beating off of this attack. The governor's horse had too many bullets in him for further

usefulness. His saddle was ruined by bullets, the scabbard of his sword was bent, and he was the last mounted officer in that fight."

28. "would surely be our doom if captured" : E.B. Quiner Scrapbooks: Correspondence of the Wisconsin Volunteers, 1861-1865, Volume 10, 25th Infantry, Number 320, Wisconsin Historical Society.

29. "the superior numbers of the enemy" : Official Records, Series 1, Volume 38, Part 3, Page 506, Report No. 557 of Brig. Gen. John W. Sprague.

30. "was immediately taken advantage of by them" : Official Records, Series 1, Volume 38, Part 3, Page 511, Report No. 558, Colonel John J. Cladek, July 26, 1864.

31. "nearly all captured" : Official Records, Series 1, Volume 38, Part 3, page 511, No. 559, Report of Lieut. Col. William A. Henry, September 9, 1864.

32. "had my hat in his hand" : Samuel Wragg Ferguson Papers, Mss. 1416, 1576, Louisiana and Lower Mississippi Valley Collections, LSU Libraries, Baton Rouge, La., Part 5, Page 1.

33. "to cause them to fall back" : Official Records, Series 1, Volume 38, Part 3, Page 516, Report No. 561 of Major John W. Fouts, Sixty-third Ohio Infantry.

34. "and was captured": Official Records, Series 1, Volume 38, Part 3, Report No. 562 of Lieutenant-Colonel J.M. Rusk, July 26, 1864, Page 521.

35. "the courage of a lion" : Cincinnati Daily Commercial, Vol. XXV, No. 21, August 2, 1864, Page 1, Column 5, "Left Wing 16th Army Corps, Colonel Sprague's Brigade, Near Atlanta, Ga, July 23, 1864.

36. "a new line was formed at the jail" : Cincinnati Daily Commercial, Vol. XXV, No. 21, August 2, 1864, Column 5, Left Wing 16th Army Corps, Colonel Sprague's Brigade Near Atlanta, Ga, July 23, 1864.

37. "ready for retreat or advance" : John A. Nourse Papers, Detailed history of the Chicago Board of Trade Battery, 1862-1865, written in diary form, Chicago History Museum, Research Center, Page 91.

38. fired 59 rounds during the battle : Official Records, Series 1, Volume 38, Part 3, Page 536, Report No. 569 of Lieut. Henry Shier, July 26, 1864.

39. "not more than three wagons were lost" : Cincinnati Daily Commercial, Vol. XXV, No. 21, August 2, 1864, Column 5, Left Wing 16th Army Corps, Colonel Sprague's Brigade Near Atlanta, Ga, July 23, 1864.

40. "no stop for any obstruction" : John A. Nourse Papers, Detailed History of the Chicago Board of Trade Battery, 1862-1865, written in diary form, Chicago History Museum, Research Center, Page 92.

41. and would shortly die : "Isaiah R. Rose," by Betty K. Rose, in Reflections Along The Muskingum, Lower Muskingum Historical Society, Waterford, Ohio, Volume 36, No. 3, July-August-September 2010, Page 7.

42. "cautiously into town" : Official Records, Series 1, Volume 38, Part 3, Page 510, Report of John J. Cladek, 35th New Jersey, July 26, 1864.

43. "taken house by house" : Samuel Wragg Ferguson Papers, Mss. 1416, 1576, Louisiana and Lower Mississippi Valley Collections, LSU Libraries, Baton Rouge, La., Part 5, Page 1.

44. "the enemy pay dearly" : Official Records, Series 1, Volume 38, Part 3, Page 510, Report of John J. Cladek, 35th New Jersey, July 26, 1864.

45. "from the front" : Cincinnati Daily Commercial, Vol. XXV, No. 21, August 2, 1864, "Sherman's Army", column 5, accessed through Genealogybank.com.

46. "should fall into rebel hands" : Official Records, Series 1, Volume 38, Part 3, Page 517, Report 561.

47. best for the guns to retreat : Official Records, Series 1, Volume 52, Part 1, Page 108, Report of Lieut. Trumbull D. Griffin, Chicago Board of Trade Battery, of operations July 22.

48. "from Colonel Sprague's brigade" : Cincinnati Daily Commercial, Vol. XXV, No. 21, August 2, 1864, Column 5, Left Wing 16th Army Corps, Colonel Sprague's Brigade Near Atlanta, July 23, 1864.

49. "the balance of the brigade" : Official Records, Series 1, Volume 38, Part 3, Pages 516-517, Report No. 561 of Major John W. Fouts, 63rd Ohio.

50. "how sad and savage a thing war is" : Cincinnati Daily Commercial, Vol. XXV, No. 21, August 2, 1864, Column 5, "Sherman's Army."

51. "could not be conquered" : Sprague recounted this story almost 30 years later in an account of the Battle of Decatur that he wrote from Tacoma in September 1892 for a reunion of the 63rd in Dayton, Ohio. See the Oregonian [Portland, Oregon], December 26, 1893. "Still another gone: Death of General J.W. Sprague"

52. "he entirely satisfied their curiosity" : History of the 72nd Indiana Volunteer Infantry of the Mounted Lightning Brigade, written and

compiled by B.F. McGee and edited by Wm. R. Jewell, S. Vater & Co., 1882, Page 350-352. The 72nd Indiana's regimental history goes on to note that, "We have more than once had occasion to speak of the distrust with which Gen. Sherman treated our division; but the fight at Decatur fully demonstrated that he thought we were of some account after all."

53. "enlisted for the war?" : Life in Dixie During the War, by Mary A.H. Gay, Mercer University Press, 2001, Pages 138-139.

54. as it retreated north : John A. Nourse Papers, Detailed History of the Chicago Board of Trade Battery, 1862-1865, written in diary form, Chicago History Museum, Research Center, Page 92.

55. "on the Roswell road" : Official Records, Series 1, Volume 38, Part 3, Page 506, Report No. 557 by Brig. Gen. John W. Sprague.

56. "driven out of the town" : Official Records, Series 1, Volume 38, Part 3, Page 519, Report of Major J.W. Fouts, Sept. 5, 1864.

57. almost 30 years later in 1892 : Oregonian (Portland, Oregon), December 26, 1893,. "Still another gone: Death of General J.W. Sprague".

58. northward out of Decatur : Official Records, Series 1, Volume 38, Part 3, Page 513, Report of Col. Wager Swayne, No. 560.

59. "in sight of the town" : Official Records, Series 1, Volume 38, Part 3, Page 507, Report of Colonel J.W. Sprague.

60. "attempts to strike our rear" : Official Records, Series 1, Volume 38, Part 2, Page 516, Report of Major Gen. John M. Schofield.

61. by Wheeler's troops : Official Records, Series 1, Volume 38, Part 2, Report of Brigadier-General J.W. Reilly, First Brigade, 23rd Army Corps, Sept. 10, 1864, Page 705.

62. "to General Hardee's position" : Official Records, Series 1, Volume 38, Part 3, Page 953, Report of Major General Joseph Wheeler, October 9, 1864.

63. his girlfriend back home : Well Mary: Civil War letters of a Wisconsin volunteer, edited by Margaret Brobst Roth, The University of Wisconsin Press, 1960, Page 83.

64. "all but his underclothes" : Cincinnati Daily Commercial, Vol. XXV, No. 21, August 2, 1864, "Left Wing 16th Army Corps", Column 5, accessed through Genealogybank.com.

65. "and may have died" : Confederate Veteran magazine, Vol. 1, No. 4, April 1893, page 118.

66. "about one hundred and fifty" : My Dear Nellie: The Civil War Letters of William L. Nugent to Eleanor Smith Nugent, edited by William M. Cash and Lucy Somerville Howorth, University Press of Mississippi, 1977, Pages 189-190.

67. "it was too much shaken up" : In the Saddle: Exploits of the 5th Georgia Cavalry During the Civil War, by Timothy Daiss, Schiffer Publishing Ltd., 1999, Page 109. The historian weeps that Chester did not leave a longer account.

68. "during that time" : A Georgia Farm Boy in Wheeler's Cavalry, Civil War Times Illustrated, Volume VII, Number 7, November 1968, Page 40.

69. "joined in the rejoicing" : Life in Dixie During The War, by Mary A.H. Gay, Mercer University Press, 2000, Page 140.

70. "by the soldiers and citizens" : Wisconsin Historical Society, E.B. Quiner Scrapbooks: Correspondence of the Wisconsin Volunteers, 1861-1865, Volume 10, 25th Infantry, Number 320.

71. "would probably be for their injury" : Cincinnati Daily Commercial, Vol. XXV, No. 21, August 2, 1864, "Left Wing 16th Army Corps", Column 5, accessed through Genealogybank.com.

72. "used with effect upon the enemy" : Official Records, Series 1, Volume 38, Part 3, Page 507, Report No. 557 of Brig. Gen. John W. Sprague, September 3, 1864.

73. and First Lieut. William W. Hyzer : Official Records, Series 1, Volume 38, Part 3, No. 569, Page 537, Report of Lieut. Henry Shier, July 26, 1864.

74. "they cherish his memory" : Cincinnati Daily Commercial, Vol. XXV, No. 21, August 2, 1864, "Left Wing 16th Army Corps", Column 5, accessed through Genealogybank.com.

75. "and caught him" : The Battle of Decatur, July 22, 1864, DeKalb Historical Society, June 7, 2003, Page 17.

76. "his cool judgment and excellent dispositions" : Official Records, Series 1, Volume 38, Part 3, Page 371, report of G.M. Dodge, August 11, 1864.

77. "and defeated Wheeler's Cavalry" : The Battle of Atlanta by Grenville M. Dodge, A Paper Read Before The New York Commandery, Page 39.

78. "on July 30, 1864." : "The Fight For The Wagons," by David Evans, Civil War Times, February 1988, Volume XXVI, Number 10, Pages 21-22. For another account of the Battle of Decatur, see also Evans' "Sherman's Horsemen" Union Cavalry Operations in the Atlanta Campaign, Indiana University Press, 1996, Page 91.

Notes to Chapter 7: Aftermath, Part 1

1. "my war-stricken home" : Life in Dixie During the War, by Mary A.H. Gay, Mercer University Press, 2001, Page 150-152.

2. they stopped and entrenched. : Official Records, Series 1, Volume 38, Part 3, Page 524, Report of Lieutenant Colonel J.M. Rusk.

3. "towards the main army two miles" : Wisconsin Historical Society, E.B. Quiner Scrapbooks: Correspondence of the Wisconsin Volunteers, 1861-1865, Volume 10, 25th Infantry, Number 320.

4. 242 killed, wounded and missing : Official Records, Series 1, Vol. 38, Part III, Page 504, Report of Brig. Gen. John W. Sprague, No. 557, Sept. 3, 1864.

5. a total loss to the 63rd of 91. : Official Records, Series 1, Volume 38, Part 3, Page 519, Report of Major J.W. Fouts, September 5, 1864.

6. one was taken prisoner : Wisconsin Historical Society, Report of Lt. Col. J.M. Rusk, Quiner Scrapbooks: Correspondence of the Wisconsin Volunteers, 1861-1865, Volume 10, Page 334.

7. and 37 men missing : Official Records, Series 1, Volume 38, Part 3, Page 511Report of Lieut. Col. William A. Henry, No. 559, Sept. 9, 1864.

8. "were obliged to fall back" : Official Records, Series 1, Volume 52, Part 1, Page 109, Report of Lieut. Trumbull D. Griffin, Chicago Board of Trade Battery, of operations July 22.

9. "I doubt it." : John A. Nourse Papers, Detailed History of the Chicago Board of Trade Battery, 1862-1865, written in diary form, Chicago History Museum, Research Center, Page 92-93.

10. a reduction of 48 percent : Official Records, Series 1, Vol. 38, Part III, Page 509, Report of Brig. Gen. John W. Sprague, No. 557, Sept. 3, 1864.

11. in a field hospital on August 3 : For a listing of the soldiers of the 63rd Ohio see Official Roster of the Soldiers Of The State of Ohio In The War Of The Rebellion, 1861-1866, Volume 5, The Werner PTG. & MFG. Co., Akron, O., Page 381. See also "List of Killed, Wounded and Missing in the 2d Brigade, Colonel John W. Sprague's 4th Division, 16th Army Corps, at Decatur, Georgia, Friday, July 22, 1864" in the Cincinnati Daily Commercial, Vol. XXV, No. 21, August 2, 1864, Column 5, accessed on GenealogyBank.com. Also see Meigs County Ohio and Her Soldiers In The Civil War, by Lois Helmers, iUniverse Inc., 2009, Page 105.

12. list from the 63rd Ohio : Cincinnati Daily Commercial, Vol. XXV, No. 21, August 2, 1864, Column 5, "List of Killed, Wounded and Missing in the 2d Brigade, Colonel John W. Sprague's, 4th Division, 16th Army Corps, at Decatur, Georgia, Friday, July 22, 1864."

13. "the enemy received a greater loss" : Official Records, Series 1, Volume 38, Part 3, Report No. 562, Page 524.

14. in his official reports : Official Records, Series 1, Volume 38, Part 3, Report No. 562, Page 521.

15. a total of 100 casualties : Wisconsin Historical Society, Report of Lt. Col. J.M. Rusk, Quiner Scrapbooks: Correspondence of the Wisconsin Volunteers, 1861-1865, Volume 10, Page 334.

16. 15 were killed outright : Wisconsin Historical Society, Quiner Scrapbooks: Correspondence of the Wisconsin Volunteers, 1861-1865, Volume 10, 25th Infantry, Page 321.

17. 44 wounded and 25 missing : Wisconsin Historical Society, E.B. Quiner's Military History of Wisconsin, Chicago, 1866, 25th Infantry, Chapter 33, Page 741.

18. would amputate his right arm. : Roster of Wisconsin Volunteers, Page 281, https://archive.org/stream/rosterofwisconsi02wisco#page/281/mode/1up] ; Baird Holm's First Century, by Michael G. Lessman, Baird Holm LLP, November 2007, Page 9.

19. reported his capture to the Federals : Wisconsin Historical Society, Report of Lt. Col. J.M. Rusk, Quiner Scrapbooks: Correspondence of the Wisconsin Volunteers, 1861-1865, Volume 10, Pages 333.

20. the 25th Wisconsin's other casualties included : This list of the 25th Wisconsin's casualties at the Battle of Decatur was compiled from the following sources: Roster of Wisconsin Volunteers, War of The Rebellion, 1861-1865, Volume 2, Madison, Wisconsin, Democrat Printing Company, State Printers, 1886, Page 282 ; The Military History of Wisconsin, E.B. Quiner, Clarke & Co., Chicago, 1866, Page 741; Wisconsin Losses in the Civil War, Charles E. Estabrook, (Madison, Wis.: Adjutant General's Dept.?, 1915). Online facsimile at http://www.wisconsinhistory.org/turningpoints/search.asp?id=1697), Wisconsin Historical Society; Report of Lt. Col. J.M. Rusk to Wisconsin Governor James T. Lewis, Quiner Scrapbooks: Correspondence of the Wisconsin

Volunteers, 1861-1865, Volume 10, Pages 333-334, Wisconsin Historical Society.

21. "with grape and cannister" : A Badger Boy in Blue: The Civil War Letters of Chauncey H. Cooke, Wayne State University Press, Detroit, 2007, Page 112.

22. and 37 men missing (captured.) : Official Records, Series 1, Volume 38, Part 3, Report No. 559 of Lieut. Col. William A. Henry, Page 512.

23. two companies became prisoners : Official Records, Series 1, Volume 38, Part 3, Page 511, Report of Colonel John J. Cladek.

24. August Phillipe, Company C, wounded : Record of Officers and Men of New Jersey in the Civil War, 1861-1865, Volume 2, John L. Murphy, Steam Book And Job Printer, 1876, Pages 1054, 1062, 1065, 1067, 1091.

25. eight men were wounded : Official Records, Series 1, Volume 52, Part 1, Page 110, Report of Lieut. Trumbull D. Griffin, Chicago Board of Trade Battery, of operations July 22; Historical Sketch of the Chicago Board of Trade Battery, Horse Artillery, Illinois Volunteers, Chicago, 1902, Pages 67-80; Diary of John A. Nourse, Chicago History Museum Research Center, Page 93.

26. "Good boys all" : John A. Nourse Papers, Detailed History of the Chicago Board of Trade Battery, 1862-1865, written in diary form, Chicago History Museum, Research Center, Page 95. Editor's note: With the end of the war, in 1865 the bodies of members of The Chicago Board of Trade Battery who had been killed in the war were recovered and returned to Chicago where, on January 7, 1866, they were reinterred in a solemn funeral ceremony at Rosehill Cemetery,

the city's largest cemetery. The Chicago Republican, January 6, 1866, "Interment of the Bodies of Members of the Chicago Battery Companies", Page 2, Column 4, accessed on Genealogybank.com on November 9, 2017.

27. "less than a hundred killed and wounded" : Campaigns of Wheeler and His Cavalry, 1862-1865, edited by W.C. Dodson, Hudgins Publishing Company, Atlanta, Georgia, 1899, Page 211.

28. "about seventy killed and wounded" : My Dear Nellie: The Civil War Letters of William L. Nugent to Eleanor Smith Nugent, edited by William M. Cash and Lucy Somerville Howorth, University Press of Mississippi, 1977, Page 190.

29. losses to be 150 casualties : Decision In The West: The Atlanta Campaign of 1864, University Press of Kansas, Page 412.

30. The list includes : Campaigns of Wheeler and His Cavalry, 1862-1865, edited by W.C. Dodson, Hudgins Publishing Company, Atlanta, Georgia, 1899, Page 371

31. northwest of the town : History of the 72nd Indiana Volunteer Infantry of the Mounted Lightning Brigade, written and compiled by B.F. McGee and edited by Wm. R. Jewell, S. Vater & Co., 1882, Page 350.

32. "promoted to brigadier general" : Official Records, Series 1, Volume 38, Part 3, Page 385; "Still another gone: Death of General J.W. Sprague," Oregonian, December 26, 1893.

33. "seemingly almost hopeless one" : The Battle of Atlanta, by Major General Grenville M. Dodge, in a paper read before the New York Commandery, Page 39.

34. details of the fight and casualty lists : Cincinnati Daily Commercial, Vol. XXV, No. 19, July 30, 1864, accessed through Genealogybank. com.

35. wading the Chattahoochee on July 10 : Frank Leslie's Illustrated Newspaper, No. 463, Vol. XVIII, August 13, 1864, Page 332, accessed through Archive.org.

36. Sherman's headquarters on July 19 : Harper's Weekly, Vol. VIII, No. 400, August 27, 1864, Page 557, accessed through Archive.org.

37. hung for war crimes in November 1865 : National Park Service, https://www.nps.gov/ande/learn/historyculture/camp_sumter_ history.htm_For some details about the fate of those from the 63rd Ohio who were captured at Decatur and sent to Andersonville, see Official Roster of the Soldiers of the State of Ohio In The War of the Rebellion, 1861-1866, Volume 5, Akron, Ohio, The Werner Ptg. And Mfg. Co., 1887, beginning on Page 383. See also Meigs County Ohio and Her Soldiers In The Civil War, by Lois Helmers, iUniverse, 2009.

38. "without a challenge" : "Isaiah R. Rose," by Betty K. Rose, in Reflections Along The Muskingum, Lower Muskingum Historical Society, Waterford, Ohio, Volume 36, No. 3, July-August-September 2010, Page 7.

39. "My health is good" : Newark Daily Advertiser, August 27, 1864, Page 2, Column 4, "Capt. Dusenberry at Charleston"

40. taken from the Reading Eagle newspaper of July 30, 1907: "87th PA officer escaped from prison after being captured at 2nd Winchester": Part 2, Cannonball, by Scott Mingus, York Daily Record, June 18, 2016, used with permission of the author.

41. a later biography notes : The New Jersey Coast In Three Centuries, William Nelson, Editor, Vol. III, The Lewis Publishing Company, 1902, Page 107, 108.

42. in The New York Times on January 17 : http://www.nytimes. com/1865/01/17/news/escaped-correspondents-safe-arrival-nash-ville-messrs-richardson-brown-tribune.html

43. medical care and food : Baird Holm's First Century, by Michael G. Lessmann, November 2007, Page 9. Manuscript provided to the author by Baird Holm LLP.

44. "into whose power he fell" : Claim For Minors Pension and Claim of Guardian of Orphan Children for Pension, Hamilton County, Ohio, May 8, 1868, accessed on Fold3.com on November 23, 2017.; The History of Fuller's Ohio Brigade, 1861-1865: Its Great March, with Roster, Portraits, Battle Maps and Biographies, by Charles H. Smith, Press of A.J. Watt, Cleveland, Ohio, 1909, Page 363; Widow's Claim for Pension, December 27, 1866, State of Ohio, Montgomery County, accessed on Fold3.com on November 23, 2017.

45. "in the hot sun and burn" : Well Mary: Civil War letters of a Wisconsin volunteer, edited by Margaret Brobst Roth, The University of Wisconsin Press, 1960, Page 91.

46. were being routinely ignored : Sultana, by Alan Huffman, Harper, 2009, Page 180.

47. "perishing with them" : Loss Of The Sultana And Reminiscences Of Survivors, by Rev. Chester D. Berry, Darius D. Thorpe Printer And Binder, Lansing, Mich., 1892, Pages 7-9.

48. 1,800 died on the Sultana : The Sultana Tragedy: America's Greatest Maritime Disaster, by Jerry O. Potter, Pelican Publishing Company, 1992, preface.

49. on the Sultana : Loss Of The Sultana And Reminiscences Of Survivors, by Rev. Chester D. Berry, Darius D. Thorpe Printer And Binder, Lansing, Mich., 1892, Page 42.

50. when the Sultana blew up : Official Roster of the Soldiers of the State of Ohio In The War of the Rebellion, 1861-1866, Volume 5, Akron, Ohio, The Werner Ptg. And Mfg. Co., 1887, Pages 404, 407; Loss Of The Sultana And Reminiscences Of Survivors, by Rev. Chester D. Berry, Darius D. Thorpe Printer And Binder, Lansing, Mich., 1892, Page 400.

Notes to Chapter 8: Young, Lovely, Brave and True: The Life and Death of Howard Forrer

1. Sarah Forrer's diary, [2 Sept. 1862], quoted in Frances I. Parrott, "Sons and Mothers," [undated], Forrer-Peirce-Wood Collection (hereafter cited as FPW), 32:4, Dayton Metro Library, Dayton, Ohio. The FPW Collection does not include Sarah's diary, although her granddaughter Frances Parrott quotes it frequently in the aforementioned article "Sons and Mothers."

2. Forrer Genealogical Data, FPW, 7:12.

3. Howard Forrer: Invitations, Calling Cards, etc., FPW, 6:10.

4. History of Dayton, Ohio (Dayton, OH: United Brethren Publishing House, 1889), 292-294.

5. Samuel Forrer to Mary Forrer, 24 Aug. 1862, FPW, 1:10.

6. Douglas Harper, "Northern Draft of 1862," in *Online Etymology Dictionary*, https://www.etymonline.com/columns/post/draft, accessed 20 Nov. 2017.

7. *History of Dayton, Ohio*, 295.

8. *History of Dayton, Ohio*, 298-299; recruitment ad for the 1st Ohio Volunteer Infantry, *Dayton Journal*, 23 Oct. 1862.

9. Sarah Forrer to Mary Forrer, 24 Aug. 1862, FPW, 4:5.

10. Luther Bruen to Samuel Forrer, 27 Aug. 1862, FPW, 33:10.

11. Sarah Forrer to Mary Forrer, 2 Sept. 1862, FPW, 4:5.

12. Sarah Forrer to Mary Forrer, 3 Sept. 1862, Forrer-Peirce-Wood Collection (hereafter cited as FPW), 4:5, Dayton Metro Library, Dayton, Ohio.

13. *History of Dayton, Ohio* (Dayton, OH: United Brethren Publishing House, 1889), 296; David E. Roth, "Squirrel Hunters to the Rescue," *Blue and Gray Magazine* 3, no 5 (Apr./May 1986), http://www.cincinnaticwrt.org/data/ohio%20in%20the%20war/1862%20Defense%20of%20Cincinnati/iii_squirrel.pdf.

14. *History of Dayton, Ohio*, 296.

15. David Tod, 2 Sept. 1862, quoted in Roth.

16. H. Eugene Parrott's diary, 2 Sept. 1862, FPW, 31:1.

17. Sarah Forrer's diary, [2 Sept. 1862], quoted in Frances I. Parrott, "Sons and Mothers," [undated], FPW, 32:4.

18. Sarah Forrer to Mary Forrer, 3 Sept. 1862, FPW, 4:5.

19. Sarah Forrer's diary, [3 Sept. 1862], quoted in F. I. Parrott, FPW, 32:4.

20. H. Eugene Parrott's diary, 3 Sept. 1862, FPW, 31:1.

21. *History of Dayton, Ohio*, 297.

22. Sarah Forrer's diary, 5 Sept. 1862, quoted in F. I. Parrott, FPW, 32:4.

23. Sarah Forrer to Mary Forrer and Augusta Bruen, 7 Sept. 1862, FPW, 4:5.

24. Sarah Forrer to Mary Forrer and Augusta Bruen, 7 Sept. 1862, FPW, 4:5.

25. H. Eugene Parrott's diary, 4 Sept. 1862, FPW, 31:1.

26. Sarah Forrer's diary, 5 Sept. 1862, quoted in F. I. Parrott, FPW, 32:4.

27. Sarah Forrer to Mary Forrer and Augusta Bruen, 7 Sept. 1862, FPW, 4:5.

28. Sarah Forrer's diary, 7 Sept. 1862, quoted in F. I. Parrott, FPW, 32:4.

29. Sarah Forrer's diary, [?] Sept. 1862, quoted in F. I. Parrott, FPW, 32:4.

30. H. Eugene Parrott's diary, 5 Sept. 1862, FPW, 31:1.

31. H. Eugene Parrott's diary, 5 Sept. 1862, FPW, 31:1.

32. H. Eugene Parrott's diary, 6 Sept. 1862, FPW, 31:1.

33. H. Eugene Parrott's diary, 7 Sept. 1862, FPW, 31:1.

34. H. Eugene Parrott's diary, 8 Sept. 1862, FPW, 31:1.

35. Sarah Forrer to Mary Forrer and Augusta Bruen, 10 Sept. 1862, FPW, 4:5.

36. H. Eugene Parrott's diary, 9 Sept. 1862, FPW, 31:1.

37. Roth.

38. H. Eugene Parrott's diary, 10 Sept. 1862, FPW, 31:1.

39. Sarah Forrer to Mary Forrer and Augusta Bruen, 10 Sept. 1862, FPW, 4:5.

40. H. Eugene Parrott's diary, 11 Sept. 1862, FPW, 31:1.

41. H. Eugene Parrott's diary, 12 Sept. 1862, FPW, 31:1.

42. *History of Dayton, Ohio,* 297.

43. H. Eugene Parrott's diary, 13 Sept. 1862, FPW, 31:1.

44. Howard Forrer to Elizabeth (Forrer) Peirce, 16 Sept. 1862, FPW, 6:8.

45. Sarah Forrer to Mary Forrer and Augusta Bruen, 21 Sept. 1862, FPW, 4:5.

46. Sarah Forrer to Mary Forrer, 4 Nov. 1862, Forrer-Peirce-Wood Collection (hereafter cited as FPW), 4:5, Dayton Metro Library, Dayton, Ohio.

47. Sarah Forrer's diary, 11 Nov. 1862, quoted in Frances I. Parrott, "Sons and Mothers," [undated], Forrer-Peirce-Wood Collection (hereafter cited as FPW), 32:4, Dayton Metro Library, Dayton.

48. Sarah Forrer to Mary Forrer, 24 Sept. 1862-2 Oct. 1862 [several letters], FPW, 4:5.

49. Sarah Forrer to Mary Forrer, 28 Sept. 1862-23 Oct. 1862 [several letters], FPW, 4:5.

50. Sarah Forrer to Mary Forrer, 5 Oct. 1862, FPW, 4:5.

51. Sarah Forrer to Mary Forrer, 23 Oct. 1862, FPW, 4:5.

52. Samuel Forrer to Mary Forrer, 9 Nov. 1862, FPW, 1:10.

53. Sarah Forrer's diary, 11 Nov. 1862, quoted in F. I. Parrott, FPW, 32:4.

54. Sarah Forrer's diary, [late July] 1863, quoted in F. I. Parrott, FPW, 32:4.

55. Sarah Forrer's diary, 11 Nov. 1862, quoted in F. I. Parrott, FPW, 32:4.

56. Sarah Forrer's diary, 12 Jan. 1863, quoted in F. I. Parrott, FPW, 32:4.

57. Sarah Forrer's diary, [Jan. 1863], quoted in F. I. Parrott, FPW, 32:4.

58. Howard Forrer to Henrietta Peirce, 21 Feb. 1863, FPW, 6:9.

59. Howard Forrer to Jeremiah H. Peirce, 17 Mar. 1863, FPW, 6:8.

60. Howard Forrer to Henrietta Peirce, 9 June 1863, FPW, 6:9.

61. Janet B. Hewett, ed., *Supplement to the Official Records of the Union and Confederate Armies, Part II – Records of Events*, vol. 53 (Wilmington, NC: Broadfoot Publishing Co., 1997), 277.

62. Sarah Forrer's diary, 9 Aug. 1863, quoted in F. I. Parrott, FPW, 32:4.

63. Sarah Forrer's diary, 2 Sept. 1863, quoted in F. I. Parrott, FPW, 32:4.

64. Sarah Forrer's diary, 25 Nov. 1863, quoted in F. I. Parrott, FPW, 32:4.

65. Sarah Forrer's diary, 29 Dec. 1863, quoted in F. I. Parrott, FPW, 32:4.

66. Sarah Forrer's diary, 14 Feb. 1864, quoted in F. I. Parrott, FPW, 32:4.

67. Sarah Forrer's diary, 27 Dec. 1867, quoted in F. I. Parrott, FPW, 32:4.

68. Mary Affleck to Sarah Forrer, 24-25 July 1864, Forrer-Peirce-Wood Collection (hereafter cited as FPW), 35:3, Dayton Metro Library, Dayton, Ohio.

69. Sarah Forrer's diary, 14 Feb. 1864 and 27 Dec. 1867, quoted in Frances I. Parrott, "Sons and Mothers," [undated], FPW, 32:4.

70. Howard Forrer's diary, 18 Feb.-2 Mar. 1864, FPW, 6:13; Janet B. Hewett, ed., *Supplement to the Official Records of the Union and Confederate Armies, Part II – Records of Events*, vol. 65 (Wilmington, NC: Broadfoot Publishing Co., 1997), 277.

71. Howard Forrer's diary, 18-23 Feb. 1864, FPW, 6:13.

72. Howard Forrer's diary, 24 Feb.-2 Mar. 1864, FPW, 6:13.

73. Howard Forrer's diary, 24-25 Apr. 1864, FPW, 6:13.

74. Hewett, 277.

75. Howard Forrer's diary, 17-20 May 1864, FPW, 6:13

76. Sarah Forrer to Samuel Forrer, 20 June 1864, FPW, 4:2.

77. Mary Affleck to Sarah Forrer, 24-25 July 1864, FPW, 35:3.

78. "The Army Before Atlanta: The Battle of the 22d," Cincinnati Gazette, 29 July 1864.

79. Samuel Forrer to Sarah Forrer, [after 29 July] 1864, FPW, 1:8.

80. *Official Roster of the Soldiers of the State of Ohio in the War of the Rebellion, 1861-1866*, vol. V (Akron: Werner Co., 1887), 383; "John W. Sprague," *Wikipedia*, accessed 10 Apr. 2012, http://en.wikipedia.org/wiki/John_W._Sprague; Samuel Forrer to Mary Forrer, 9 Nov. 1862, FPW, 1:10.

81. *Official Roster of the Soldiers of the State of Ohio in the War of the Rebellion, 1861-1866*, vol. V (Akron: Werner Co., 1887), 383; Samuel Forrer to Mary Forrer, 9 Nov. 1862, FPW, 1:10.

82. *Official Roster of the Soldiers of the State of Ohio in the War of the Rebellion, 1861-1866*, vol. VI (Akron: Werner Co., 1887), 478, 469; The War

of the Rebellion: A Compilation of the Official Records of the Union and Confederate Armies, Series I, Vol. 38, Part I-Reports (Washington, DC: Government Printing Office, 1891), 107.

83. Samuel Forrer to Sarah Forrer, [after 29 July] 1864, FPW, 1:8.

84. Lizzie Morton, "Lines Suggested by the Death of Ajt. Forrer – July 22, 1864," Forrer-Peirce-Wood Collection (hereafter cited as FPW), 6:12, Dayton Metro Library, Dayton. (Miss Morton allegedly witnessed the death of Howard Forrer, although it seemed later that she had him confused with one of the other soldiers who died nearby. Nevertheless, these lines ring true.)

85. Sarah Forrer's diary, 27 Dec. 1867, quoted in Frances I. Parrott, "Sons and Mothers," [undated], FPW, 32:4.

86. Quincy [war correspondent], "Beautiful Tribute," 10 Aug. 1864, *Western Christian Advocate*, in Howard Forrer: Obituaries, FPW, 6:15.

87. Benjamin St. James Fry to Samuel Forrer, [circa 22 July-1 Aug.] 1864, published in the *Dayton Journal*, 2 Aug. 1864, in Howard Forrer: Obituaries, FPW, 6:15.

88. "Battle of Atlanta," *Wikipedia*, accessed 17 Apr. 2012, http://en.wikipedia.org/wiki/Battle_of_Atlanta; "Wheeler's Cav. at Decatur," *Historical Marker Database*, accessed 17 Apr. 2012, http://www.hmdb.org/Marker.asp?Marker=8887; *The War of the Rebellion: A Compilation of the Official Records of the Union and Confederate Armies* (Washington, DC: Government Printing Office, 1891), Series I, Vol. 38, Part I-Reports, 74; *The War of the Rebellion*, Series I, Vol. 38, Part II-Reports, 854.

89. J. W. Fouts, official report, 5 Sept. 1864, in *The War of the Rebellion*, Series I, Vol. 38, Part III-Reports, 519.

90. J. W. Fouts, official report, 26 July 1864, in *The War of the Rebellion*, Series I, Vol. 38, Part III-Reports, 517.

91. Quincy [war correspondent], "Beautiful Tribute," 10 Aug. 1864, *Western Christian Advocate*, in Howard Forrer: Obituaries, FPW, 6:15.

92. Benjamin St. James Fry to Samuel Forrer, [circa 22 July-1 Aug.] 1864, published in the *Dayton Journal*, 2 Aug. 1864, in Howard Forrer: Obituaries, FPW, 6:15.

93. "Swanton House," *Historical Marker Database*, accessed 17 Apr. 2012, http://www.hmdb.org/marker.asp?marker=9364; "Benjamin Swanton House," in "Preservation," DeKalb County History Center website, accessed 17 Apr. 2012, http://www.dekalbhistory.org/dekalb_history_center_preservation_historic-complex.htm.

94. A.C. Fenner to Samuel Forrer, 11 Jan. 1865, Forrer-Pierce-Wood Collection, 6:12, Dayton Metro Library, Dayton

95. Sarah Forrer's diary, 27 Dec. 1867, quoted in Frances I. Parrott, "Sons and Mothers," [undated], FPW, 32:4.

96. Sarah Forrer to Mary Forrer, 31 Aug.-27 Sept. 1864 [several letters], FPW, 4:6; Inflation Calculator, http://www.westegg.com/inflation/.

97. Sarah Forrer to Mary Forrer, 12 Sept. 1864, FPW, 4:6.

98. Sarah Forrer to Mary Forrer, 31 Aug.-27 Sept. 1864 [several letters], FPW, 4:6.

99. A. C. Fenner to Samuel Forrer, 11 Jan. 1865, FPW, 6:12.

100. Mary Affleck to Sarah Forrer, 18 June 1865, FPW, 35:3.

101. Mary Affleck to Sarah Forrer, 18 June 1865, FPW, 35:3; Fanny Kemble, "The Hour of Northern Victory," in *The Spectator: A Weekly Review of Politics, Literature, Theology, and Art* (London: John Campbell), vol. 38 (1865), 6 May 1865, 497. The date of the original publication was May 6; the date of the poem was April 25.

102. Mary Affleck to Sarah Forrer, 18 June 1865, FPW, 35:3.

103. Maj. Gen. Thomas to Samuel Forrer, 25 Sept. 1865, FPW, 6:12.

104. Gates P. Thruston to Samuel Forrer, 13 Oct. 1865, FPW, 6:12; Will T. Hale, *A History of Tennessee and Tennesseans* (Chicago: Lewis Pub. Co., 1913), accessed 15 May 2012, http://files.usgwarchives.net/tn/davidson/bios/thruston307nbs.txt; Inflation Calculator, http://www.westegg.com/inflation/.

105. U.S. Treasury Department to Samuel Forrer, Certificate # 192284, 23 Oct. 1865, FPW, 6:12.

106. Inflation Calculator, http://www.westegg.com/inflation/.

107. Sarah Forrer's diary, 27 Dec. 1867, quoted in Frances I. Parrott, "Sons and Mothers," [undated], FPW, 32:4.

108. "The Lamented Howard Forrer," *Dayton Journal*, 14 Nov. 1865, pg. 2.

Notes to Chapter 9: The Life And Death of Solomon Spitler

1. Details about the family of Solomon Spitler : Personal communication of Paula Spitler to the author, January 2017; General Affidavit of John Spitler, May 12, 1890, Department of the Interior,

Bureau of Pensions. Provided to the author by Paula Spitler, January 2017.

2. wound up enlisting : The Colonel's Diary, by Colonel Oscar L. Jackson, Page 107.

3. "best respects to them" : Taken from "House of Spittler-Spitler," compiled by Gale Honeyman, provided to the author by Paula Spitler, January 2017.

4. their enlistment bounties : The Colonel's Diary, by Oscar L. Jackson, pages 107-108.

5. "handsomest things I ever saw" : The Colonel's Diary by Oscar L. Jackson, Page 111.

Notes to Chapter 10 The Civil War of John C. Fleming

1. give us such a picture : The Civil War in Letters, A Newberry Library Transcription Project, Newberry Library, Chicago, John C. Fleming Letters, online at http://publications.newberry.org/civilwarletters/

2. Battle figures for Stones River : The Civil War Trust, Stones River/ Murfreesboro, https://www.civilwar.org/learn/civil-war/battles/stones-river

3. an account of the battle to his father : The Civil War in Letters, A Newberry Library Transcription Project, Newberry Library, Chicago, John C. Fleming Letters, Jan. 9, 1863, online at http://publications. newberry.org/civilwarletters/items/show/794

4. two letters from this period : The Civil War in Letters, A Newberry Library Transcription Project, Newberry Library, Chicago, John C.

Fleming Letters, July 25, 1864, http://publications.newberry.org/civilwarletters/items/show/850, and August 3, 1864, http://publications.newberry.org/civilwarletters/items/show/851

5. in Rosehill Cemetery in Chicago : History of Chicago: From 1857 until the fire of 1871, by Alfred Theodore Andreas, 1885.

6. an early "skyscraper" : The trade journal The Iron Age of May 11, 1899, carries a story called "The Carnegie Interests" which on Page 28 reports that "The Carnegie Steel Company, Limited, were organized July 1, 1892, for the purpose of consolidating under one management the business of the various iron and steel works in Pittsburgh which were owned and operated by Andrew Carnegie and his partners." John C. Fleming is listed as one of the organizers. ; The Iron Age, Volume 55, May 9, 1895, carries an article on Page 982, "The Carnegie Steel Company at Chicago", which illustrates that Fleming was one of Carnegie's top executives: "The Carnegie Steel Company's Chicago offices have been removed from the Home Insurance Building to suite 1016 to 1022 inclusive, in the Marquette Building, corner of Adams and Dearborn streets. The Marquette has just been completed and is the finest office building in Chicago. The Carnegie Steel Company furnished the steel for this building, and up to that time it was the largest structural contract they had ever taken, requiring 4500 tons. Their quarters in this building are commodious, the space taken being 80 x 22 feet, extending along nearly half the Dearborn street front on the tenth floor. They are divided into several rooms, comprising a private office for Manager John C. Fleming, a general office, a workroom for typewriters, &c, and a telegraph and telephone room. The building being finished in mahogany, the desks and other furniture have been specially made of the same wood, presenting a remarkably rich effect. The manager's room is 22 feet square, laid with a specially finished hardwood floor.

The telephone and telegraph room is connected with Pittsburgh, Philadelphia and New York by a private telegraph wire as well as by long distance telephone, enabling business to be conducted as quickly and conveniently as if the mill and the branch office were located in the same block. The Chicago branch was established by John C. Fleming in 1884, being the first agency opened by this great concern. It was regarded as an experiment at the time, so much so that the company assumed no obligation as to rent and contracted for only one-third of Mr. Fleming's time. Under his management the business grew rapidly, and the Chicago branch became a very important part of the establishment. That its importance is so recognized is shown by the opening of this fine suite of offices, superior in many respects to the general offices of most manufacturing concerns." A 1900 settlement of a dispute between Andrew Carnegie and his estranged former business colleague Henry Clay Frick shows John C. Fleming as a bondholder in the Carnegie Company with bonds valued at $451,000, equivalent to millions in today's dollars. [The Inside History of the Carnegie Steel Company: A Romance of Millions, by James Howard Bridge, University of Pittsburgh Pres, 2014, Page 356]

Notes to Chapter 11: Aftermath, Part 2: New beginnings, new lives

1. driven away by Garrard's troopers : Official Records, Series 1, Volume 38, Part 5, Page 303, correspondence by General J.M. Schofield to Major General Sherman, July 30, 1864.

2. north of Decatur : History of the 72nd Indiana Volunteer Infantry of the Mounted Lightning Brigade, written and compiled by B.F. McGee and edited by Wm. R. Jewell, S. Vater & Co., 1882, Page 367-368

3. "to love their country" : History of the 72nd Indiana Volunteer Infantry of the Mounted Lightning Brigade, written and compiled by B.F. McGee and edited by Wm. R. Jewell, S. Vater & Co., 1882, Page 370.

4. went into camp : See Special Field Orders No. 104, Army of the Ohio, Official Records, Series 1 Volume 38 Part 2, page 521, September 8, 1864.

5. chased after Hood : Decision In The West: The Atlanta Campaign of 1864, by Albert Castel, University Press of Kansas, Page 553; The Union Army: A History of Military Affairs In The Loyal States 1861-1865, Volume 3, Page 64, Federal Publishing Company, Madison, Wis., 1908.

6. "to the Gate City" : The Colonel's Diary, by Oscar L. Jackson, Page 162.

7. several weeks later : The Union Army: A History of Military Affairs In The Loyal States 1861-1865, Federal Publishing Company, Madison, Wis., 1908, Volume 3, Page 64.

8. on October 19, 1863: The Union Army: A History of Military Affairs In The Loyal States 1861-1865, Volume 3, Page 64, Federal Publishing Company, Madison, Wis., 1908.

9. "are soldiers every inch" : Trenton State Gazette, July 25, 1865, Volume LXXXIII, Issue 169, Page 3, accessed on GenealogyBank.com

10. downstream to Louisville : The Colonel's Diary, by Colonel Oscar L. Jackson, Old South Books, Page 222.

11. returned home to Ohio : The Union Army: A History of Military Affairs In The Loyal States 1861-1865, Volume 2, Page 398, Federal Publishing Company, Madison, Wis., 1908.

12. during the Civil War : George Stoneman: A Biography of the Union General, by Ben Fuller Fordney, McFarland & Company Inc. Publishers, 2008, Page 100.

13. "of their long, colorful, and eventful career" : A Soldier to the Last: Maj. Gen. Joseph Wheeler in Blue and Gray, by Edward G. Longacre, Potomac Books Inc., Washington, 2007, Page 168.

14. "will decide the fate of Atlanta" : Decision In The West: The Atlanta Campaign of 1864, by Albert Castel, University Press of Kansas, 1992, Page 484.

15. Averysboro and Bentonville : Campaigns of Wheeler & His Cavalry, 1862-1865, edited by W.C. Dodson, Hudgins Publishing Company, Atlanta, Georgia, 1899, Page 363.

16. "I bid you farewell" : Confederate Veteran magazine, Vol. 1, No. 2, February 1893, Page 62; Campaigns of Wheeler and His Cavalry, 1862-1865, edited by W.C. Dodson, Hudgins Publishing Company, Atlanta, 1899, Pages 359-360.

17. must have been Thomas's father : Claim For Minor's Pension, No. 96,659, Brief In The Case of William Daugherty; Affidavit of Charles Daugherty, April 8, 1865, accessed on Fold3.com, December 9, 2017.

18. the start of the Atlanta Campaign : Widow's Claim for Increase of Pension, Meigs County, Ohio, December 3, 1866, accessed on Fold3.com on December 4, 2017; Claim For Increase Of Widow's Pension, Nov. 22, 1865. An August 27, 1867, document from the Department of the Interior's Pension Office notes discrepancies in the birth dates listed for the children in Mary Ann's affidavits. In a subsequent letter, Mary Ann wrote that she had given the original dates from memory because she had been told by a pension agent that

they were not material. She later provided exact dates from documents. She also wrote that the infant Alma Savannah had died in May 1865.; Official Roster of the Soldiers of the State of Ohio in the War of the Rebellion, The Werner Ptg. & Mfg. Co., Akron, Ohio, Page 394]

19. until her own death in December 1906 : Pensioner Dropped, U.S. Pension Agency, Milwaukee, Wis., Certificate No. 50556; Claim for Increase of Widow's Pension, certificate No. 50556, accessed on Fold3.com.

20. lived on until 1909 : Official Roster of the Soldiers of the State of Ohio in the War of the Rebellion, 1861-1865, Volume 5, Page 397. Claim For Widow's Pension, With Minor Children, No. 134,491; Affidavit of Samuel Coffee, December 31, 1866, accessed on Fold3.com on December 10, 2017; A List Of The Union Soldiers Buried At Andersonville, by Dorence Atwater, The Tribune Association, 1866, Page 46.

21. lived until January 1923 : Roster of Wisconsin Volunteers, War of The Rebellion, 1861-1865, Volume 2, Madison, Wisconsin, Democrat Printing Company, State Printers, 1886, Page 295; Affidavits of Mary M. Gribble, September 2, 1864, and September 5, 1864; Registration with the Allegheny Board of Health; Drop Report – Pensioner, all accessed on Fold3.com on December 9, 2017.

22. with a minor child : Claim For Minors' Pension, No. 93908, accessed through Fold3.com on November 5, 2017.

23. passed away on September 10, 1909 : Roster of Wisconsin Volunteers, War of The Rebellion, 1861-1865, Volume 2, Madison, Wisconsin, Democrat Printing Company, State Printers, 1886, Page 293; Application For Pension of Widow of Deceased Soldier, State of Illinois, August 30, 1864, accessed on Fold3.com on December 8,

2017. Drop Order and Report for Amy Huntley, Department of the Interior, Bureau of Pensions, Sep. 30, 1909.

24. a new guardian, a William H. Smith : Official Roster of the Soldiers of the State of Ohio in the War of the Rebellion, 1861-1865, The Werner Ptg. & Mfg. Co., Akron, O., Volume 5, Page 414; Claim For Minor's Pension, Charles Milligan, Case No. 117368; Application of Guardian of Minor Children In Order To Obtain Army Pension, April 17, 1868; Widow's Claim For Pension, August 5, 1864; Affidavit of Elizabeth Davis and Sarah Hoylton, April 17, 1868, all accessed on Fold3.com, December 12, 2017.

25. the only surviving member of the family : Roster of Wisconsin Volunteers, War of The Rebellion, 1861-1865, Volume 2, Madison, Wisconsin, Democrat Printing Company, State Printers, 1886, Page 296. (Charles Richie's name appears as Richie in the roster but as either Richie or Richey on later pension documents.) Annual Report of The Trustees Of The Soldiers' Orphans' Home of Wisconsin For The Fiscal Year Ending September 30, 1867, contained in Annual Message of the Governor of Wisconsin, Delivered to the Legislature In Joint Convention, Thursday January 9, 1868, Together With The Annual Reports Of The State Officers, For The Fiscal Year Ending September 30, 1867, Page 616; Statement of Eliza Richey, January 30, 1868, accessed on Fold3.com on December 6, 2017. Pensioner Dropped, Department of the Interior, Bureau of Pensions, Certificate No. 83402, May 25, 1914, accessed on Fold3.com on December 6, 2017.

26. Mary remarried in April 1866 : Claim for Widow's pension, accessed via Fold3 at https://www.fold3.com/image/304190900

27. and Adelbert was 13 : Claim of Guardian of Orphan Children for Pension, Hamilton County Ohio, May 8, 1868, accessed on Fold3. com on November 23, 2017.

28. west of Oshkosh : Civil War Veterans of Winnebago County Wisconsin, Volume 1, Page 17, by David A. Langkau. Heritage Books, 2012.

29. "a letter from Mary" : Well Mary: Civil War letters of a Wisconsin volunteer, edited by Margaret Brobst Roth, The University of Wisconsin Press, 1960, Page 83.

30. "and clear conscience" : Well Mary: Civil War letters of a Wisconsin volunteer, edited by Margaret Brobst Roth, The University of Wisconsin Press, 1960, Page 91-92.

31. "since he has been here" : Well Mary: Civil War letters of a Wisconsin volunteer, edited by Margaret Brobst Roth, The University of Wisconsin Press, 1960, Page 107.

32. "going home this evening" : Well Mary: Civil War letters of a Wisconsin volunteer, edited by Margaret Brobst Roth, The University of Wisconsin Press, 1960, Pages 107-108.

33. "feel proud of their mouldering bodies" [Well Mary: Civil War letters of a Wisconsin volunteer, edited by Margaret Brobst Roth, The University of Wisconsin Press, 1960, Page 111.

34. two of her three children : Well Mary: Civil War Letters of a Wisconsin Volunteer, edited by Margaret Brobst Roth, The University of Wisconsin Press, Madison, 1960, Page 4 and Page 154.

35. "who is getting along splendidly" : The Colonel's Diary, by Oscar L. Jackson, Page 144.

36. "fellow citizens at home" : The History of Fuller's Ohio Brigade, 1861-1865, by Charles H. Smith, Pres of A.J. Watt, Cleveland, Ohio,

1909, Pages 349-351. Biographical Directory of the United States Congress, 1774-2005, U.S. Government Printing Office, Page 718.

37. at Kay's Hotel in Trenton : Newark Daily Advertiser, Friday, September 9, 1864, Page 3, accessed on GeneaologyBank.com.

38. for Lincoln and Johnson" : Cited in Centinel of Freedom, Newark, New Jersey, Tuesday October 11, 1864, Volume LXVI, Issue 15, Page 2, accessed through GeneaologyBank.com.

39. "thereof the sum of $335" : Colonels In Blue: Union Army Colonels of the Civil War, by Roger D. Hunt, Stackpole Books, Mechanicsburg, Penn., 2007, Page 195.

40. at the age of 59 : New York Herald, April 6, 1884, accessed on Genealogybank.com.

41. was killed in action in Decatur : A Badger Boy In Blue, The Civil War Letters of Chauncey H. Cooke, Wayne State University Press, 2007, introduction Page 10.

42. "The Indian and The Negro" : A Badger Boy In Blue, The Civil War Letters of Chauncey H. Cooke, Wayne State University Press, 2007.

43. and Ethel A. : C.W. Butterfield's History, Grant County, Wisconsin, Western Historical Company, 1881, Page 1042-1043.

44. from Essex County : Legislative Manual, State of New Jersey, 1905, by T.F. Fitzgerald, Page 208.

45. New Jersey veterans group in 1892 : Our Secret Societies, Trenton Evening Times, July 24, 1892, Page 7, accessed on Genealogybank.com.

46. in the 1890s. : Newark Grand Army Men at Gettysburg, New York Tribune, September 25, 1895, accessed on Genealogybank.com.

47. the Police Board of Newark : Philadelphia Inquirer, May 10, 1900, Volume 142, Issue 130, Page 4, accessed on Genealogybank.com.

48. "the benefits of the rules of war" : Samuel Wragg Ferguson Papers, Mss. 1416, 1576, Louisiana and Lower Mississippi Valley Collections, LSU Libraries, Baton Rouge, La., Part 5, Page 2.

49. "the man I had fought so often" : Samuel Wragg Ferguson Papers, Mss. 1416, 1576, Louisiana and Lower Mississippi Valley Collections, LSU Libraries, Baton Rouge, La., Part 3, Page 3.

50. "undergoing much fatigue" : Samuel Wragg Ferguson Papers, Mss. 1416, 1576, Louisiana and Lower Mississippi Valley Collections, LSU Libraries, Baton Rouge, La., Part 1, Page 1.

51. "must shore up their home" : Mary Gay: Sin, Self, and Survival in the Post-Civil War South, by Michelle Gillespie, in "Georgia Women: Their Lives and Times", Volume 1, edited by Ann Short Chirhart and Betty Wood, The University of Georgia Press, 2009, Page 210.

52. "swallowed up in oblivion" : Life in Dixie During The War, by Mary A.H. Gay, Mercer University Press, 2000, Preface.

53. "unpublished letters and diaries" : Margaret Mitchell's Gone With The Wind Letters, 1936-1949, edited by Richard Harwell, Macmillan Publishing Co. Inc., New York, 1976, Page 36.

54. "drawn directly from Gay's memoir" : Mary Gay: Sin, Self, and Survival in the Post-Civil War South, by Michelle Gillespie, in "Georgia Women: Their Lives and Times", Volume 1, edited by Ann

Short Chirhart and Betty Wood, The University of Georgia Press, 2009, Page 201.

55. has been lost : An Uncompromising Secessionist: The Civil War of George Knox Miller, Eighth (Wade's) Confederate Cavalry, edited by Richard M. McMurry, The University of Alabama Press, 2007, Page 240-241.

56. at his home in Talladega : An Uncompromising Secessionist: The Civil War of George Knox Miller, Eighth (Wade's) Confederate Cavalry, edited by Richard M. McMurry, The University of Alabama Press, 2007, Page 273.

57. the year before : History of Baird Holm LLP, accessed on the firm's website, July 30, 2017, http://www.bairdholm.com/about.html

58. his son's home in Omaha : Baird Holm's First Century, by Michael G. Lessmann, November 2007, Page 11. Manuscript provided to the author by Baird Holm LLP; Civil War High Commands, by John Eicher and David Eicher, Stanford University Press, 2002, Page 393.

59. formed Nourse-Taylor Lumber Company in 1903 : The Lumber Trade Journal, Volume 55, June 15, 1909, Page 15.

60. "character generally accorded to John A. Nourse" : The Lumber World, April 15, 1910, Page 16.

61. in 1913, aged 68 : John A. Nourse Papers, Detailed History of the Chicago Board of Trade Battery, 1862-1865, written in diary form, Chicago History Museum, Research Center.

62. hard war time experiences : My Dear Nellie: The Civil War Letters of William L. Nugent to Eleanor Smith Nugent, edited by William M.

Cash and Lucy Somerville Howorth, University Press of Mississippi, 1977, Pages 239-241.

63. away in Freehold in 1918 : The New Jersey Coast In Three Centuries, William Nelson, Editor, Vol. III, The Lewis Publishing Company, 1902, Page 108.

64. "business and visit friends" : Milwaukee Journal-Sentinel, June 13, 1943, Page 19, Column 1, "Few on Hand for GAR Rally," accessed on GenealogyBank.com, November 26, 2017.

65. on Thanksgiving Day in 1916, aged 74 : "Isaiah R. Rose," by Betty K. Rose, in Reflections Along The Muskingum, Lower Muskingum Historical Society, Waterford, Ohio, Volume 36, No. 3, July-August-September 2010, Page 7.

66. Rose's war time service : Who Do You Think You Are: Kelly Clarkson, viewable online at https://www.treelines.com/story/927-who-do-you-think-you-are-kelly-clarkson; https://www.youtube.com/watch?v=uAD9TsQEsrw

67. a candidate for Congress. : "Uncle Jerry": Life of General Jeremiah M. Rusk, by Henry Casson, Madison, Wis., Junius W. Hill, 1895, Page 158.

68. "signs of coming trouble were incessant" : "Uncle Jerry": Life of General Jeremiah M. Rusk, by Henry Casson, Madison, Wis., Junius W. Hill, 1895, Page 184.

69. the Milwaukee area's biggest manufacturer : Wisconsin Labor History Society, About the Bay View Tragedy, http://www.wisconsin-laborhistory.org/resources/bay-view/

70. wanted to be Secretary of War : "Uncle Jerry": Life of General Jeremiah M. Rusk, by Henry Casson, Madison, Wis., Junius W. Hill, 1895, Page 463.

71. "which fell riddled with bullets" : "Gen. J.M. Rusk is Dead", The Milwaukee Journal, November 21, 1893, Page 1, Column 5.

72. "characteristics of the typical American..." : "Gen. Rusk In His Grave", The Milwaukee Journal, Friday, November 24, 1893, Page 1, Column 1; Elkhart Weekly Review, November 30, 1893.

73. marry and have two children : C.W. Butterfield's History, Grant County, Wisconsin, Western Historical Company, 1881, Page 885.

74. "an attorney in Minneapolis."[Encyclopedia of Biography of Minnesota, by Judge Charles E. Flandrau, Volume 1, Chicago, The Century Publishing And Engraving Company, 1900, Page 150, 151

75. and corporate attorney : History of the City of Minneapolis, Minnesota, Part 1, by Isaac Atwater, Munsell & Company, Publishers, 1893, Page 436, 437][Magazine of Western History, Volume IX, November 1888-April 1889, New York, Magazine of Western History Publishing Co., Page 544.

76. "they are not the Negroes' master' " : The History of Fuller's Ohio Brigade, 1861-1865, by Charles H. Smith, Press of A.J. Watt, Cleveland, Ohio, 1909, Page 347; "The Personnel of the Freedmen's Bureau in Arkansas," by Randy Finley, in The Freedmen's Bureau and Reconstruction: Reconsiderations, edited by Paul Alan Cimbala and Randall M. Miller, Fordham University Press, 1999, Page 94.

77. "and not as people" : "The Personnel of the Freedmen's Bureau in Arkansas," by Randy Finley, in The Freedmen's Bureau and Reconstruction: Reconsiderations, edited by Paul Alan Cimbala and Randall M. Miller, Fordham University Press, 1999, Page 96.

78. the Northern Pacific Railway : "Still another gone: Death of General J.W. Sprague," Oregonian, December 26, 1893.

79. to fight the Civil War : Jay Cooke, Private Banker, by Henrietta M. Larson, Harvard University Press, 1936, Page 254.

80. "and one of the best known men in the Pacific Northwest" : "Still another gone: Death of General J.W. Sprague," Oregonian, December 26, 1893.

81. "he was treated with great respect" : Tacoma Its History and Its Builders, by Herbert Hunt, The S.J. Clarke Publishing Company, Chicago, 1916, Page 216.

82. "the pleasure and honor of attending the reunion" : Report of Proceedings of Ohio Brigade Reunion, Columbus, Ohio, October 3 and 4, 1878, Chase & Cassil Publihers, 1879, Page 62.

83. was elected mayor of Tacoma : Tacoma Its History and Its Builders, by Herbert Hunt, The S.J. Clarke Publishing Company, Chicago, 1916, Page 295-296.

84. the Tacoma Chamber of Commerce : "Still another gone: Death of General J.W. Sprague," Oregonian, December 26, 1893; Tacoma News, December 26, 1893.

85. as a candidate for the U.S. Senate : "Still another gone: Death of General J.W. Sprague," Oregonian, December 26, 1893.

86. told his honored comrades : "Still another gone: Death of General J.W. Sprague", Oregonian, December 26, 1893

87. the medal issued on January 18, 1894 : Congressional Serial Set, General Staff Corps and Medals of Honor, 66th Congress, Document No. 58, Pages 383, 384.

88. "retold the story of this fight" : "Still Another Gone: Death of General J.W. Sprague," Oregonian, December 26, 1893.

89. Cora, Addie, Marenus and Charles : C.W. Butterfield's History, Grant County, Wisconsin, Western Historical Company, 1881, Page 925.

90. its supremacy in world affairs : "Fightin' Joe" Wheeler, by John P. Dyer, Louisiana State University Press, 1941, Pages 247-301.

91. "I forgot where I was" : Confederate Veteran magazine, Volume 14, No. 7, July 1906, Page 300; "Fightin' Joe" Wheeler, by John P. Dyer, Louisiana State University Press, 1941, Page 352.

92. "after her great mistake in 1861" : Fightin' Joe" Wheeler, by John P. Dyer, Louisiana State University Press, 1941, Page 386.

93. "would have captured the Union troops" : Reunion of the Twenty-Fifth Regiment of Wisconsin Volunteer Infantry, 1887, Page 5, accessed at Wisconsinhistory.org, November 8, 2017.

94. "throughout the world" : Reunion of the Twenty-Fifth Regiment of Wisconsin Volunteer Infantry, 1887, Page 10, accessed at Wisconsinhistory.org, November 8, 2017.

95. "When the 25th comes marching home" : Reunion of the Twenty-Fifth Regiment of Wisconsin Volunteer Infantry, 1887, Page 16-17, accessed at Wisconsinhistory.org, November 8, 2017.

96. "when the gallant McPherson fell" : Reunion of the Twenty-Fifth Regiment of Wisconsin Volunteer Infantry, 1887, Page 18, accessed at Wisconsinhistory.org, November 8, 2017.

97. in the 1878 reunion : Report of Proceedings of Ohio Brigade Reunion, Including Addresses, Correspondence, Etc., Held at Columbus, Ohio, Chase & Cassil Publishers, Mt. Vernon, Ohio, 1879.

98. "won a star for me" : Oregonian, December 26, 1893, "Still Another Gone: Death of General J.W. Sprague".

99. on October 5-6, 1897, in Corning, Ohio : Marietta Daily Leader, September 24, 1897, Volume 3, Page 4, Column 2, accessed on Genealogybank.com on Nov. 9, 2017.

100. "braved all sorts of perils together" : Trenton Evening Times, October 26, 1890, "Our Secret Societies, " "Veteran Organizations".

101. and then held a banquet : New York Herald, October 23, 1890, "Veterans Swap Yarns: First Reunion since the War of the Thirty Fifth New Jersey Volunteers".

102. a banquet, business meeting and sightseeing : Jersey Journal, Jersey City, N.J., July 22, 1897, cited in Geneaologybank.com.

Index